CHINESE - WESTERN COMPARATIVE LITERATURE THEORY AND STRATEGY

Issued by the Comparative Literature Division
of the
Comparative Literature and Translation Centre
The Chinese University of Hong Kong

CHINESE - WESTERN COMPARATIVE LITERATURE THEORY AND STRATEGY

edited by
John J. Deeney

with Preface by Horst Frenz
and Foreword by A. Owen Aldridge

The Chinese University Press
Hong Kong

International Standard Book Number: 962-201-228-0

Distributed by
The University of Washington Press
Seattle and London

Typesetting by Goldwind Photo Typesetting Co., Hong Kong
Printed by Hoi Kwong Printing Co., Hong Kong

CONTENTS

CONTENTS

PREFACE

Horst Frenz

For an outsider deeply concerned with the study of comparative literature, the Hong Kong Conference on East-West Comparative Literature is a reminder of the earlier debates which took place in the American universities decades ago. How do we define comparative literature? What does the term mean, and should we not find a better one? What are the methods of comparing works of literature from different countries—of genres, movements, trends, motifs, themes and characters? And what are the criteria for investigating the relationship between literature and such human endeavors as fine arts, music, philosophy? Most of these issues have been settled, and we have progressed beyond the discussion of principles and methods.

Since the background of most of the earlier American comparatists was European, it is not surprising that the study of comparative literature in the United States started out to be Europe-oriented. It took some time before the course of comparative literature studies was steered in different directions, and I am happy to say that the once frequent argument that we must not spread ourselves too thin—i.e. confine ourselves to the West—is hardly ever heard among my American colleagues today. Inherent in this early emphasis on the "western" world was a curious phenomenon—the absence of American literature in comparative studies. This, too, has changed, and we now find numerous investigations (and courses in institutions of higher learning) which treat American literary works from a comparative perspective.

I make these observations in order to point out that Chinese comparatists have been able to avoid two major obstacles to the development of our discipline—they have readily accepted the term East-West comparative literature, and Chinese literature has been assumed to be basic to a comparative approach. At the Chinese University of Hong Kong, a close working relationship between the Department of Chinese, the Department of English and the Comparative Literature Division is considered essential, and this symposium has become an important contribution to humanistic studies.

What comparatists in the East—as well as in the West—will have to contend with is that in the area of literary criticism there will probably never be a consensus of opinion. As in the past, schools of criticism—such as New Criticism, Structuralism, Formalism, Semiotics—will continue to vie with each other, and I have serious doubts that there will ever be a critical theory which will be congenial to Asian and western comparatists alike.

One other point needs to be made. Too often we in the West like to think of Asian literature rather than literatures, of Asian culture rather than Asian cultures. Conversely, Asians frequently view Western literature and culture as a unit. Such assumptions are fallacious. Rather, we must speak of Asian philosophy, religion and literature in the plural. I am reminded of the comments by the late Charles A. Moore, who maintained that thinking of the Far East as a philosophical unit is "unrealistic, unfair, and certainly untrue to the facts," even if there are certain tendencies Asian philosophers have in common. A similar statement can be made about the field of Asian letters.

Finally, the remarkable success of this symposium brings to mind suggestions for future scholarly discussions in such areas as the relations between Chinese and other national literatures and cultures, inter-Asian studies and the practice and theory of translation. To judge from this first Conference, subsequent symposia will go a long way to solidify the study of East-West comparative literature in Asia.

FOREWORD

A. O. Aldridge

If one were required to isolate the key-note of this significant conference, it might be found in the modest subtitle of Heh-hsiang Yuan's opening address, "An Inquiry into Possibilities." As he suggests, the investigation of relations between the literatures of the eastern and western hemispheres has not reached the stage where conclusions can be more than tentative. Although there is no reason for abandoning the view that the clusters of literatures in these two areas developed for the most part independently, many parallels between them are, nevertheless, being gradually discovered. As the motivating spirit in the organizing of the conference, Yuan stressed the need for guiding principles and concrete objectives in order to preserve cooperative efforts at research from degenerating into aimless floundering.

Of the seven papers presented here, four take up the general concept of adapting western methods of literary criticism to eastern texts, and each of the other three offers a concrete illustration of the application of a particular method.

I fully agree with Yuan's emphasis on cultural pluralism, but instead of using the great diversity in cultural traditions as an argument against affinity studies, as he seems to do, I would use it as a reason for rejecting the frequently expressed goal of attaining a common poetics for evaluating literary and artistic works in the two hemispheres. Taking England and Japan as examples, it is obvious that esthetic differences represent a major ingredient in their cultural identities. Even within individual cultures such as the English or the Japanese there exists a considerable degree of esthetic pluralism: some writers and artists in either culture, for example, advocate balance and symmetry;

others favor irregularity and asymmetry. Esthetic standards within single cultures, moreover, change with the times. Much has been made of the absence of the epic—a long narrative in poetic form —in the Chinese tradition; and many epics exist in the West. Some western critics such as Edgar Allan Poe, however, argue that the epic genre is deficient esthetically—that the essence of poetry is destroyed by length—that a long poem is a contradiction in terms. Superficially, Poe's structures seem to be a vindication of the Chinese tradition and as such an argument in favor of a common poetics, but actually his attitude merely serves to illustrate the lack of esthetic agreement in the West.

Yuan is certainly right in objecting to studies which "impose" established western models on the East, or which draw attention to elements in eastern literatures resembling those in the West in a merely superficial manner. It is, nevertheless, possible to discern resemblances in literary works in two cultures without seeking to impose one upon the other. Indeed the imposing of models has nothing to do with pointing out affinities or resemblances in style, structure, mood or idea between two works which have no other connection. The discerning of analogies without question of influence has been widely used as an instrument for drawing together the literatures of the West, and it may be legitimately used in the broader context of East-West relations. It may also be used from the perspective of the West as well as the East, that is, in showing how western works resemble those in the East as well as in the reverse direction.

As an example of superficial and misleading affinities, Yuan cites a comparison of the feeling for nature in the English poet Wordsworth and that of a Chinese poet, T'ao Yuan-ming, objecting that the comparison overlooks fundamental differences in their conception of the manner in which a separation between mind and body may be obtained. Yuan, nevertheless, accepts Anthony Thorlby's vindication of the principle of esthetic awareness in recognizing not identical, but merely similar elements in kindred genres. Yuan quotes approvingly, and properly so, in my opinion, the following passage from Thorlby:

There need be no factual connexion between the

two examples, but the comparatist must know how to juxtapose them. If he goes far afield for his comparisons, this is not in order to prove any thesis of universal philology or historical evolution or structural esthetics, but primarily for the pleasure of the thing, to broaden the basis of his experience, as an adventure.

Irving Babbitt, in a classic diatribe against romanticism, favorably compared the dependence upon nature in Taoist philosophy to the primitivism of Jean-Jacques Rousseau. This affirmation of similarity may be even farther afield than that between Wordsworth and T'ao Yuan-ming, but it has been widely accepted in the United States. Both Wordsworth and Rousseau are ordinarily regarded as romantic writers, but their resemblances to each other are probably much less striking than the affinities of either one to Taoist philosophy.

Professor Yuan reveals his awareness of the distrust of comparative literature manifested by some professors of the national literatures, whether Chinese and Japanese in the East, or French and German in the West. This may explain his theory that an inherent contradiction weakens the discipline. As I interpret his remarks, he finds two contradictions or contrasts: one between the relative homogeneity of the "Western heritage dimension" and the tremendous diversity in the rest of the world, resulting in the relative ease of studying writings belonging to the former, and the considerable problems involved in expanding studies to include the "global dimension"; the second between the need of "narrowing down the scope of our pursuit" in order to define its objectives and that of broadening its province to include all parts of the world. One cannot emphasize too strongly the contrast between what is known as the West and what is known as the East. The West, as Yuan indicates, is more or less unified and homogenous with its Judeo-Christian tradition in religion and its Greco-Roman tradition in literature. The East in the present conference has usually meant China, but in the broadest sense it also includes the cultures of the Near East, India, Japan and the Pacific. The global dimension must also take into consideration the cultures of Africa.

The literary contrast between East and West resides more in the linguistic differences between the various nations in each area than it does in divergent esthetic views. Indeed there has been a remarkable unanimity in the attitudes of one part of the world towards the literary masterpieces of the other; critics from the East have not argued that some western masterpieces have been overvalued, and sought to place others with more resemblance to eastern works in their place; nor have critics from the West reacted in a similar fashion towards eastern works. The obvious cultural diversities between East and West, in my opinion, do not call for any limitation in the materials and methodologies of comparative literature beyond those required by reason and good sense. Instead the emphasis should be in the other direction, that is, in considering as valid sources for investigation all literatures, major and minor, throughout the globe. I believe in a broadening rather than in a narrowing down of "the scope of our pursuit."

Obviously there is a tremendous difference between the subject matter which can be embraced by an entire intellectual discipline and that which a single scholar may hope to encompass. Many western professors who are not sympathetic to comparative literature have expressed sentiments similar to those of Yuan's colleague who argued that since a Chinese scholar cannot master all the writers and works of a single dynasty he had no time to devote to any other literature. The answer is to be found in selectivity. No single comparatist can deal with entire literatures any more than a single stonecutter of the Middle Ages could erect an entire cathedral. The comparatist is not an expert on every literature, and he should not be expected to have even a superficial knowledge of all literatures. Instead the comparatist specializes in certain narrowly circumscribed areas of particular literatures. He has a general knowledge of the major literary works in a variety of national cultures, together with a familiarity of the various methods of research, but his individual research projects are for the most part as limited and precise as those of his colleagues in single literatures. Comparative literature is a cooperative enterprise covering a vast and diverse area, and it is to be explored or conquered in narrow segments. In the days of exploration, it would have been impossible for any single European navigator to

cover in a lifetime the entire geographic expanse of the two
American continents, but in the twentieth century any tourist
can visit by jet airplane all of the major centers of population in
three or four months. We may hope for a similar future progress
toward universal coverage in the study of literature.

Any single comparatist would be justified, if he wishes, in
discarding "some of the less significant authors and their works"
in favor of the "important literatures," in Yuan's words, but from
the perspective of literary study as an academic discipline, there
exist no value hierarchies for admission. If literature is defined as
the communication by means of written symbols when the
purpose is to provide esthetic pleasure as well as convey a message,
then all works, both major and minor, ancient and modern, must
be accepted as legitimate objects of study, and no national literature has a privileged or superior position. This does not mean,
however, that one must ignore the historical record, which indeed
reveals that some literatures embody centuries of rich tradition
whereas others are only now in the process of emerging. Nor does
it mean that one cannot affirm values or erect standards of judgment. When a biologist maintains that ants and elephants are completely equal as legitimate material for study, for example, he is
not placing ants and elephants on the same level, or suggesting
that they have equal strength or intelligence. Nor is he maintaining
that every individual biologist should devote equal attention to the
two disparate species. He is merely affirming that all living or-
ganisms are the province of his intellectual discipline. The individual comparatist similarly chooses the individual works or theoretical problems to which he wishes to give special attention, but he
still recognizes that the province of his discipline is universal. Yuan
indeed implies assent to this principle by quoting Harry Levin's
proposition that the comparatist must assume "an equal belief in
the equal validity of all traditions constituting the unity of knowledge."

Yuan's special concern is to determine whether or not it is
possible to arrive at a definition of "Comparative Literature East-
West," and his major contribution consists in successfully formulating a working definition, if not an absolute one. One can hardly
challenge the statement that comparative literature East-West

comprises "a branch of literary study which compares literary works of both the East and the West beyond the confines of national boundaries, seeking mutual understanding through exchange and comparison of ideas, denying not the uniqueness of a national tradition but giving its manifestation a new dimension and making Comparative Literature a universal medium of communication."

Significantly this definition speaks of comparing individual works of the East and the West rather than comparing the two cultures. Indeed comparative literature East-West at its best consists of treating the art of written communication with appropriate examples drawn from the two hemispheres. It is not primarily a medium of communication, but rather an analysis of forms of communication which resemble each other. Some critics have been reluctant to attribute to the discipline the function of promoting mutual understanding, perhaps one of the reasons for Douwe Fokkema's objection in the subsequent discussion to the combining of moral enthusiasm with scientific methodology. I agree that the fostering of international understanding is not one of the primary functions of literature, but, on the other hand, it cannot be denied that individuals who are acquainted with an alien culture—even on a superficial level—show much greater receptivity towards that culture than they would otherwise. I am not, of course, referring to political relationships, since it has been empirically proved that culture and politics do not necessarily go hand in hand. Cultural similarities are powerless to prevent civil wars, shifting alliances, and ideological splits such as the one between capitalism and communism which at present separates eastern and western Europe as well as the two Chinas.

Because of the discreteness of culture and ideologies, I question the view that "cultural and philosophical diversities" have given rise to the historically divergent views which have been expressed about comparative literature, particularly those associated with the so-called French and American schools. The method which stresses influence and reception, or *rapports de fait*, and considers comparative literature as a branch of literary history happened to be the first to develop, and French scholars were at the time the most productive. The method which admits in addition, or rather recommends, the study of resemblances or affinities rather than source-influence relationships, and which discerns these resemblances by means of *rapprochment* or placing one passage in juxtaposition with another developed subsequently. At first the major practitioners were Americans, but eventually many Europeans followed their example. Neither method bears the imprint of French or American culture or philosophy. At present the two methods are practised indiscriminately by citizens of both France and the United States as well as of other countries in every part of the world. Scholars choose one or the other method not according to their cultural background but according to the nature of the problem in which they are interested. These fundamental methods have more recently been succeeded—but not superseded—by other techniques stressing linguistics and ignoring history. The latter techniques are, of course, well represented in the present conference. Those who pursue any of these methods are merely using available tools, not revealing cultural or philosophical conditioning. Incidentally, the method of relating literature to other disciplines such as sociology, psychology and the arts—which Yuan considers the primary characteristic of the American school—was originally rejected by American purists, including many eminent scholars. When universities as a whole developed the interdisciplinary approach to knowledge, however, nearly all American comparatists accepted this philosophy for their own area as well as the university at large.

Before treating the method which Yuan offers as the most efficacious for treating East-West relations, I should like to comment briefly on his reservations concerning comparatism as it has been practised in the past. He is right that the methodology associated with the French school has only limited application to East-West relations; not, in my opinion, because an emphasis upon material information implies the neglect of esthetic values, but because until recent times direct historical connections between the two cultures were either entirely lacking or merely fragmentary. There still remain, however, significant *rapports de faits* to be investigated. The nineteenth-century German poet, Heinrich Heine, for example, reported Goethe's self-satisfaction in hearing that scenes from his novel *Werther* were being depicted on porcelain in China, and Heine in turn gloated upon hearing that an edition of his own poems had been published in Japan. Yuan at first seems to be even more intransigent towards the American school, on the grounds that its involvement of multiple disciplines renders the study of East-West relations so complex as to be impossible. He later relaxes his opposition, however, by observing that "for a Chinese scholar, the study of literature often involves the study of philosophy and art." He also accepts the axiom of the convertibility of poetry and painting, the theme, moreover, of the subsequent paper of Wai-lim Yip.

Yuan's preferred method seems to be a combination of the French and American methods. He proposes that the scholar isolate a cause and effect relationship in one literature and investigate the cultural and philosophical elements bearing upon the relationship. He would then isolate a similar cause and effect in another literature and pursue an identical investigation of relevant cultural and philosophical elements. Finally, he would bring the two pairs together for comparison, pointing out the parallel elements. I heartily approve of the combination of history of ideas and literature in this method, but I am afraid that its other features would drastically limit the possibilities of comparison. It would not be easy to find examples in either an eastern or a western literature of a cause and effect relationship which could be paired with one in the opposing literature; the demonstration of the parallels would be cumbersome; and the conclusions would probably be sociological or anthropological rather than literary.

Although this method may have been used successfully in Yuan's illustration of the investigation of ancient myths, to adopt it as an exclusive or even preferred method of research would almost bring comparative studies to a standstill. In my opinion, it is significant enough to isolate any extensive parallelism in theme, style or portrayal of human condition without requiring in addition the demonstration of similar causes and effects.

Yuan's example of close parallelism, Gogol's *The Inspector General* and Lao She's *Looking Westward to Ch'ang-an*, the latter "almost a copy" of the former, provides a superb model for East-West research; yet the parallelism is not based upon the causes and effects leading to the creation of either work, but upon the internal resemblances in plot and characterization. As Yuan observes, the ideological backgrounds of the two works are diametrically opposite, but they reflect social reality in an identical manner; in treating them, therefore, the critical emphasis should be generic rather than sociological. There would also seem to be a good case to be made that Lao She wrote under the direct influence of his Russian predecessor, but even so it is the thematic and narrative resemblances which are essential. The same is, of course, true about the parallels between Lao She's *City of Cats* and Jonathan Swift's *Gulliver's Travels*. Little need be said about the backgrounds of these works, for they have almost nothing in common. What counts is that both may be interpreted as dystopias, allowing for the portrayal of extensive thematic and generic parallels.

At this point a distinction needs to be made between the stylistic and the thematic elements which comprise literary genres. Style consists of mechanical or technical components such as rhyme schemes, metaphors, internal divisions or narrative voice, most recognizable and essential in such forms as the sonnet and the *haiku*. Theme consists of conceptual elements such as mixing of tragedy and comedy, character development or portrayal of reality, most recognizable and essential in such forms as the *bildungsroman* or the Utopia. To be sure, there is considerable overlapping, but usually either the technical or the conceptual dominates in particular genres. Yuan seems reluctant to admit studies which emphasize parallels in style without taking into consideration cultural differences, and he is also wary of attempts at periodization based on stylistic criteria.

It is probably impossible to devise a valid system of periodization which incorporates both eastern and western literatures before the twentieth century. Yuan observes, however, a concrete parallelism in the creation myths of both civilizations. Investigation of ancient mythologies may be extended to include myths and folklore of later centuries. Some fascinating parallels emerged during the conference, suggesting that this area may well be a fruitful one for subsequent scholarship.

The analysis of themes is closely related to the history of

ideas, a methodology which Yuan recommends as a means of discerning affinities between different cultures and the basic aspirations of man. Here again, I believe it is possible and desirable to separate the study of literary texts from the study of cultures. An author or a text, for example, may express ideas completely alien to the culture or climate of opinion in which he lives. Our mission as literary scholars is not primarily to compare cultures (a function of anthropology), but to observe parallels in ideas, themes and manifestations of the lyric, dramatic and narrative modes. Yuan is closer to the mainstream of our discipline when he agrees that comparative literature "is not comparison of different national literatures by setting one against another" than when he seeks new light "on the cause-effect relationship between two literatures."

In broaching the topic of criticism, Yuan seems to disengage himself from the prevailing effort of eastern scholars to affirm and to establish a common poetics for East and West. Certainly he warns against the dangers of misunderstanding and misrepresentation inherent in forcing western models upon Chinese works. I heartily concur with this caveat; indeed, as I have previously said, there is no more need for a common poetics than for a common religion. Nothing approaching a critical consensus exists in the West—opposing, even antithetical, theories compete with each other—and in recent years new ones have appeared and faded away with astonishing frequency. There would be no advantage in transposing this anarchy to the East. Classical Chinese criticism, moreover, as Yuan observes, comprises both intuitive and emulative branches. These are loosely parallel to a similar dichotomy in western neoclassicism. The Confucian emulative goals of moral integrity embodied in unity of form and content have their counterparts in Aristotelian principles of unity and imitation; whereas the concept of intuitive appreciation corresponds to European eighteenth-century notions such as *je ne sais quoi* and judging literary works by pointing out beauties and faults. It is not surprising, therefore, that the general discussion following Yuan's presentation developed into a debate over the relative merits of impressionistic and objective criticism in which opinion was not divided along geographic lines; some scholars from the West defended impressionistic judgments, and others from the East argued for objectivity. The obvious conclusion is that neither the East nor the West has a monolithic approach to literature, and that the study of East-West relations cannot be based upon a single system of criticism.

In Chinese culture the inherent relationship between literature and the fine arts is probably more clearly established than in the West. As Yuan points out, the study of Chinese literature traditionally involves the study of painting, calligraphy and seal-carving. In the West, the concept of the resemblance between painting and poetry was accepted as commonplace from classical times until the late eighteenth century when Lessing pointed out an essential difference—that poetry describes consecutive action while sculpture portrays special relations confined to a particular moment of time. Wai-lim Yip, in summarizing the contrary arguments of Herder, Pound and others, relates the controversy to Chinese esthetic theory and poetic practice. His examples of arrested action or static description in Chinese poetry and of the passage of time in Chinese landscape painting are convincing arguments against the absolute application of Lessing's theory. Similar examples may be cited in western art, such as Picasso's "Guernica."

Going beyond these concrete illustrations, however, Yip maintains that poetry and painting are esthetically unified in the sense that both transcend the physical to arouse a feeling of something beyond or outside. In Ezra Pound's expression, the two means of communication possess a common bond or "inter-recognition," a type of energy or power which creates an esthetic state in the viewer or reader. In short, Yip believes that poetry and the plastic arts have an identical esthetic function. This is saying a great deal. Indeed, it is much too much to be defended in the limited scope of a conference paper. Yip's theories are based upon a particular esthetic, that of the Pound-Eliot coterie; certainly, they may fit the poetry of this school and of many Chinese exemplars as well, but they do not, as he suggests, apply to all poetry, all painting or all music in the West. These theories concern a certain type of lyric poetry, sometimes called pure poetry, which indeed has affinities to abstract painting, but there are many other forms of poetry, including narrative, which, as Yip correctly affirms, Lessing had in mind. As lyric poetry resembles abstract painting and sculpture, so narrative and satirical forms resemble representational art. Because of Yip's emphasis on pure poetry, the discussion of his paper turned into a debate over absolute versus relative standards in esthetics. It is significant that the participants were about equally divided, but again not along East-West lines. The discussants on both sides, however, seemed to believe that some single principle should be found to explain all poetry rather than recognizing that there are many kinds of poetry and that each kind has its own standards. Some is discursive, some abstract, some concrete and some intellectual, whether in the West or the East. Poetry, like the arts, has its genres and sub-genres, and although all of them may be related and provide, as Yip declares, correspondences with the others, it does not follow that all forms work esthetically in the same way.

William Tay, in his treatment of aspects of Pound's poetics, offers additional light on the concept of static description. According to Pound, the metro poem records "the precise instant when a thing outward and objective transforms itself, or darts into a thing inward and subjective." In conformity with the notion of epiphany which he shared with Joyce, Pound maintains that "certain facts give one a *sudden insight* into circumjacent conditions, into their causes, their effects, into sequence, and law." Tay reveals that Pound believed that poetic language should comprise concrete, noun qualities and that, like the *haiku* and Chinese classical poetry, it should emphasize the technique of juxtaposition and the suppressing of linguistic connectives. As an illustration of his theories of the pictorial nature of the epigram, Pound found close similarities between the Anglo-Saxon *Seafarer* and Li Po's *Exile's Letter*. Pound developed these poetic theories, as Tay explains, not only for their esthetic values, but for their pragmatic ones as instruments for the education of the public, revitalizing the reader's imagination by shocking and upsetting him. Paradoxically, he succeeded esthetically, but not pragmatically, failing to create an audience for his work or his philosophy. Unfortunately for Pound, there were no William Tays to expound his work during his lifetime. Tay, however, is by no means sympathetic to the opinion of Pound and Eliot that modern life represents little but futility and anarchy.

One concrete example of a form of literary criticism adopted by both East and West is that which affirms, in Yuan's words, that "cultural values are the product of social and economic conditions." This view is held by Marxist critics in both East and West, although it is, of course, not universally accepted in either area. Since it is the official ideology of the People's Republic of China, however, it is quite understandable that the conference organizers should request Douwe Fokkema to treat the Marxist theory of literature with special reference to mainland China. Since his analysis is precise, comprehensive and reasonably objective, it is surprising that it should have been subjected to rather harsh attacks during the discussion period, particularly on the grounds that he made insufficient distinctions between the attitudes of Soviet Russia and mainland China, and that he failed to consider Marxists who live outside the communist hegemony.

Given the broad scope of his topic and his limited time, simplification was inevitable. It is true that Fokkema did not concentrate on criticism such as it is found in the writings of Marx and Engels, or in such modern spokesmen as George Lukács and Lucien Goldmann, but rather on the official attitudes towards literature inculcated by political states. The latter topic, however, is the one announced in Fokkema's title. The attacks to which he was subjected may have been provoked by his introduction setting forth a methodology which he claims belongs to "the scientific study of literature." In attributing to himself the invulnerability of science, he was guilty of one of the critical attitudes which he finds objectionable among the Marxists. In his way, Fokkema was prescribing the same doctrine of a single truth and a single approach to it which flawed Yip's analysis of artistic correspondences.

Although the study of literature may be made relatively precise and systematic, it can never attain the objectivity of science any more than the study of esthetics can isolate absolute or eternal values. Fokkema's analysis, moreover, clearly shows a bias against the system he is examining. It is reflected in such phrases applied to Marxism as "truth should be represented in only a selective way" and "applicability will be decided by ideological and political contingency." It would be possible to take almost any other social-ideological system, however, and discover weaknesses similar to those discovered by Fokkema. The above phrases, for example, could certainly be applied to various sects of institutionalized Christianity or to governments dependent upon a capitalistic economy. A recent book published in the United States by Edward W. Said, entitled *Orientalism*, comes close to doing just that. It portrays European and American scholarship devoted to the Near East or the Arab World as deliberately reflecting a will to cultural domination and repression. Fokkema is somewhat unfair to Marx and Engels in suggesting that neither has written extensively about literary problems while citing three times their *Über Kunst und Literatur*. Marx himself, through the wide range of quotations in his various works, reveals himself as a connoisseur of world literature.

The title of Donald Wesling's paper on one of the recent modes in western criticism suggests that it represents a defense of the theories of Jacques Derrida. To the contrary, Wesling actually adopts a sceptical attitude toward this post-structuralist phenomenon, observing that "Derrida does not just complicate, enormously, the relation between language and the practical world of things and actions, he writes as if there is no relation whatsoever." In reference to East-West comparative literature, Wesling subjects some of the articles in the *New Asia Academic Bulletin*[1] to Derrida's method of deconstruction and grants to the method a degree of validity in exposing methodological inconsistencies, even

[1]This special issue on East-West Comparative Literature was published by New Asia College, The Chinese University of Hong Kong (1978), and was guest edited by the Hong Kong Comparative Literature Association. It has now appeared in book form under the title, *China and the West*, ed. William Tay, Ying-hsiung Chou, and Heh-hsiang Yuan (Hong Kong: The Chinese University of Hong Kong Press, 1980; distributed by the University of Washington Press). Most of the essays also appear in Chinese under the title, *Chung-hsi pi-chiao wen-hsüeh lun-chi* 中西比較文學論集 (A Collection of Essays on Chinese-Western Comparative Literature), edited by the same scholars (Taipei: Shih-pao wen-hua, 1980).

though the same common sense approach which Wesling uses in
his own analysis would expose these same logical deficiencies.
Wesling also reveals the fallacies in Derrida's theories concerning
the supposed anti-logocentrism of Chinese written characters. He
grants that prevalent attitudes which perceive a basic philosophical
East-West opposition need to be destroyed, but concludes that
the "undoing will not be accomplished merely by bringing French
fashions to the Far East."

The final two papers brought into focus the question of
structuralism, and a fiery debate ensued in the discussion period
over the validity of the method. It was generally accepted that
both Professor Chang and Professor Chou had presented well-
organized and sophisticated examples of the method, but
questions were raised concerning the value of structuralism itself.
My personal feeling is that it is as useless to debate methods of
criticism as it is to argue over religion. On both subjects, it is
impossible to get anyone to change his mind. Innovators adhere
to their innovations and traditionalists cling to their traditions.
I would merely observe that criticism is subject to more fads or
new methods than any other branch of literary study, and that it
is a risky business for a young scholar to invest years of his
formative period acquiring a vocabulary and techniques which
may be superseded before he has established himself in the pro-
fession. I agree with Chang that his four stories about tigers need
to be classified into more specific genres than the category of
animal stories, but it is perhaps not necessary to follow the
systems of Barthes or Todorov to do so. Indeed, Chang concludes
after explaining Barthes at length that the latter's system "is not
adequate enough for universal applications." He has better luck
with Todorov's discriminations of the uncanny, the fantastic and
the marvelous, but even here he is obliged to invent a new de-
nominator, the fantastic-marvelous. Since Chang modestly admits
that any approach "has to run the risk of confining the description
to certain features while ignoring the others," I venture to suggest
that it would be possible to classify his stories by means of traditional terminology without recourse even to Todorov. According
to traditional terminology, all of the stories could very well be
labeled either fable, parable or allegory. The story of the tiger

who shows gratitude for having a thorn removed is a fable, defined as a narrative in which animals represent human beings to point a moral. The story of the bride snatched by a tiger from an impending marriage and delivered to another suitor to whom she had been promised is a simple parable, defined as a narrative designed to illustrate any principle, here the moral one that promises must be kept. The story of the tiger who changes into a beautiful woman is an allegory with overtones of myth. The tiger skin represents evil or a tribal taboo. The two stories of a man changed into a tiger and then back into a man are examples of the fantastic, a category reserved for stories and themes completely devoid of moral and allegorical overtones, in which events not to be explainable by natural causes are accepted as plausible by the reader.

From the perspective of Chinese literature, Chang's contribution consists in establishing some order in the classification of national fiction; from the perspective of comparative literature it consists in drawing attention to motifs which exist also in the West. The story of the grateful tiger is exactly parallel to a story told by Aulus Gellius, a Roman author of the second century A.D. In this story a gladiator named Androclus is confronted in the Circus Maximus by a lion who turns in a flash from ferocious to docile. Androclus then reveals that he had previously plucked out a splinter from this same lion's paw and that they had subsequently lived and eaten together in the same cave for three years. This became the basis of a twentieth-century play, *Androcles and the Lion*, by George Bernard Shaw. The story of the tiger who turns into a beautiful woman is related to the theme of the demonic woman in western literature, particularly to the story related by Flavius Philostratus, a quasi-contemporary of Gellius, concerning Lamia, a beautiful woman who turns into a snake. Both the tiger and the snake may be allegories for evil.

The elaborate analysis in the paper by Ying-hsiung Chou of *hsing* as a rhetorical device has relevance merely to Chinese literature, but his additional treatment of bird motifs in *Southeast Fly the Peacocks* opens up the possibilities of comparison with the mythologies of other nations. This famous narrative has at least one major resemblance to western literature apart from the theme of the double-suicide, which was widespread in the Renaissance, and taken up by Shakespeare in *Romeo and Juliet*. In the Chinese poem, Lan Chih and her husband are buried in adjoining graves from which two trees eventually grow and their branches intertwine to form a canopy. In one of the stories of Ovid's *Metamorphoses*, a married couple, Philemon and Baucis, offer hospitality to two gods, Zeus and Hermes, who reward them by turning their hut into a temple in which they serve as priests. When they die, they are buried in front of the temple and are turned into trees. The two sets of lovers are, of course, not entirely parallel; the Chinese characters commit suicide in youth, and the Latin ones die from old age, but the symbol of the adjoining trees commemorates the fidelity and devotion of both couples.

The single concept which seemed to unite all of the sessions of the conference was that of the approach to truth. Wai-lim Yip argued for eternal values and esthetic absolutes even though stressing as models literary texts which many other critics would reject. Fokkema flatly denied the existence of esthetic absolutes, but insisted that literary criticism can attain to scientific objectivity, a position which was tacitly, if not overtly, accepted by the two advocates of structuralism, Chang and Chou. Yuan stood alone on the other side by recognizing impressionistic along with prescriptive or imitative criticism, and accepting the validity of a wide number of methodological approaches to the study of literature. Yuan is right. I accept esthetic relativism, with due regard to the *consensus gentium*, and I do not believe that the study of literature can be made scientific, although statements made about it should be precise and verifiable. Students of East-West relationships in particular should emphasize the historical, the concrete and the specific in revealing parallels and similarities where they exist, but they should be on guard against the superficial and the irrelevant. If our goal is the expanding of knowledge and understanding, our approach must be eclectic, polysystematic and, above all, factual.

Obviously no consensus was attained at the conference, although certain implications seemed to be generally accepted: that the study of East-West relations is a worthy enterprise; that there is no preferred manner of going about it; and that it is beset by

the same difficulties which exist in the study of national literatures as well as additional ones.

EAST-WEST COMPARATIVE LITERATURE:
AN INQUIRY INTO POSSIBILITIES

Heh-hsiang Yuan

In discussing the subject of comparative literature East-West, our primary concern is with three questions: (a) What do we compare? (b) How do we compare? (c) What possible results do we expect? The first question demands the setting forth of a definition; the second requires the formulation of proper methodology; the third anticipates certain demonstrable achievements. The close relationship between these three questions is such that any answer to one inevitably affects that of the other, and that the successful finding of one answer would eventually lead to those of the other two and, subsequently, guide the comparatists of both the East and the West to a new horizon of their discipline.

Prior to any attempt to set forth a definition of comparative literature East-West, and to test its validity governing the study of the subject matter, we must guard ourselves against certain prejudices. We must first make an effort to counter two antithetical tendencies, one fostered by western or westernized (eastern) comparatists who treat the study of comparative literature East-West as largely an affinity study, by either imposing already established western models on eastern literatures, or by finding in eastern literatures types of literary expressions that superficially resemble those of the West; the other, resulting from provincial-minded indigenous native scholars who unilaterally and unequivocally rule out any possibility of comparison between the literatures of the East and the West. One attitude is caused by ignorance of cultural pluralism, which produces literary diversity, and compels scholars and students of comparative literature to take into consideration cultural relativism in their academic pursuit. The other is caused by cultural chauvinism which elects to abandon the opportunity of crossing national and cultural boundaries in order to establish a greater understanding of divergent literatures and their sources. Nothing can do more harm to the cause of comparative literature than the persistent pursuit of either one of the above two courses.

Superficial comparison not only distorts the national and cultural spirit of a literature, and violates its integrity and indigenous virtue, but also creates misunderstanding of its esthetic values. Zaehner's dispute of Huxley's conception of mystical experience in *Mysticism, Sacred & Profane* is a good warning against such comparison. To equate T'ao Yuan-ming's Taoist naturalness to Wordsworth's romantic nature betrays similar miscomprehension as the former describes how the state of oblivion can be reached by will without having to separate the mind and the body, the individual and his environment, while the latter presets the condition of transcendence as physical removal from the scene in order to attain the blissful state of existence. This difference explains why T'ao Yuan-ming could resolve the contradiction between the ideal and the real in his drinking poems, whereas Wordsworth could only lament the unbridgeability between the two in his poem, *Lines Written a Few Miles above Tintern Abbey*.

Blind hostility opposing any effort to build communication between two different cultures through the study of their literatures in a comparative way is also ungrounded. The purity of a national literature can never be contaminated through a comparative study of other national literatures. This cultural chauvinism should be condemned as it is incompatible with literary cosmopolitanism, which is a prominent characteristic of comparative literature.

By cosmopolitanism, I mean the combination of the sense of pluralism and the attitude of tolerance. Comparative literature is not attached to any national literature though its study is related to different national literatures. As national literature may be defined within linguistic, political-historical and cultural confines, in our particular case it seems more justified to stress the linguistic and cultural elements in setting up its definition. The linguistic separation between the East and the West, though making East-West comparative literature study more difficult than study of literatures within the same linguistic family, does not create misrepresentation in our discipline if the languages involved are isolated from their philosophical implications and are understood correctly. But this is hardly possible as the relevance of linguistics to philosophy is significant and as linguistic theory often incorporates "solutions" to philosophical problems.[1] In the study of the classical or early period of Chinese history and literature, one has to delve into the evolutionary development of the Chinese language.[2] Thus in the comparative study of different national literatures, cultural relevance and national heritage must not be ignored. Such intimacy between culture or philosophy and literature finds strong evidence in the Chinese literary outlook as Y. P. Mei suggested:

> Chinese Literature, like the symphonic composition, presents a unity of pattern, significance, and spirit. Fundamentally the spirit of Chinese philosophy ... is also the underlying spirit of Chinese literature. ... Chinese philosophy exercises its influence over Chinese literature sometimes directly and sometimes indirectly through the total cultural milieu.[3]

It also finds examples in John Donne's poetry, in Milton's poetic works, and in the whole range of literary works in the middle ages and Renaissance period in the West.

It is obvious that different national or cultural heritages

[1] See Jerrold J. Katz, "The Philosophical Relevance of Linguistic Theory," *The Philosophy of Language*, ed. J.R. Searle (Oxford: Oxford University Press, 1977, 4th impression). Kuo Shao-yü, *Yü-wen t'ung-lun* 語文通論 (n.d.; rpt. Hong Kong: Tai-p'ing, 1978).

[2] See Ma Hsü-lun 馬敍倫, "Yen-chiu Chung-kuo ku-tai-shih pi-hsü liao-chieh Chung-kuo wen-tzu" 研究中國古代史必須瞭解中國文字, in *Ma Hsü-lun hsüeh-shu lun-wen chi* 馬敍倫學術論文集 (Hong Kong: Chung-hwa, 1963).

[3] Y. P. Mei, "Man and Nature in Chinese Literature," *Proceedings of Indiana University Conference on Oriental-Western Literary Relations*, ed. by Horst Frenz & G. L. Anderson (Chapel Hill: North Carolina University Press, 1955).

often make comparative literature study difficult. Differing literary traditions more than often elude our apprehension. But if we accept divergence without imposing any value judgment, without any discrimination, cultural variety and differences would then only constitute interesting subjects for exploration rather than prejudices for exploitation. A comparatist should realize that distinction is not division, that "in order to obtain adequate notions of any truth," he must "intellectually separate its distinguishable parts" without breaking their inter-relatedness. As Anthony Thorlby has remarked,

> the comparatist need only accept one self-evident principle of aesthetic awareness, which is valid in all arts: that to see one poem, or one picture, or one building is to have little feeling for its qualities. To see another example of the 'same' thing, which being another work of art is of course not the same but only 'comparable,' is to take the first step towards recognizing what is in each case good, original, difficult, intended. There need be no factual connexion between the two examples, but the comparatist must know how to juxtapose them. If he goes far afield for his comparisons, this is not in order to prove any thesis of universal philology or historical evolution or structural aesthetics, but primarily for the pleasure of the thing, to broaden the basis of his experience, as an adventure.[4]

This broadening of experience, this adventure, by nature, is humanistic; it constitutes a field that is "so vast and vague, so centrally located and tangentially defined" that one "can never be sure where its frontiers lie."[5] Such a subject calls for discussion that seeks common grounds for all traditions by pushing through the cultural and philosophical limits towards the speculative

[4] Anthony Thorlby, "Comparative Literature," *YCGL*, No. 18 (1969), p. 79.

[5] Harry Levin, "New Frontiers in the Humanities," *Contexts of Criticism* (New York: Antheneum, 1963), pp. 3-14.

horizons of the various nations represented in the discipline. A comparatist must assume an equal belief in the equal validity of all traditions constituting the unity of knowledge.[6] A comparatist must stand between two national traditions, be positive but not partial towards either one. He must not adhere to a single national tradition; this "negative freedom" must liberate him from rigid conventions and allow him an opportunity for a "creative openness" to new possibilities. Such an international attitude to the study of literature provides a comparatist "a richer storehouse of examples," enriches the study of any single national literature, and widens the intellectual contact among scholars and students of all nations.

The specific purpose of formulating a definition in any subject is to narrow down the scope and content of what one is going to investigate. Two elements are, therefore, to be considered: firstly, certain basic criteria upon which an examiner is to make his selection of the subject matter; the other, subsequent to the choice, proper methodology which will ensure the success of the investigation. Professor René Wellek, in describing the present state of comparative literature study, suggested that our discipline "has not been able to establish a distinct subject matter and a specific methodology."[7] His objection to certain existing definitions of comparative literature is that they make comparative literature "a mere sub-discipline." Briefly scanning through the different definitions advocated by different schools, we discover that the general factors included in the definition of comparative literature are: history, relationship (including interrelationship, influence or imitation, reception), linguistics (language, diction, style), political-geographical elements, thematology, literature and other arts. Our particular query in this case remains the definition, if one is obtainable, of comparative literature East-West.

The French School designated comparative literature as a branch of literary history, studying the international spiritual

[6] Levin, passim.

[7] René Wellek, "The Crisis of Comparative Literature," *Concepts of Criticism* (New Haven: Yale University Press, 1955, 8th printing), p. 282.

relationships among European nations, or as a study of *rapports de fait* between Byron and Pushkin, Goethe and Carlyle, Walter Scott and Alfred de Vigny (Carré); or as a study of the mutual relationship between classical Greek and Roman literatures (Homer and Virgil), the debt of modern literature to ancient literature (Keats to Homer, Eliot to Dante), and the links between various modern literatures (Van Tieghem); or as a study surveying the exchanges of themes, ideas, books or even feelings between two or several literatures, indispensably linked to knowledge of languages and bibliographies (Guyard). Such conception of comparative literature has very limited application in East-West comparative literature studies. The study of comparative literature is more than a mere amassing of material information, which act neglects the value of the esthetic aspects of the literary works compared. The study of spiritual relations among different national literatures can only be applied to influence and reception relationship in East-West comparative literature studies.

Standing at the opposite end to the French School in its definition of comparative literature is the American School, whose prescription would make even more difficult the study of East-West comparative literature. The broad scope and the multiple disciplines involved (arts, music, architecture, politics, economics, sociology, philosophy, religion, etc.) would make a literary purist, Chinese or western, feel frustrated at the vicissitudes of the subject matter. In an unfortunate way, this concept fortifies a traditional Chinese scholar's antagonism and sometimes even prejudice against comparative literature. There is just not enough time. Ke Ch'ing-ming 柯慶明 of National Taiwan University once made the remark that as there were so many writers and works to study even within a single dynasty, how would it be possible for a Chinese scholar to devote time to the study of other literatures? Even though he himself is very sympathetic toward and interested in comparative literature, and has read broadly in Western literature and literary theories, the point is well taken. It is perhaps wise in this case for a scholar to exercise some discretionary choices, relying on the research results of certain trustworthy scholars in various fields, discarding some of the less significant authors and their works, thus giving time to the study of the important literatures of other nations, provided he can abandon professional jealousy and personal bias.

The criticism against individual insufficiency resulting from the involvement of multiple disciplines is valid if one demands a comparatist to know all fields of knowledge and know them well. This is indeed impossible. However, it is possible to know certain related fields well. For instance, for a Chinese scholar, the study of literature often involves the study of philosophy and art (painting, calligraphy, seal-carving), though the latter two are treated not as independent disciplines but as integral parts in a unified humanistic discipline. Evidence of this is found in the classical education of ancient times.[8] We see in the present day curriculum of a Chinese department, courses in *I Ching* (Book of Changes), *Lao-Chuang* (Lao-tzu and Chuang-tzu), *Shih Chi* (Sze Ma Ch'ien's History), *Tso Chuan* (Spring & Autumn Annals), and others, ranging from philosophy to history. The disagreement exists not in the involvement of multiple disciplines but in the treatment of them.

The Pichois (Basel) and Rousseau (Aix) suggestion that comparative literature is analytical description, methodical and differential comparison limits the access to comparative literary studies on grounds of cultural relevance. However, the idea that the discipline is also a synthetic interpretation of inter-linguistic or inter-cultural literary phenomena posits a problem for East-West comparative literature as synthetic interpretation in Pichois' and Rousseau's sense presumes a basis of cultural or linguistic affinity (western culture and western language), and such affinity seldom exists between the East and the West.

Weisstein has stressed the necessity of defining the "links in the chain of the phenomena" of national, comparative and world literature, suggesting that national literature "needs to be defined in a way that is binding for comparative literature, since by its very nature, it refers to the units which form the basis" of the comparative literature discipline.[9] Bearing this urge in mind, we

[8] See Liu Po-chi 劉伯驥, *Liu-i t'ung-lun* 六藝通論 (Taipei: Chung-hua, 1956).

[9] Ulrich Weisstein, *Comparative Literature and Literary Theory* (Bloomington: Indiana University Press, 1973). ch. 1.

can agree with Professor Aldridge that comparative literature is not comparison of different national literatures by setting one against another; it rather provides a method of broadening one's perspective in the approach to single works of literature, and looks beyond the narrow boundaries of national frontiers in various national cultures, and attempts to see the relations between literature and other spheres of human activity.[10]

Whatever definition we adopt, an inherent contradiction in the nature of our discipline remains unsolved. The attempt to define the subject of comparative literature is aimed at narrowing down the scope of our pursuit in order to clearly define its objectives. Such objectives in East-West comparative literature, at this stage however, defy any definition as they constitute more than the comparison of authors of one "Sprachraum" with authors of another speech area, which approach, as Clements mentioned, is used "for study of individuals or literatures within a more encompassing Western Heritage dimension."[11] Though he did add that such intention could also be applied to East-West comparative literature study and eventually in "global dimension," the actual realization of the aim would not be possible until after considerable deliberations and efforts be devoted to bringing together divergent views on literatures of the East and the West. To resolve cultural and philosophical diversities which give birth to divergent views calls for the most flexible description and the broadest scope for our discipline. These two contradictory tendencies have made the definition of East-West comparative literature very difficult, if not impossible. At this stage, we perhaps should not attempt to set a definition for East-West comparative literature; instead, we should only describe what we are doing. We should substitute the prescriptive statement "what comparative literature is" with a descriptive question "what is comparative literature?" To answer the question, certain methodological approaches may be helpful.

[10]See A. Owen Aldridge, *Comparative Literature: Matter & Method* (Urbana: University of Illinois Press, 1969).

[11]Robert Clements, *Comparative Literature as Academic Discipline: A Statement of Principles, Praxis, Standards* (New York: MLA, 1978), p. 10.

Among the several methodological possibilities attempted by comparatists in East-West comparative literature studies, influence and analogy or affinity studies are perhaps most popular. Aldridge linked influence study with the studies of analogy, affinity and tradition and thus, according to Prawer, gave priority to the discussion of the latter three before assessing the role of influence study.[12] He defined affinity study as the study of "resemblances in style, structure, mood or idea between works which have no other connection."[13] Prawer suggested that he had two "main kinds of studies" in mind, respectively exemplified by the works of James Liu and H. R. Jauss. One drew "parallels between the literatures of China and of Europe" on the basis of "chivalrous tradition and dramatic conventions"; the other, between concepts which, in spite of their different evolutionary notions, could be linked to "social and political upheavals."[14] The former, in East-West comparative literature studies, seems unfortunately to be in the vogue. Parallels drawn on certain affinitive characteristics in style without taking into consideration cultural and philosophical differences often misrepresent the essence of the works compared.[15] Stylistic study of literary works of different cultural traditions belongs to technical study, and to extend the study of parallels to "phenomena pertaining to two different civilizations," as in East-West comparative literature, means more than technical study. Jauss' example, to me, provides a better possibility.

It is possible to study parallels by first studying each separately, and finding out first, in each case, the cause-effect relationship from a "preceding" event to a "succeeding" one; then going to contiguous incidences to look for the cultural or philo-

[12] S. S. Prawer, *Comparative Literary Studies: An Introduction* (London: Gerald Duckworth & Co., 1973), ch. 4.

[13] Aldridge, p. 3.

[14] Prawer, pp. 53-54. In a similar sense, R. H. Blyth in *Zen in English Literature and Oriental Classics* (N.Y.: Dutton, 1960) compared Wordsworth's poetic stages to Zen, Pantheism and Orthodoxy.

[15] See H. H. Yuan, "East-West Communication and Cooperation," *Comparative Literature Studies*, 15, No. 2 (June 1978).

sophical elements linking them together; and finally putting the two "parallels" to a comparison. This is to combine the study of history of ideas with the study of literature as systematic patterns of abstract thought. The 19th century Russian "comparatist," Alexander Nikolaevitch Veselovsky, suggested:

> We take a parallel series of similar facts for verification. Here it is possible that the relationship of a given preceding and a given succeeding phenomenon may not repeat itself, or, if it occurs, then the items contiguous to it will be different, and vice versa, a similarity may appear between more distant items of the series. Accordingly, we reduce or expand our concept of the causality: each new parallel series may bring with it a new alteration of the concept. The more verifications there are, the greater is the probability that the generalization formulated will approach the exactitude of a law.[16]

What is aimed for is not, as the original author expected, a scientific exactitude, but rather a workable principle governing parallel study in East-West comparative literature. Assuming that all literatures belong to human cultural activities, among which certain natural affinities can be found, parallel study will be based on a firmer foundation, embracing not merely "superficial resemblance," but also philosophical, political or cultural contiguity. Hans Gustav Guterbock in his study of the "Oriental Forerunners of Hesiod"[17] compared the Hurrian gods to the Greek gods—Anu to Ouranos, Kumarbi to Kronos, and Tesub to Zeus, and brought out the parallels between the Hittite myth and Hesiod's "Theogony." Both myths, to him, deal with the "Kingship in Heaven" in striking similitude. Whatever links scholars found between the

---

[16]A. N. Veselovsky, "On the Methods and Aims of Literary History as a Science," *YCGL*, No. 16 (1967), p. 38.

[17]See Hans Gustav Güterbock, "The Hittite Version of the Hurrian Kumarbi Myths: Oriental Forerunners of Hesiod," *American Journal of Archaeology*, No. 52 (1948), pp. 123-34.

Greek myth and the Hittite one are not definitive. What interests us here is the reflection of historical events in the myths of the replacement of one generation of gods by that of another. The display of succession in a primitive society, whether oriental or occidental, seems to be the same.

Hans Frankel made comparisons between Lope de Vega and Su Tung-p'o and other western and Chinese poets and painters on the axiom of the convertibility between poetry and painting— poems are figureless paintings/paintings are wordless poems— pointing out the culminative historical development of these arts. The development of *tz'u* in Chinese literature, combining music, painting and poetry, has its historical and cultural backgrounds; so has the artistry of Milton, which also embraced the three elements.[18] The parallel is not in terminology (metaphysical or baroque), but in literary phenomena, in the historical causes and cultural temperaments which have effected such literary expressions. Such parallel study may be worthwhile.

C. H. Wang regarded culture as the formulative force of the concept of heroism in an epic,[19] thus allowing Chinese literature to have its epic heroes but not epics. His argument that the cultural emphasis on *Wen* 文 and the traditional antagonism to weaponry have made epic impossible in Chinese literature, would be convincing if the Chinese had never gone through a stage of primitive living as the Greeks, the Egyptians or the Babylonians. Perhaps a comparative study can be made of the "Iliad" and the "Weniad" according to the stages of the development of the respective societies. We could say that in the "Iliad" the social stage is one in which human beings were still locked in the battle between the intellect and the emotion, with the latter playing a dominant role; thus the savagery of killing and of dragging an enemy's body outside the city walls was not considered inhuman but demonstrative of the warrior's prowess; while in the other, the intellect had already won the battle, and the civil treatment of man was deemed

[18] See Milton's shorter poems ("On Time," "Upon A Circumcision," "At a Solemn Music").

[19] C. H. Wang, "Towards Defining a Chinese Heroism," *JAOS*, 95, No. 1 (1975), pp. 25-35.

a vital sign of a cultivated society. Possibilities still exist.

On the same comparative basis, we can pursue a parallel study of literary phenomena of nations of the East and the West with similar political orientation. Such approach can either be applied to the study of literary movements or to individual works in Socialist and Marxist countries. Dave Laing cited, for instance, the "Let A Hundred Flowers Bloom" movement in China in 1955 and the succeeding mobilization of "the arts in support of the Great Leap Forward in 1958" as a "development very similar to the 'literature of fact' and 'shock workers of literature' during the first Soviet Five Year Plan," in which time "authors and artists were dispatched to the factories and the countryside both to record the struggle for production through their own work and to encourage and collect the art of the masses."[20] The criticism against Hao Ran 浩然 and the "rule of the three contrasts," after the fall of Chiang Ch'ing 江青 and her "Gang," is reminiscent of the "attacks on Zhdanov's socialist realism in the Soviet Union during the period following Stalin's death."[21] Posterity will find interesting parallels between Russia's "destalinist movement" in literature and China's "demaoist tendency" in the same area. The field is wide open for more detailed studies and, I am convinced, promises fruitful results. Within this range of "movement," with "political," "social" and "cultural" inter-relatedness as its formative aspect, numerous works can be studied.

Works with different ideological backgrounds may also provide good instances for parallel scrutiny. Laing described Lu Hsun's two short essays "on public reactions to a mother's suicide and the hypocritical Western attitude towards animals" as significant "critique of ideologies of everyday life," which "looks forward to Roland Barthes' *Mythologies*, which performs a similar

[20] *The Marxist Theory of Art: An Introduction* (Hassocks, Sussex: The Harvester Press, 1978), p. 77.

[21] "Give prominence to positive characters among all the characters, to heroes among the positive characters, to the principal hero among heroes. Create special environment, character and personality and use all kinds of artistic media to make the proletarian heroes stand out. Reveal the heroes' communist spirit" (Quoted in Laing, p. 79).

task within a very different class society."[22] Lao She's 老舍
Looking Westward to Ch'ang-an 西望長安 is almost a copy of
Gogol's *The Inspector General.* A question may be raised: what
kind of social environment and what kind of ideological temperament would produce such literary works? The ideological backgrounds of the two works are so diametrically apart, yet the works
are so identical in their reflection of social reality. Such parallel
study may expand the boundaries of our discipline.

Parallel study is often related to influence study which
Weisstein considers "the key concept in Comparative Literature
study."[23] This, however, would not necessarily apply to the study
of East-West comparative literature, particularly in the case of
Chinese-western literary studies. Anthony Thorlby considers influence study "a minor variation of conventional literary history,
and one which suggests a largely secondhand interest on original
authors and works."[24] He suggests that this method rests on two
assumptions: (1) "an author's reception and reputation in one
country constitutes a natural unit of knowledge, circumscribed
and complete in itself"; (2) "in this way the essentially factual
bias of literature's international importance is established." And
his objection to both (the concept of country and that of fact) is
that they are "characteristic of a certain late nineteenth-century
attitude of mind to which it does not seem necessary to tie Comparative Literature for all time."[25] I agree that we should not restrict comparative literature study to a certain approach popular
and valid only in a limited time span, but I also feel that we cannot dismiss the relevance of such an approach. Influence study
certainly is valuable for the study of the artistic growth of modern
Chinese poets, playwrights and novelists.[26] Weisstein cautioned

[22] Laing, p. 72.

[23] Weisstein, p. 29 and ch. 2, passim.

[24] Thorlby, p. 76.

[25] Thorlby, p. 76.

[26]
    See Hou Chien, "Irving Babbitt & the Literary Movements in Republi-
can China," *Tamkang Review,* IV, No. 2 (April 1973), 1-23; Yu Kwang-
chung, "American Influence on Post-War Chinese Poetry in Taiwan," *Tam-*

against setting any qualitative distinction between the "active" (giving) and the "passive" (receiving) factors in influence study. This is quite difficult to observe in the study of the artistic growth of contemporary Chinese poets as they are clearly on the receiving end of the line. The position unfortunately vindicates the severe criticism by the traditionalists against contemporary Chinese poetry. They argue that for any poetic work to be unique, it must be creative in order to be excellent; contemporary Chinese poetry is too imitative, too Western and, therefore, cannot rival classical Chinese poetry, nor compete with Western poetic works. The creative transmutation that will transform western influenced poetic works and give them a sense of originality is still hard to find. Gleams of hope, however, can be seen in Yip Wai-lim's idea of "the use of models," and in both Yu Kwang-chung and C. H. Wang's laborious attempts to infuse classical elements into their poetic works.

Creative transmutation in East-West comparative literature study does not mean innovation or inventiveness; it means first subordination of inventiveness to a critical and selective appreciation of national tradition; then, secondly, assimilation of foreign elements into the national tradition, to broaden its scope and give it new strength to reach a higher level of complexity and achievement, and ultimately to transcend the narrow confines of nationality, making comparative literature the medium of universal understanding.

Treating influence study in its broadest sense means more than the study of the "emitter-receiver" relationship between one author and another, or one national literature and another; it means a study of the reverberation of cultural, philosophical, religious or ideological influences among literary works of different nations. The idea that cultural values are the product of social and economic conditions certainly has placed individual talents and national traditions in a new light. Despite the fact that many, including myself, will question the true literary quality of

kang Review, V, No. 1 (April, 1974), 1-9; and Chang Pi-lai 張畢來, Er-shih nien-tai hsin wen-hsueh fa-jan shih 廿年代新文學發史 (Peking: Tso-chia, 1956), sections 2-3.

a work being investigated under this "principle," and that so much depends on the intellectual integrity of an observing critic, the approach still offers possibilities of comparison that may illuminate works produced of "comparable social conditions" in different countries.

Other areas of possibility include studies of style, periodization, inter-relationship between literature and history of ideas, and literary criticism. The study of style can sometimes be linked to influence study and to periodization, as evidenced in the stylistic study of contemporary Taiwan poetry and in the study of classicism and modernism in art and literature.

Two kinds of stylistic study can bear fruitful results in East-West comparative literature study. The synchronic aims at searching for the idiosyncratic elements of literary works which are not related to one another, and then bringing those elements together to form fundamental principles which bring these unrelated works into some sort of relationship. Ernst Curtius related how script or calligraphy had affected literary style in Islamic literature; that the metaphors of writing had made the style ornamental.[27] He suggested that "the medieval Latin and the Eastern ornamental styles could meet and mingle only in Spain. They help to form that playful Spanish Mannerism which is known as Gongorism and Conceptism."[28] James Liu's study of the dramatic conventions of the Elizabethan and Yuan plays[29] can be convincing if one regards it only as a comparative study of style; however, the best one can say about the similarity is that it is purely coincidental. Similarly to treat all classical forms of art "as more naturalistic, less rigid, and more relaxed" and apply these characteristics to the art works of Greece in the fifth century B.C., India in the fifth century A.D., China at the end of the sixth century and Europe in the fifteenth

[27] Ernst Robert Curtius, *European Literature and The Latin Middle Ages*, tr. by Willard R. Trask (Princeton: Princeton University Press, 1973), pp. 340-47.

[28] Curtius, p. 343.

[29] See James J. Y. Liu, *Elizabethan and Yuan: A Brief Comparison of Some Conventions in Poetic Drama* (London: China Society, 1955).

century[30] is acceptable as long as they are not construed as period style. There is no Baroque period in either Chinese art or literature, though there may be works in different periods with such idiosyncracy that reminds us of the Baroque style.

The diachronic traces the evolutionary development of literary or artistic style in a lineal sense. It is partly historical as its initial step is to collect facts; it is also analytical and synthetic as both analysis and synthesis constitute subsequent stages of the study. Analysis helps to identify and to sort out relevant materials before subjecting them to critical scrutiny; synthesis attempts the union of the underlying themes or ideas and their expressive techniques in literary works.[31]

Whatever approach is adopted, we should guard against the arbitrary designation of terms and the careless identification of group style with period style. Charles Rosen argues that the concept of a style can only have a purely pragmatic definition, and it can at times be so fluid and imprecise as to be useless.[32] The second case is often caused by "confusion of levels." Rosen considers that "dangerous" as it arbitrarily sets the scope of the context of works, artistic or literary, without distinguishing between "the style of a small group and the more 'anonymous' style of an era." He expresses his conviction by the following example:

> To compare High Renaissance painting, envisaged as
> the works of a small group of artists in Rome and

---

[30] See J. Leroy Davidson, "Style—East and West," in Theodore Bowie's *East-West in Art* (Bloomington: Indiana University Press, 1966).

[31] Explications of these points are found in G. L. Hendrickson, "The Origin and Meaning of the Ancient Characters of Style, *American Journal of Philology*, 26, No. 3 (1905), 249-290; Annemarie Mahler, "Art and Visual Imagery: A Methodology for the Study of Medieval Styles," *YCGL*, No. 21 (1972), pp. 7-14; Liu Yung-chi 劉永濟 ed., *Wen-hsin tiao-lung chiao-shih* 文心雕龍校釋 (Taipei: Cheng-chung, 1957); and Lu K'an-ju 陸侃如 and Mou Shih-chin 牟世金, *Liu Hsieh he Wen-hsin tiao-lung* 劉勰和文心雕龍 (Shanghai: Shanghai Ku-chi, 1978).

[32] See Charles Rosen, *The Classical Style: Haydn, Mozart, Beethoven* (London: Faber & Faber, 1971), I & II.

Florence and an even smaller group of Venetians, with
Baroque painting, conceived as international and as
stretching over more than a century and a half, could
only lead to methodological chaos, however fruitful
the individual observations it may suggest.[33]

Thus comparative study of style may not be, as some of us feel,
so free of danger.

The problem with periodization in East-West comparative
literature study lies in the search for "common denominators."
What would be acceptable criteria for the period division in both
Chinese (or eastern) and western literatures? Van Tiegham, for
instance, divided the development of European literature into four
"Cosmopolitan Ages";[34] such division assumes the affinity of all
literatures (European) in religious faith and Latin culture (piety,
chivalry, popular legends), common source of thought in the
Greek and Latin thinkers (subscribing to the same ideals, interested in reviving the ancient concepts and also rivaling with
them), dissemination of French cultural tastes and rationalist
cosmopolitanism, and 19th century wars, emigration and Romanticism. Such affinities (among European literatures) just do not
exist between the East and the West, with perhaps the exception
of the last one. Cheng Chen-to 鄭振鐸 divided the development of
Chinese literature into three major periods, based on the "natural
development and tendency of literary history," the introduction
of Buddhist literature, and the first emergence of *K'un* drama 崑劇
and novel.[35] The two are certainly not comparable. Bate, in his
Criticism: The Major Texts, had two major divisions with romantic
individualism (imagination and emotion) and transcendentalism
as the dividing mark separating the mimetic and the expressive
tradition and other modern traditions. Kuo Shao-yü 郭紹虞, in
History of Chinese Classical Literary Criticism 中國古典文學理論

[33] Rosen, p. 20.

[34] The four ages are: (a) Middle Ages—religious faith, (b) 16th century,
the Renaissance, (c) 18th century, and (d) 19th century.

[35] See Cheng Chen-to, *Ch'a-tu pen Chung-kuo wen-hsüeh shih* 插圖本中國
文學史 (Hong Kong: Shang-wu, 1973).

批評史 divided Chinese literary criticism into eight periods, ranging from 221 B.C. to 1840 A.D. But his division is based on (a) the independent development of critical concepts and theories, and (b) the ideological (social development) coloration of these concepts. Again they are not comparable.

Even in the simple use of terms, comparison in East-West literary study requires explanation. Bate, for instance, refers to classicism as "the principles and values that characterized the art and thought of ancient Greece" and the studies revolving around that "core."[36] It has a basic premise that art is an imitation of nature embodied with a universal principle (logos, idea), which concept implies that an external "reality" is the supreme ultimate; while the Chinese term points to (a) the study of ancient texts discovered, by pure accident, in the walls of the Temple of Confucius at Ch'ü Fu 曲阜 in Shantung Province about 90 B.C., and (b) the movement by some T'ang Dynasty literary revivalists who advocated the recovery of the classical prose style in the writings of the pre-Ch'in-Han period.[37] It is obvious that the referential terms used here are not comparable. We can, therefore, understand the criticism made by purists against such studies in East-West comparative literature.

On the other hand, one should perhaps make room for students of East-West comparative literature who are writing their dissertations and thus tend to pontificate a bit in their argument. Bearing in mind the possibility that such endeavor may eventually lead to greater understanding of the subject matter and produce meaningful results, we should encourage such attempts with studied advice. We can perhaps look at the development of literature in its philosophical context, combining the technical aspects with the reflective abstract ideas. The creation myths, eastern and western, are very much similar; the metamorphosis of man and his world can be found in Chinese, Indian and Greek mythologies

[36] See Walter Jackson Bate, *Preface to Criticism* (Garden City, N.Y.: Doubleday, 1959), "Introduction."

[37] Ch'ien Tung-fu 錢冬父, *T'ang Sung ku-wen yun-tung* 唐宋古文運動 (Shanghai: Chung-hua, 1965).

almost alike,[38] indicating a universal tendency toward interpretive mythology among the ancients. The interpretation of nature read in Renaissance western literature finds a counterpart in the writings of many Chinese wise men, that nature as a rationally ordered and harmonious entity working according to fixed laws and principles suggests a meaningful process, in which all parts are integrated with the living whole.

Myths, as discussed earlier, can be another fertile ground for exploration in East-West comparative literature study. Joseph Campbell suggested that traditional mythologies had the following functions:[39]

1. The mystical or metaphysical—to reconcile "consciousness with the preconditions of its own existence";

2. The cosmological—to formulate and render "an image of the universe in keeping with the science of the time";

3. The sociological—to maintain and to validate "some specific social order, authorizing its moral code as a construct beyond human criticism or human emendation";

4. The psychological—to shape "individuals to the aims of their various social groups, bearing them on from birth to death through the course of a human life."

Functions 1 and 2 are almost universal in all mythologies, whether eastern or western; functions 3 and 4, though universal in abstract pattern, vary with each national tradition and cultural tempera-

[38] See Samuel Noah Kramer, ed., *Mythologies of the Ancient World* (Garden City, N.Y.); Yang K'uan 楊寬, "Chung-kuo shang-ku shih tao-lun" 中國上古史導論, in *Ku-shih pien* 古史辨 (Hong Kong: Tai-p'ing, 1963), vol. 7, chs. 2-3.

[39] Joseph Campbell, "Mythological Themes in Creative Literature & Art," *Myths, Dreams, and Religion*, ed. by Campbell (N.Y.: Dutton, 1970).

ment.

In both oriental and occidental traditional systems, "the authorized mythological forms are presented in rites to which the individual is expected to respond with an experience of commitment and belief." It is the response and its conditioning factors, experience and belief, decided by the cultural and religious backgrounds, that dictate what forms the manifestation shall take. Campbell gave the example of the three variants of a "single mythic theme"—the ultimate origin of all. The Indians gave the term of Brahman (Brihadaranyaka Upanishad 1.4.10); the Hebrews, Yahweh; the Greeks, Logoi;[40] and we may add another term, Tao. It is obvious, from observation of the interpretation of each, that each represents a particular mode of experience—significantly different from the other—of "the mystic dimension of man's being." The Hebrew term is theological and religious, presented historically; the Greek term, humanistic, treated neither historically nor proto-historically but symbolically; the Indian and the Chinese, ontological, interpreted philosophically. Thus the archetypes of myths should be recognized "not as merely irrational vestiges of archaic thought, but as fundamental to the structuring of human life, and, in that sense, prophetic of the future as well as remedial of the present and eloquent of the past."[41]

Another area of study which may bear fruitful results in East-West comparative literature is the combined study of history of ideas and literary development, in which the relationship of literature and other systematic patterns of abstract thought must provide certain affinities between different cultures, as the basic aspirations of man, eastern or western, are very much alike. Thus there is a certain sense of relatedness among literatures of different nations. For instance, in studying eighteenth-century Russian literature, we will do well if we acquire a good knowledge of the intellectual movements in England and France at the same time. When we study early twentieth-century Chinese literature, we shall benefit from a thorough acquaintance with French and English romanticism, Russian nihilism and Communism. Such

[40] Campbell, passim.

[41] Campbell, p. 170.

understanding sheds light on the cause-effect relationship between two literatures, effects mutual verification, and ultimately leads to a concept of world view of literature. However, we must bear in mind that in such an approach, we need not literary anecdotes, nor do we need Boswells or Carlyles, as individuals do not constitute the major subject of our study.

We can certainly say that, in the above sense, East-West comparative literature is a branch of literary study which compares literary works of both the East and the West beyond the confines of national boundaries, seeking mutual understanding through exchange and comparison of ideas, denying not the uniqueness of a national tradition but giving its manifestation a new dimension and making comparative literature a universal medium of communication.

Criticism remains perhaps the most baffling yet most "frequented" area in East-West comparative literature study. Comparatists working in this area who are known to us are James Liu, C. H. Wang, Wai-lim Yip, Andrew Plaks, Yen Yuan-shu, William Tay, Ying-hsiung Chou, Chang Han-liang, Douwe Fokkema and many others. All have produced brilliant works, yet all have been criticised by traditional Chinese scholars as being fallacious in their interpretations.

I admit that the major problem facing those of us who adopt (and even adapt) Western critical theories in analyzing and evaluating Chinese literary works is applicability. Misjudgment can be a factor that beguiles such critics. When a critic disregards the peculiar cultural milieu, and forces a western model on a Chinese work, misunderstanding and misrepresentation occur. For instance, the stylistic analysis of Chinese poetry which breaks down the whole contextual structure of a poetic line according to western linguistic composition, often misplaces the esthetic value of the work, as textual analysis tends to emphasize compositional merit, which is technical, while Chinese poetics stresses esthetic appreciation of an intuitive nature. A discussion of poetic works in subject-object, subject-verb relationships does not suffice in appraising the greatness of Li Po or Tu Fu's poetry.

Classical Chinese criticism is both intuitive and emulative— intuitive in appreciation and emulative in function. Intuitive criticism is hard to define, as it stresses "inspirational appreciation without verbal communication" 意會而不言傳. In *Ch'ang-lang Shih-hua* 滄浪詩話, in *K'un-hsüeh chi-wen* 困學記聞, the Zen concept of sudden enlightenment is adopted in criticizing literature.[42] Intuitive criticism illuminates the dichotomy of the internal and the external, the subjective and the objective, the form and the content, treating all as a unifying and unified whole. It is Buddhist, taking the permeating existence of Buddha-nature in all things to imply the "spirit" 神韻 embodied in literary works. It is also Taoist in analogizing the "unspeakable nature of esthetic beauty" with Lao-tzu's "The Tao that can be described is not the true Tao" 道可道非常道.

But, in a sense, intuitive criticism constitutes a paradox as a critical method. On the one hand, it attempts to fulfill a technical function which can and should be able to answer the queries posed by science (in the sense of analysis and precision); on the other hand, it also wishes to instill a sense of appreciation which complies with the demand of esthetics. Often, it fails both. Indeed, beauty is not to be measured by degrees of precision, nor to be analyzed by scientifically formulated standards. The esthetic sense of beauty of

> Twisting and turning, the mountain path seems to have
>   come to an end;
> Amidst the shading willows and the blooming flowers,
>   there appears another village.

山廻巒轉疑無路，柳暗花明又一村。

can only be appreciated by one who has that added richness in experiencing the truth of

> Tomorrow, and tomorrow, and tomorrow
> Creeps in this petty pace from day to day,

---

[42] See Kuo Shao-yü, *Chung-kuo shih te shen-yün, ke-tiao chi hsing-ling shuo* 中國詩的神韻、格調及性靈說 (Taipei: Hua-cheng, 1975). "詩家之景如藍田日暖，艮玉生煙，可望而不可即" (Tai Shu-lun 戴叔倫 in *K'un-hsüeh chi-wen*).

To the last syllable of recorded time,
And all our yesterdays have lighted fools
The way to dusty death.

This inherent contradiction in intuitive criticism may be resolved by personal experience of what esthetic theory inadequately defines as beauty. As Anthony Thorlby suggests, "this experience provides a kind of permanent touchstone as to what is, and what is not, worth knowing. Knowledge which is not inspired by, and does not inspire, any sense of personal participation may, with regard to the study of literature, justifiably be regarded as pointless."[43]

We make room for intuitive criticism on the ground that "truth must mean something more than factual knowledge." Analytical facts, with all their scientific verification, do not suggest eternal truth; without the "breath of new insight" they eventually become fossilized facts and beguile us from "a proper grasp of the subject."

The emulative concept of criticism reveals itself more in the moral philosophy of the Confucian school than in actual critical texts. The emphasis on the correspondence between one's conduct based on moral conviction and his writing or literary production as manifestation of this conviction is evidenced in Confucius' comment on his pupils. This again shows a desire to unify the idea and the expression, the content and the form, the internal and the external. A sense of kinship may be found between the Chinese emulative concept and the Aristotelian theory of magnetism and the Neo-platonic idea of emination. The literary concepts subsequently developed by western authors offer exemplary cases. The departure from this classical critical tradition in modern western critical concepts offers desirable inspiration to comparatists who are interested in the study of East-West comparative criticism. The horizon of Chinese literary criticism may be expanded by the inclusion of sociological, psychological, archetypal and other approaches. Similarly, western literary criticism may be enriched by the magic touch of intuitive appreciation.

[43]Thorlby, p. 76.

In our search for possibilities, we face an irreducible challenge. Like the medieval knights (if knights we be), we have been shown the Grail, veiled in the mystery of cultural peculiarities, philosophical biases, personal habits, methodological uncertainties and many other unpredictable elements; now we must unveil it.

TOWARDS A STRUCTURAL GENERIC THEORY
OF T'ANG *CH'UAN-CHI*

Han-liang Chang

In the traditional scholarship of Chinese fiction, the absence
of a rigorous narratology based on the structure and function of
language has partly resulted in a vague concept of narrative as
genre, and limited its classification to inadequate thematic taxonomy.[1] Ever since Li Fang's 李昉 compilation of *T'ai-p'ing kuang-
chi* 太平廣記 in the Sung Dynasty, scholars have attempted purely
empirical taxonomies on the basis of observed motif similarities
among the texts, which, however, usually remain unmotivated
raw material.

A classic example of imprecise narrative taxonomy is found
in the authorized *Ssu-k'u ch'uan-shu* 四庫全書 (The Imperial
Manuscript Library), where its editor Chi Yün 紀昀 loosely divides
Chinese fiction into three categories: (1) Miscellaneous Writings

---

[1] Some scholars might have reservations over my use of "narrative" and
"Narratology." Andrew H. Plaks, in an illuminating article on Chinese "narrative" theory, argues that one might "question the entire validity of maintaining the term "Narrative" as a generic or modal category for a diverse class of
literary materials in the first place" for the reason that there is no epic in
China. However, he admits that "running through both of these cultural
systems [Western and Chinese] we can still perceive the shared outlines of a
narrative category which includes materials that represent human experience
in terms of a more or less continuous succession of changing situation in
time." Indeed, both the "storytelling function" in the West and the function
of "transmission" of fact in China share the same function of relating discrete
events in a sequential order. See Andrew H. Plaks, "Issues in Chinese
Narrative Theory in the Perspective of the Western Tradition," *PTL: A
Journal for Descriptive Poetics and Theory of Literature*, No. 2 (1977), pp.
340, 342-343.

敘述雜事, (2) Records of Marvels 記錄異聞, and (3) Anecdotes 綴輯瑣語. One is baffled by the arbitrary distinctions made among "Miscellaneous Writings," "Marvels" and "Anecdotes," which might be grouped under one heading.[2]

An authoritative classification of T'ang short stories, which has exerted influence on later historians and critics, has been made by the Japanese scholar Shionoya On 鹽谷溫. In his *Chung-kuo wen-hsüeh kai-lun* 中國文學概論 [Lectures on Chinese Literature], Shionoya classifies T'ang fiction into four types: (1) unorthodox biographies, (2) stories of knights-errant, (3) love stories and (4) stories of the uncanny.[3] The reader can only be confused by Shionoya's multiple standards simultaneously used in classifying narrative. Apparently, he classifies narrative according to the matter or raw material that is dealt with. But one fails to see the common ground on which unorthodox historical facts, knights-errant, love and the uncanny can be regarded as one logical type of identical semantic function. A close examination clearly indicates the confusion of his criteria, which involve at least the following: (1) verisimilitude to reality (type 4), (2) verisimilitude to orthodox history as narrative (type 1), (3) the identity of heroes or characters (type 2) and (4) the relationship between characters, i.e. between men and women (type 3).

While the use of several thematic and formal systems of coordinates in genre description is possible and sometimes much-needed, a set of interlocking systems cannot be articulated unless each of them is functionally motivated. The classical distinction

---

[2]The classification is most misleading for under the heading of "Miscellaneous Writings" is listed *New Anecdotes of Social Talk*, but under the heading of "Anecdotes" are *Records of Strange Things, Accounts of Marvels,* and *The Yuyang Miscellany*, etc. See Chou Shu-jen 周樹人, *Chung-kuo hsiao-shuo shih-lüeh* 中國小說史略 (Shanghai, 1931; rpt. Taipei: Ming-lun, 1969), p. 20. English renderings of the terms are from Lu Hsun, *A Brief History of Chinese Fiction*, trans. Yang Hsien-yi and Gladys Yang (Peking, 1959; rpt. Westport, Conn.: Hyperion, 1973), p. 7.

[3]Shionoya On, *Chung-kuo wen-hsüeh kai-lun* 中國文學概論 (Lectures on Chinese Literature), trans. Sun Liang-kung 孫俍工 (Taipei: K'ai Ming, 1970), p. 354.

between the lyric, the narrative and the dramatic is made in terms of the manner as opposed to, but not as well as, the matter of presentation. Sir Philip Sidney's seemingly confused division of poets into "sundry more special denominations . . . the Heroic, Lyric, Tragic, Comic, Satiric, Iambic, Elegiac, Pastoral and certain others" conforms, however, to "the matter they deal with" *or* "the sorts of verses they liked best to write in."[4] Shionoya's problem is that his classification is not motivated, it is a random taxonomy instead of a codified genre classification.

The confusion of motif-index and genre classification is as old as the Sung Dynasty. In *chüan* 426-433 of *T'ai-p'ing kuang-chi* some eighty stories are listed under the general heading of "Tigers." We shall now submit four stories to comparison to see how a common motif is far from being adequate in putting them into one category. The stories are (1) *Chang Yü-chou* 張漁舟, (2) *Chung-ch'ao tzu* 中朝子, (3) *Chang Fung* 張逢 and (4) *Ts'ui T'ao* 崔韜, whose plots are summarized as follows.

Chang Yü-chou. Fisherman Chang Yü-chou lives in a cottage. One morning he wakes up to find a tiger in the cottage, with a thorn in its left paw. Chang picks out the thorn for the tiger. The latter "prostrates" itself to express gratitude. Later, to return the favor, the tiger catches boars, deer, and even brings "silk web" for Chang.

Chung-ch'ao tzu. A courtier's orphaned son is brought up by his uncle. The young man asks his uncle for his daughter's hand in marriage. The uncle promises Chung-ch'ao tzu, with the condition that the latter should first pass the civil service examination. Chung-ch'ao tzu makes a pledge with his uncle that he will come back and marry his cousin after three years. If he does not show up by then, his uncle is free to marry her to anyone else. Having passed the examination and made himself known in public service, the hero returns, but four years have lapsed since his departure. On his way back to his uncle's house, the hero is overtaken by night and finds shelter in a deserted house. Before dawn, he sees a tiger throw a young woman onto the doorstep. This woman is

---

[4]Philip Sidney, *An Apologie for Poetrie*, ed. Evelyn S. Shuckburgh (Cambridge: Cambridge Univ. Pr., 1915), p. 12. The spelling has been modernized.

no other than his cousin. The next morning, Chung-ch'ao tzu takes her back to her father. Amazed, his uncle says, "Since you did not show up in time, I have promised your cousin's hand to someone else. The wedding was supposed to be held yesterday evening. Shortly after mid-night, she was snatched away by a tiger. . . ." The hero's wish of marriage is finally fulfilled.

Chang Fung. One evening, Chang Fung takes a walk in the mountain area. Totally relaxed, he takes off his clothes and finds tumbling and rolling on the ground quite amusing. He gets up to find that he has changed into a tiger. Driven by hunger, he devours a certain Scriviner Cheng, then suddenly realizes what has happened. He recovers his clothes, tumbles and rolls on the ground again, and changes back to a man. Years later, at a banquet, he tells his strange experience to the other guests. One of them happens to be Cheng's son. To avenge his father's death, Cheng Junior tries to kill Chang but is prevented by the other guests.

Ts'ui T'ao. On a trip, Ts'ui T'ao stops over at Jen Yi Mansion. The caretaker advises him not to stay there for the night. Ts'ui ignores him. At midnight, he is awakened by a tiger. To his surprise, the tiger takes off its skin and becomes a beautiful woman. The woman explains that she has put on a tiger skin for the sake of convenience, and that she wants to be Ts'ui's wife. The next morning, Ts'ui throws the tiger skin into a well in the backyard and takes the woman away. Years later, with his wife and son, Ts'ui chances to pass by the same mansion and stays there. Finding the tiger skin still in the well, Tsui smiles at his wife and says, "The skin you wore is still here." His wife puts it on, becomes a tiger again, and devours Ts'ui and his son.

The four stories are all listed under the heading "Tigers." But a more detailed examination reveals that a similar motif is far from being adequate in attributing them to the same genre. *Chang Yü-chou* is apparently an animal fable. *Chung-ch'ao tzu* is a purely human adventure story, in which the tiger serves only as the function of an agent, or at most, Frye's "emblematic talisman."[5] As to the other two stories, they are stories of meta-

---

[5] Northrop Frye, *Fables of Identity* (New York: Harcourt, 1963), pp. 25-26.

morphosis, whose reference to reality is two-fold: natural and supernatural. Even these are different from each other in two ways. Firstly, *Chang Fung* is almost entirely free from moral lesson, whereas, *Ts'ui T'ao* has to do with the concept of taboo, its establishment and violation and the consequential punishment. Secondly, in *Chang Fung* there is only one leading character, while in *Ts'ui T'ao* two equally important characters are involved. This second difference makes *Chang Fung* a story of one-actant string and *Ts'ui T'ao* a two-actant string; consequently the patternings of motifemes in both stories diverge.[6]

Last but not least, the four stories require a recognition of different levels of verisimilitude on the part of the reader. The world in *Chung-ch'ao tzu* is one level, namely human reality. The world in *Chang Yü-chou* is very probably a supernatural one, characteristic of the fairytale. Although the grateful tiger is not portrayed as capable of human language, it behaves like a man. The problem of credibility related to the pragmatic aspect of the speech act does not exist. Credibility is lost in the moral lesson that dominates the story. As to the two stories of metamorphosis, they border on Todorov's fantastic and uncanny. Ts'ui T'ao's attitude towards the caretaker and his wife and his death, not to mention the interpreter's imposed message, renders the story an uncanny one or even an allegory. *Chang Fung* resists a natural or a supernatural interpretation and verges towards the fantastic. Therefore, judging from the reader's response and literary pragmatics, the four stories should be classified into at least three types, and cannot be fully explained by the unmotivated motif "tiger."

Similar examples are found everywhere in *T'ai-p'ing kuang-*

---

[6]Motifeme is Alan Dundes's term for Propp's function. Dundes argues that in a structural investigation of the folktale, the patterning of motifemes rather than the patterning of motifs becomes the object of the study. In Dolezel's model, motifeme is a proposition predicating act (Act) to actant (Ant): M = Ant + Act. The motifeme proposition assumes the form of a sentence. Examples of motifeme strings are: (a) one-actant strings: "The hero returned"; "The hero passed the test"; (b) two-actant strings: "The hero defeated the villain." See Lubomir Dolezel, "From Motifemes to Motifs," *Poetics*, No. 4 (1972), pp. 59-60.

chi. An irrelevant motif seems to be a sufficient reason for the compilers to put *Nan-k'e t'ai-sho chüan* 南柯太守傳 under the heading of "Insects" (*chüan* 475), *Jen-shih chuan* 任氏傳 under the heading of "Foxes" (*chüan* 452), and *Li Chang-wu chuan* 李章武傳 under the heading of "Ghosts" (*chüan* 346). Completely ignoring each writer's mode of articulation of the given motif, the compilers have made the anthology a "motif-index," not unlike that of Stith Thompson.

However, as Jonathan Culler argues, a genre is not simply an unmotivated taxonomic class, and a theory of genres "must attempt to explain what features are constitutive of functional categories which have governed the reading and writing of literature."[7] Since literature is an act of communication through the medium of language, a genre theory should take into account the language structure and function in the process of reading and writing. By focusing on the linguistic structure, a generic enquiry is concerned with the text itself, without reference to the creative act of the writer or the experience of the reader. By focusing on the linguistic function, it is concerned with the writer's creative experience and activity which give birth to the work and the reader's receptive experience and behavior.[8]

[7] Jonathan Culler, *Structuralist Poetics* (Ithaca and New York: Cornell Univ. Pr., 1975), p. 137.

[8] See Roman Ingarden, "Phenomenological Aesthetics: An Attempt at Defining Its Range," *The Journal of Aesthetics and Art History*, No. 33 (1975), pp. 256-260. Recently, Ingarden's dichotomy between subject and object has been challenged, especially by the reader-oriented critics, who hold that an object-focused approach is a fallacy. See, for example, Earl Miner, "The Objective Fallacy and the Real Existence of Literature," *PTL*, No. 1 (1976), pp. 1-31. Mention must also be made of the fact that linguistic communication is a form of social interaction and that literary communication is a subsystem of linguistic communication embedded in sociocultural contexts. Todorov's pragmatics can be appropriately described as the "internal pragmatics," as Professor Elrud Ibsch suggests. See, for example, Siegrid J. Schmidt, "On the Foundation and the Research Strategies of a Science of Literary Communication," *Poetics*, No. 7 (1973), pp. 7-35 and especially pp. 22-31. Todorov's ignoring the sociocultural context of genres as modes of literary communication has been pointed out by Maria Corti in her *An Introduction to Literary Semiotics*, trans. Margherite Bogat and Allen Mandelbaum (Bloomington: Indiana Univ. Pr., 1978), pp. 158-159.

In other words, a generic study can be either objective (object or text-oriented) or subjective (subject or writer and reader-oriented). With the objective approach, the critic holds that meaning is the result of logical operations defined in the text itself, and sets as his task investigating the language medium's phonological, syntactic and semantic aspects immanent and signified by the text. The subjective approach is concerned with the function of medium, i.e. the interactions that take place among sender, message and receiver in the act of communication. The critic investigates the writer's *écriture* or mode of writing, the function that the latter "gives his language, [the] set of institutional conventions within which the activity of writing can take place,"[9] or the reader's "ability to naturalize it [this mode of writing] and to recognize the common world which serves as point of reference."[10] Thus the subjective study includes writing and reading in the act of communication, both involving language as medium and a set of institutional conventions. A genre study then should be based on any of the three entities or on all three. These two approaches make contradictory claims and deny validity to each other, but they belong to sub-systems interactive within a broad literary system.

A recent tendency in the subject-focused approach shows that more attention has been paid to the receiver's perception rather than the sender's performance of the text. In his paper presented to the 1973 Bellagio Symposium on the problems of literary history, Wolfgang Iser points out:

> Once the time-honored opposition [between fiction and reality] has been replaced by the concept of communication, attention must be paid to the hitherto neglected recipient of the message. Now if the reader and the literary text are partners in a process of communication, and if what is communicated is to be of any value, our prime concern will no longer be the *meaning* of the text (the hobbyhorse ridden by the critics of

[9] Culler, p. 134.

[10] Culler, p. 135.

yore) but its *effect*. Herein lies the function of literature, and herein lies the justification for approaching
literature from a functionalist standpoint.[11]

The stress laid on the reader's response to the text, though
hermeneutic in outlook, is not alien to the structuralist. In fact,
both the structuralist and the hermeneutic critic assume that the
literary work is an event achieved by the interaction of author,
text and reader.[12] Roland Barthes, in his decoding of the Balzac
text "Sarrasine," defined the literary text as the readerly *(lisible)*
versus the writerly *(scriptible)*.[13] By turning a readerly text into
the writerly and making the reader an active producer instead of a
passive consumer of the text, Barthes implies the intersubjectivity
between reader and writer in the act of literary communication.
        The general accommodation of structuralism to hermeneutics
can be represented by Todorov's approach to the fantastic as
narrative genre. Defining a genre as "the codification of discursive
properties"[14] of a given society, Todorov argues that these properties can be examined in terms of the semantic, the syntactic, the
verbal and the pragmatic aspects of language.[15] The fantastic, for
example, is codified by the pragmatic aspect that governs the
reader's reconstruction of the fictional referent. In other words,
the genre can be understood by the attitudes and expectations
of the users of language (i.e. the author, the characters and the

[11]Wolfgang Iser, "The Reality of Fiction: A Functionalist Approach to
Literature," *New Literary History*, No. 7 (1975), pp. 8-9. The article is
Chapter III of his *The Act of Reading* (Baltimore: Johns Hopkins Univ. Pr.,
1978).

[12]Maria Corti points out that in our age "structuralist criticism, which
centers on study of the text understood as an object," is one of the three
forces "working to eclipse the figure of the author in favor of the addressee."
Corti, p. 36.

[13]Roland Barthes, *S/Z*, trans. Richard Miller (New York: Hill and Wang,
1974), p. 4.

[14]Tzvetan Todorov, "L'Origine des genres," in his *Les genres des discours*
(Paris: Seuil, 1978), p. 49.

[15]Todorov, *Les genres*, p. 50.

reader) as well as their levels of identification.[16] A sample study based on Todorov's generic model and focusing on the interaction of the aforesaid aspects will be given later in this paper.

While a subject-oriented study is primarily concerned with the function of language, an object-oriented study must have as its point of departure an understanding of the structure of language. Among the three aspects in descriptive linguistics as independent of the situation in which the utterance is made, the phonological aspect is the least relevant to narrative study, and is thus generally overlooked. In narrative study one does not bother discussing the phoni-tonal structure of the text unless its medium is verse or partly verse, as is the case of *Yü hsien-k'u* 遊仙窟 (A Journey to the Fairy Cavern). For the phonological aspect, one might substitute, in light of traditional semiotics, the pragmatic aspect. To decode the narrative text, the critic concerns himself with the syntax and the semantics, the relations between linguistic expressions and those between expressions and the objects to which they refer.[17]

The procedure of narrative analysis, as postulated by Roland Barthes, involves *découpage* and *agencement*.[18] It is a procedure consisting of two steps: firstly, decomposing the narrative discourse into constituent elements and classifying them into levels according to their functions; secondly, examining the laws that govern the distribution and integration of the elements and their articulation towards a hierarchy. William O. Henricks further suggests the decomposing strategies of normalization and summarization, by which "components not contributing to gross plot structure (e.g. meta-narration, scene-setting assertions, etc.) are excised."[19] Before dissecting the discourse, one should have a

[16]Todorov, *Les genres*, p. 57.

[17]In recent years, objections have been raised against the semiotic tripartition of syntax, semantics and pragmatics. See János S. Petöfi, "Semantics-Pragmatics-Text Theory," *PTL*, No. 2 (1977), pp. 119-149.

[18]Roland Barthes, *Essais critiques* (Paris: Seuil, 1964), p. 216.

[19]William O. Hendricks, *Essays on Semiolinguistics and Verbal Art* (The Hague and Paris: Mouton, 1973), p. 196.

basic understanding of the nature and function of its constituents and the way they join to form a functional and meaningful proposition. The underlying assumption is a homology between sentence and discourse. The narrative text, being an articulation of parts, is analogous to the sentence, an articulation of words. A narrative is, so to speak, a large sentence in the same way that a sentence is a small discourse.[20] Reduced to its basic structure, a narrative which represents a hero (or heroes) performing action or being acted upon resembles a sentence whose subject governs the predicate. The homology is thus $A:B::a:b$.[21]

A sentence is constituted by the subject and the predicate, the former being invariably noun phrase, the latter verb phrase. But a verb phrase can be either dynamic or static. In the sentence "He is happy" or "He is a student" the predicate is static in that it serves to qualify the subject. In the sentence "He left the room" the verb is dynamic in that it changes the subject's situation. Since narrative relates human action, the most important element of a narrative proposition—in addition to the agent that performs action—is therefore the verb that depicts actions. As Todorov puts it, "The description of a state is not sufficient for narrative, it requires the development of an action, that is, change, difference."[22] Hence follows the formalist-structuralist bifurcation of plot elements into variables versus constants (Propp), static versus dynamic motifs (Tomashevsky), statics versus dynamics (Reformatsky), qualifications versus functions (Greimas), indices versus functions (Barthes). These binary pairs are projected onto the narrative discourse according to two distinct principles: the metonymical (syntagmatic, diachronic) and the metaphorical (paradigmatic, synchronic). While the dynamics are horizontally distributed to constitute narrative syntagm, the statics are vertical-

[20] Roland Barthes, "Introduction à l'analyse structurale des récits," *Communications*, No. 8 (1966), p. 3.

[21] Roland Barthes, "To Write: An Intransitive Verb?" in *The Structuralist Controversy*, ed. Richard Macksey and Eugenio Donato (Baltimore: Johns Hopkins Univ. Pr., 1970), p. 136.

[22] Tzvetan Todorov, "Les deux principes du récit," in his *Les genres du discours*, p. 64.

ly integrated into semantic paradigms.[23] The structure can be articulated, as by Barthes, as a three-level hierarchy consisting of functions, actions and narration. The distributional functions combine to form sequences in terms of either triadic (Bremond) or homologic (Todorov) relationships and refer upward to the actions of a higher level; actions in turn are integrated into the highest level of narration. The three levels are thus connected by a procedure of progressive integration.[24] A total analysis of narrative discourse presupposes, then, a thorough examination of the relationships among the syntactic and semantic elements.

The generic classification of a narrative can be thus determined by the way dynamics and statics are articulated and the relative emphasis laid on them. A popular tale is characteristically distributional, in which dynamics are foregrounded; whereas a psychological story is strongly indicial when statics are given more importance. Chatman's analysis of Joyce's "Eveline," for example, shows that among the one hundred and twenty-seven sentences, only eight phrases or sentences are kernel units, the others being catalytic or indicial and moving towards the higher semantic level.[25] The reader's attention is thus attracted to the heroine's psychology in relation to the sociocultural context, rather than the turns of action. This makes "Eveline" a psychological and symbolic story par excellence. Todorov's distinction between the two types of narrative can be illustrated by the relative dominance of dynamics and statics.[26] The mythological narrative which shows the logic of succession and transformations is dominated by dynamics distributed on the horizontal level; the gnoseological

[23] As Propp puts it, "All *predicates* give the composition of tales; all *subjects, objects* and other parts of the sentence define the theme." Vladimir Propp, *Morphology of the Folktale*, trans. Laurence Scott (Austin and London: Univ. of Texas Pr., 1968), p. 113.

[24] See the articles of Barthes, Bremond and Todorov in *Communications*, No. 8 (1966).

[25] Seymour Chatman, "New Ways of Analyzing Narrative," *Language and Style*, 2 (1969), 3-36.

[26] Todorov, *Les genres*, p. 68.

narrative in which the reader's perception is more important than the action itself is dominated by statics in semantic paradigms. Likewise, Barthes's lower form of the readerly text shows the foregrounding of the linear codes, but can be redeemed by the other vertical codes and turned into a writerly text.

The proportion of dynamics to statics is a convenient characterizer of plot types. However, such a differentiation of plot elements runs the risk of oversimplifying the complicated macrouniverse of narrative. Barthes's reduction of the narrative into five codes seems to be a more rigorous strategy in decomposing the narrative discourse. The five codes or five areas of connotative meaning are systems of knowledge possessed by the reader of a literary community and realized in his linguistic experience of the text. The hermeneutic and the proairetic codes, both syntagmatic on the horizontal axis, join to form the plot. The semic and the symbolic codes consisting of semantic elements in vertical paradigms serve respectively the functions of characterization and defining themes. The referential code shows common knowledge shared by the writer and the reader that forms the cultural verisimilitude of the work.

For all its ingenuity, a number of reservations can be raised over Barthes's model. First, the five codes are assigned to the constituents of Balzac's "Sarrasine," without being tested on any other text. The critic has left out, among other things, the first person narrator's meta-discourse, which is dominant in the lyrical narrative such as Chateaubriand's *René*. He has not encoded and decoded, again, the scene-setting assertions but has confused the narrator's referential discourse with the characters' represented discourse. Barthes should have considered what Mixail Baxtin pointed out over half a century ago: if the character's speech appears in the author's speech, there are two speech centers, complexes, messages.[27] The two examples are clear indications of not only the inadequacy of the magic number *five* but also Barthes's not attempting at a hierarchy of codes. To indicate a

----

[27] Mixail Baxtin, "Discourse Typology in Prose," in *Readings in Russian Poetics*, trans. and ed. Ladislav Matejka and Krystyna Pomorska (Cambridge, Mass.: The M.I.T. Press, 1971), p. 177.

logical order among the five codes and order them in a hierarchy, we have to resort to his earlier model, as we have shown above.

To fill out what Barthes has missed, one is free to encode and decode a given narrative into more levels. Once the constituents are encoded, one may determine the *dominanta* of the work, "its preeminent component or group of components . . . which insures the unity of the work of literature as well as its 'perceptibility,' i.e. the fact that it is recognized as a literary phenomenon."[28] The dominant is found not only in the work of an individual writer, but also in the literary canon of a given genre viewed as a whole. For instance, if the dynamic proairetic and hermeneutic codes dominate and guarantee the integrity of the narrative structure, the work falls into the category of an adventure or detective story, as is the case of a traditional *récit*. If a narrative is dominated by the static semic code, it might be a psychological novel or *bildungsroman*, characteristic of the Romantic lyrical-narrative tradition. Take for example the well-known T'ang stories *Yu Hsien-ku* and *Chou-ch'in hsing-chi* 周秦行記. Despite a common archetypal motif of the fairy queen, the first story is dominated by the narrator's meta-discourse, i.e. his lyricism; but the second is dominated by the referential code in the narrow sense of verisimilitude to orthodox history (i.e. citations to history) rather than the broader sense of cultural verisimilitude and ideological stance shared by the writer and the reader.

Lyricism put aside, the poetic conventions invoked in the first story are no less culturally encoded than the allusions to Han and T'ang history in the second story. However, poetic conventions and historical allusions represent different facets of a cultural code and can be shared to a different extent by the reader for whom these codes have a coherent significance. Therefore, the stories can be regarded as belonging to distinct sub-genres since their perceptibility is determined by varied dominants of the referential code. Likewise, in the four stories of the tiger motif alluded to earlier in the paper, different codes are foregrounded

[28] Victor Erlich, *Russian Formalism* (The Hague and Paris: Mouton, 1969), p. 199. See also Roman Jakobson, "The Dominant," in *Readings in Russian Poetics*, pp. 82-83.

that govern the reader's construction of the texts and his recognition of their degrees of verisimilitude.

In Barthes's study of "Sarrasine" we notice the shift of
importance from the writer to the reader as well as the latter's
relation to the text. This is also true of Todorov's approach to
the fantastic, a genre closest to the majority of the T'ang fictional
corpus. To demonstrate how a work's generic classification can
be determined by its pragmatics in connection with the other
structural aspects, we shall now submit to analysis a story bearing
the tiger motif in terms of Todorov's model.

Todorov's approach to the fantastic and its neighboring
genres, the uncanny and the marvelous, is based on the examination of linguistic pragmatics, i.e. the attitude and expectation of
author, characters and reader as well as their levels of identification.[29] This pragmatic property of the discursive situation is precisely what distinguishes the fantastic from the uncanny and the
marvelous. In the fantastic the character who experiences the
unnatural event is hesitant about giving a natural or supernatural
explanation of the experience. If he chooses to give a rational
explanation, the story falls into the category of the uncanny; if
he chooses to accept as real what has happened in the story, the
latter falls into the category of the marvelous. The possibility of
a hesitation between the explanation of natural causes and that of
supernatural causes creates the fantastic effect.[30] Todorov, then,
proposes three conditions that fulfill the fantastic genre:

> First, the text must oblige the reader to consider the
> world of the characters as a world of living persons and

[29] Here the pragmatic aspect involves only the first stage of the reading
process, i.e. understanding achieved through a process of signification, but
not interpretation through the process of symbolization. The critic is concerned with the meaning signified by the text. Hence, Todorov's reconstruction is not to be confused with hermeneutics. See Todorov, "La lecture
comme construction," in his *Les genres*, pp. 90-94.

[30] Tzvetan Todorov, *The Fantastic: A Structural Approach to a Literary
Genre*, trans. Richard Howard (Ithaca and New York: Cornell Univ. Pr.,
1973), pp. 25-26.

to hesitate between a natural and a supernatural explanation of the events described. Second, this hesitation may also be experienced by a character; thus the
reader's role is so to speak entrusted to a character, and
at the same time hesitation is represented, it becomes
one of the themes of the work—in the case of naive
reading, the actual reader identifies himself with the
character. Third, the reader must adopt a certain attitude with regard to the text: he will reject allegorical
as well as 'poetic' interpretation.[31]

The fulfillment of the three conditions signifies the fantastic's
encoding of the pragmatic property, that is, "the triple identification between the implicit reader, the narrator, the witness-
character, which is concerned with an attitude of the represented
narrator."[32]

Todorov calls our attention to an emblematical sentence in
Potocki's *Manuscrit trouvé à Saragosse* that summarizes this
discursive situation: "J'en vins presque a croire que des démons
avaient, pour me tromper, animé des corps de pendus."[33] [I almost
come to believe that some demons had animated bodies of hanged
men in order to trick me.] The sentence shows the ambiguous
situation of the typical fantastic. The main clause suggests the
world governed by reason, but the subordinate clause designates
the supernatural event. The adverb "presque" (almost) shows the
modalization of uncertainty. Following this example, Todorov
postulates the formula of the fantastic narrative as:

'Je' (pronom dont on a expliqué la fonction) + verbe
d'attitude (tel que 'croire,' 'penser,' etc.) + modalisation
de ce verbe dans le sens de l'incertitude (modalisation
qui suit deux voies principales: le temps du verbe, qui
sera le passé, en permettant âinsi l'instauration d'une

---

[31] Todorov, *The Fantastic*, p. 33.

[32] Todorov, *Les genres*, p. 57.

[33] Todorov, *Les genres*, p. 57.

distance entre narrateur et personnage; les adverbes de manière comme 'presque,' 'peut-être,' 'sans doute,' etc.) + proposition subordonnée dècrivant un événement surnatural.[34]

('I' (pronoun that performs action) + verb of attitude (such as 'believe,' 'think,' etc.) + modalization of this verb showing uncertainly (modalization that follows two principle ways: the verb tense, which will be the past, thus allowing for the establishment of a distance between the narrator and the character; adverbs of manner like 'almost,' 'perhaps,' 'doubtlessly,' etc.) + subordinate proposition describing a supernatural event.)

Bearing in mind Todorov's description of the model, we may now examine and categorize the given story. The story which was written by an anonymous author and entitled *Nan-yang shih-jen* 南陽士人 (The Nan-yang Scholar), can be summarized as follows. A scholar took up his residence in Nan-yang Mountain. One day, he had a stroke of fever, which lasted for ten days and nobody knew of a cure. One moonlit summer night during his illness, he went into the yard to relax. Suddenly, he heard someone knocking at the door. He got up drowsily to see who it was, and heard the man behind the door tell him that he was fated to change into a tiger. Amazed, the scholar stretched out his hand to take the dispatch and found the dispatcher's hand to be a tiger's paw. The next morning, he told this to his family and felt the fever disappearing. Then he took a walk in the mountain. When he reached the river he saw in the reflection that he had really become a tiger. Once changed into a tiger, he left the human world, wandered in the mountain, and became a beast of prey. On one occasion he ate a mulberry picker and found the human flesh to be extremely tasty, just as he had previously been told. From then on, he began to haunt the mountain trails, trying to prey upon human beings. One day just before dark, he saw a woodcutter passing by and decided to seize him. All of a sudden, he heard someone call from

[34]Todorov, *Les genres*, p. 58.

behind, "Don't do it! Don't do it!" It was a white-haired old man, who the hero knew to be a god. Although the scholar now had the appearance of a tiger, he had not completely lost his human consciousness, and therefore implored the old man for help. The old man told him that he was fated to be transformed into a tiger, but this could be ameliorated if he spared the woodcutter. His last ordeal, the old man continued, was to eat a certain Judge Wang, who would pass by a certain city. The next day, the scholar did as he had been told. Having eaten Judge Wang, he found himself changed back to a human being. He made his way back home. The whole family were astonished because he had been away for seven or eight months. After eating rice and proper food again for a month, he recovered completely. Five or six years later, he took a trip to Ch'ang-ke County, where the prefect invited him to a banquet. During the banquet, conversation rambled to strange tales of metamorphosis, which the host did not believe at all. To convince him, the scholar told about his own experience. It was a strange coincidence that the host happened to be Judge Wang's son. To avenge his father's death, the host killed the scholar.

The first thing we notice about this story is the phenomenon common to the uncanny, the fantastic and the marvelous, that the hero undergoes two levels of worldly experience, one human, the other animal. In Louis Vax's words, his context of real life is brutally intruded upon by the mysterious experience of metamorphosis.[35] The scholar is confronted for no reason by the dispatcher who predicts his transformation. No rational explanation whatsoever is given by the narrator for the unnatural event. When the old man explains to the hero "You have been made a tiger by the gods," he is not rationalizing the event on behalf of the narrator, but trying, instead, to establish the supernatural frame of reference for the hero and the audience to follow. This supernatural explanation leads the character, if not the reader, to believe what has happened. Towards the end of the story, we find the hero recounting his experience to Judge Wang's son in order to refute the latter's incredulous attitude towards the phenomenon of metamorphosis; this ironically results in his death. The

[35] See Todorov, *The Fantastic*, p. 26.

establishment of the supernatural framework excludes the possibility of attributing the story to the uncanny, and brings it near the marvelous.

Be that as it may, one might argue that the hero is subject to an illusory state of mind during his metamorphosis which can be *interpreted* as a dream process or a product of his imagination. Suppose this were true, it would be the reader's, not the narrator's, meta-discourse. Although the hero, during his transformation, is sometimes characterized as being in some way mentally deranged, he does not seem to question the "reason behind" his change. We can cite some examples in accordance with the sequential development of the text to see if the hero demands any explanation and if the author intrudes to rationalize.

The narrative opens with the situation when the hero "suddenly heard a knocking at the door" which "was not heard by the other members of his family. . . . He listened to it attentively and suddenly felt he was in a dream. Drowsily, he rose without full consciousness to see who it was." Here marks the beginning of the hero's process of transformation. The process draws to its close when the hero, "having eaten Judge Wang, became a little more conscious and remembered his way back home." Once home, he "spoke incoherently as if he were drunk." Although the above quotations, which cover the beginning and end of the metamorphosis, suggest that the hero is subject to a state of dreaminess, or even insanity, their function is only descriptive and indicial. They are symptoms of the metamorphosis; not a meta-discourse of the narrative discourse or a rationalization of the metamorphosis. As a matter of fact, there is no textual evidence whatever to show that the event is susceptible of rational explanation; nor is the implicit reader (if any) led to judge whether it is real or unreal. One must distinguish between the author's intention and the reader's interpretation. A Lévi-Straussian or Freudian interpretation is, after all, the reader's, not the author's, meta-discourse. Such being the case, we cannot attribute the story to the category of the uncanny.

Once the possibility of the uncanny is ruled out, two neighboring genres are left for us to choose: the marvelous and the fantastic, before we can suggest a third type outside of Todorov's categories. We notice in the course of narration the characters' acceptance of the supernatural. There are at least three characters who accept it: the hero himself, the son of Judge Wang, and the law man (to a minor extent). But can we readily regard the story as the marvelous simply because of the characters' final acceptance of the supernatural or unnatural? The question *seems* difficult to answer since there is no clearcut frontier between the fantastic and the marvelous. For the fantastic, "by the very fact that it remains unexplained, unrationalized, suggests the existence of the supernatural."[36] However, as far as the pragmatic aspect of genre is concerned, "the *fantastic* refers to an ambiguous perception shared by the reader and one of the characters,"[37] whereas, "in the case of the marvelous, supernatural elements provoke no particular reaction either in the characters or in the implicit reader. It is not an attitude towards the events described which characterizes the marvelous, but the nature of these events."[38]

We shall now probe into the character's perception. All the textual details clearly indicate that the author of *Nan-yang shih-jen* is not so much concerned with the mystery itself as with the hero's perception of it. The passages quoted above are intended to show his state of mind, almost to the extent of suggesting the hero's *possible* insanity and thus bringing the story near the uncanny. A closer examination would bear out the author's emphasis on the hero's perception over his physical experience. Following the sequence of action we can single out all the verbs of aspect and modality governed by the subject hero, starting from his encounter with the dispatcher. All the words showing perception and modality are in italics.

1. Suddenly, he *heard* a knocking at the door.
2. He *listened* to it and suddenly *felt* as if he was in a dream.
3. *Drowsily* and *unconsciously*, he *rose to see* who it was.
4. The man *was surprised* and *unconsciously* stretched out

[36] Todorov, *The Fantastic*, p. 52.

[37] Todorov, *The Fantastic*, p. 46.

[38] Todorov, *The Fantastic*, p. 54.

      his hand to receive it.

5. He *saw* the dispatcher's hand was a tiger's paw.

6. He unsealed the dispatch and *looked* at it.

7. He *felt* much disgusted.

8. The next morning, he vaguely *remembered* this experience.

9. He reached for the dispatch and *found* it was still there.

10. He *felt* all the more *surprised* but *seemed to find* his fever cured.

11. Suddenly, he *thought* of taking a walk outdoors.

12. Suddenly, through the reflection of water, he *saw* his head had become that of a tiger.

13. He *looked* further at his hands and feet and *found* they were distinctly those of a tiger.

14. He *thought* if he went back home like this, his wife and children would be scared.

15. *Harboring anger* and *disgrace*, he went along the trail up into the mountain.

16. Two days later, he *felt* hungry.

17. He *saw* some tadpoles.

18. He *remembered* that he *had heard* that tigers eat mud.

19. He *thought* them delicious.

20. He *saw* a hare.

21. He *felt* his body getting *lighter* and *stronger*.

22. He had acquired *a mind to kill*.

23. He *searched* from the trees above and *saw* a mulberry-picker.

24. He *watched* her from the grass and *thought*, "I *heard* that all tigers eat human beings."

25. He *thought* human flesh was really *delicious*.

26. Suddenly, he *heard* someone shouting from behind.

27. Alarmed, he *saw* a hoary-headed old man and *knew* he was a god.

28. Though his body was changed, *his heart was* still *homeward bound*.

29. He *did not see* the old man any more.

30. Suddenly, he *heard* the ringing of bells.

31. He *heard* a human voice from the sky.

32. Having *heard* this, the tiger waited along the road.
33. He *heard* the noises of men and horses.
34. He *saw* a man in red clothes . . . .
35. Having eaten Judge Wang, he *became* a little more *conscious* and *remembered* his way back home.
36. He went to the stream again and *found* he had changed back to a man.

The above quotations, rendered as literal assimilations rather than artistic translations, cover the major part of the hero's adventure of change. We find all the verb phrases verge towards noun phrases, serving almost invariably a descriptive or expository function instead of a narrative one. The narrative propositions which link up those descriptive ones are limited in number. One may venture to say that the narrative syntagm is made up largely by indices assimilating to functions, and the narrative itself, with a focus on the character's perception rather than action, is an indicial narrative rather than a functional one; a gnoseological narrative rather than a mythological one.

However, we also notice from the above quotations that although emphasis is put on the hero's perception of his change, his perception is not ambiguous. Our hero is never confronted, as Gregor Samsa is in the opening scene of Kafka's *The Metamorphsis*, with the dilemma of realness or unrealness, believing or not believing. He is indignant and feels disgraced, but never doubts. The old man's remark explains why he is changed; it does not confirm or verify his change. Therefore, whether the hero believes or not is beside the point. This makes us hesitate when we try to "classify" (a word which Todorov would not use) the present story as the fantastic.

The difficulty of classification is raised because of the problem of identification between character and reader, an essential one in the narrative's pragmatic aspect. Such an identification is a result of the attitude of the represented narrator, or in terms of Anglo-American criticism, the author's choice of point of view. Earlier in this paper we mentioned Todorov's three conditions that fulfill the fantastic, one of which is the hesitant experience shared by the reader and one of the characters, preferably the represented witness-character-as-narrator. If the narrator is represented or dramatized, not necessarily as the hero, and more often than not, a minor character one like Marlow in Joseph Conrad's *Heart of Darkness*, the reader tends to identify himself with the narrator, sharing his belief or disbelief.[39] Furthermore, the represented narrator might not be speaking the truth, as is the case of the narrator in Faulkner's "A Rose for Emily," hence the reader's doubt and hesitation. If a supernatural event is told not by a represented narrator but by an omniscient one hidden behind the curtain, the reader is left with no other choice but to believe him. In other words, in a pure fantastic narrative, "emphasis is put on the fact that we are concerned with the discourse of a character rather than with a discourse of the author."[40] That is why the narrator in the fantastic is almost invariably the first person "I," the first necessary ingredient of Todorov's formula.

This is evidently not the case of *Nan-yang shih-jen*. The narrator is the non-represented, omniscient third person. We are listening to the discourse of the author though he does not intrude, as Li Kung-tso 李公佐 in *Nan-k'e t'ai-sho chuan*, to give meta-discourse so as to render the story uncanny. There is no witness-character or represented narrator, whose discourse we might listen to with doubt. Todorov distinguishes between the narrator's and the character's discourses as follows:

> The represented (or 'dramatized') narrator is suitable to the fantastic, for he facilitates the necessary identification of the reader with the character. This narrator's discourse has an ambiguous status. . . . As the narrator's, the discourse lies outside the test of truth; as the character's, it must pass this test.[41]

As a matter of fact, there is only one important character: the hero himself, with whom the reader might otherwise identify

[39] Todorov, *The Fantastic*, p. 83.

[40] Todorov, *The Fantastic*, p. 86.

[41] Todorov, *The Fantastic*, p. 86.

himself if the former told his own story, i.e. from the first person specific point of view. Under this circumstance, the reader is obliged to "believe" what has happened to the hero, as Judge Wang's son does, though perhaps too hastily. Since the hero never doubts, nor can the reader in any way doubt.

To the extent that the narrator is not represented as the first person "I." there are hardly verbs of attitude such as "almost," "perhaps," to show the narrator's uncertainty which can be shared by the reader. If we examine in detail the quotations of the text previously numbered according to sequential development, we find only three sentences using verbs of attitude: i.e. 11, 14 and 24. The verb "thought" in sentence 11 shows the character's desire rather than attitude; that in 14 and 24 shows respectively his concern about his family and his knowledge of the tiger's carnivorous nature. They are not real verbs of attitude as the one used in the context of "I *think* I have become a tiger."

Finally, since the ambiguous vision is not presented through the character's reaction, the corresponding syntactic structure is not one consisting of a main clause describing his attitude of uncertainty and a subordinate clause describing the supernatural event. There is hardly a sentence like "I almost came to believe that some demons had animated bodies of hanged men in order to trick me." Instead, there are more sentences like "He saw the dispatcher's hand was a tiger's paw" (5), ". . . he saw his head had become that of a tiger" (12), and "He felt much disgusted" (7), etc. Similar sentences abound in the narration of the hero's un-natural adventure. Although they function to describe his perception, the relation between the main clause and the subordinate clause, between verbs of attitude and their complements or objects, does not show that the latter (subordinate clauses or objects) are to modify or to revise the former (main clause or subject) to the extent of awakening doubt. Even after normalization, complex structure suggesting the incompatibility of two worlds is not dominant, if there is any. As has been said earlier, verbs of aspect or attitude are intended to form the gnoseological structure, but not of necessity an ambiguous gnoseology. As the case is, the hero believes what he experiences, not unlike the one in the marvelous.

All these point up to one thing: the verbal, semantic and syntactic details do not completely meet the requirements of the fantastic. In spite of the fact that the character's perception of the supernatural is emphasized, which renders the story more fantastic than marvelous, other elements, such as the use of non-represented, third-person omniscient narrator, render the story more marvelous than fantastic. As Todorov remarks, "If a supernatural event were reported to us by such a narrator, we should immediately be in the marvelous."[42]

The above observations oblige us to draw the conclusion that the story is fantastic-marvelous, a transitory sub-genre in Todorov's scheme. Referring to Todorov's famous distinction between two types of narrative, we find the story a combination of the gnoseological and the mythological, with the former dominating. With the given story, we cannot take the two apart. The story not only *describes* the hero's state of equilibrium or disequilibrium in terms of statics, but also *narrates* the transition from one state to the other in terms of dynamics.[43] It goes without saying that the indicial narrative cannot narrate for its own right, unless it has turned out to be a functional narrative, with statics serving as dynamics.

The above analysis of *Nan-yang shih-jen* is focused on the interactions among the syntactic, verbal and pragmatic aspects, aiming to demonstrate how the story's generic status can be defined by the reader's construction of some textual features in relation to reality. A syntagmatic and semantic analysis has been engaged elsewhere and will not be rehearsed here.[44] A few re-

---

[42]Todorov, *The Fantastic*, p. 83.

[43]Todorov, *The Fantastic*, pp. 163-164. For the concept of cycle and equilibrium, see also Tzvetan Todorov, *The Poetics of Prose*, trans. Richard Howard (Ithaca and New York: Cornell Univ. Pr., 1977), p. 111.

[44]Chang Han-liang 張漢良, *T'ang ch'uan-ch'i Nan-yang shih-jen te chieh-kou fen-hsi* 唐傳奇南陽士人的結構分析 (A Structural Analysis of T'ang Story Nan-yang Scholar), *Chung Wai Literary Monthly*, 7, No. 6 (November 1978), 4-38. The story's syntagmatic pattern observes the Bremondian triadic logic that subjects all the functional and sequential units to a dialectic relationship, thus revealing the hero's process of degradation until death. Lévi-Strauss's structural model of myth brings to light the message: while man is supposed

marks, however, have to be made concerning the present study in particular and the structural study of T'ang narrative in general. Firstly, instead of confronting the problem of the reader from the historical point of view, one is justified in choosing the structural point of view. This implied reader's character and historical situation are not predetermined. As Iser puts it, "He embodies all those predispositions necessary for a literary work to exercise its effect—predispositions laid down, not by an empirical outside reality, but by the text itself."[45] Secondly, to analyze the "structuration" rather than the "structure" of T'ang narrative, one is obliged to put all the texts together to work towards a structural model of system that can function for the genre as a whole.[46] Our application of a western generic model to the T'ang short story has inevitably put two literary systems in confrontation and raised some hermeneutic problems yet to be solved.

to live on cooked (vegetable) food, the tiger lives on raw (animal) food; man kills when he is changed into an animal of prey; both hunting and killing are Buddhist taboos.

[45] Iser, *The Act of Reading*, p. 34.

[46] Julia Kristeva, *Le texte du roman* (The Hague and Paris: Mouton, 1970), p. 67.

THE LINGUISTIC AND MYTHICAL STRUCTURE
OF *HSING* AS A COMBINATIONAL MODEL

Ying-hsiung Chou

Confucius views *Shih ching*—and by extension poetry in general—in a pragmatic light:

Poetry can uplift. It can enhance self-contemplation. It can cultivate sociability. It can regulate resentment. From it one learns the immediate duty of serving one's father as well as the remoter one of serving one's prince. From it one learns extensively the names of birds, beasts and plants.[1]

詩可以興，可以觀，可以羣，可以怨，邇之事父，遠之事君，
多識於鳥獸草木之名。 （《論語》·「陽貨」）

Its first function, "*hsing*" (uplift), must be seen in two ways. In a social sense, it refers to the psychologically stimulating effect of poetry in one's education process, or to the coordinating function of poetic refrains in work songs.[2] Conventionally, however, *hsing* is interpreted as a rhetorical device, with one term followed by another term. K'ung An-kuo 孔安國, for instance, annotates *hsing*

---

[1] My translation, based mainly on James Legge. See *The Chinese Classics* (Hong Kong: Hong Kong Univ. Pr., 1970), vol. I, 323. The term "uplift" was first used by Chen Shih-hsiang. See *Chen Shih-hsiang wen-ts'un* 陳世驤 文存 (Taipei: Chih-wen, 1972), p. 240.

[2] Chen Shih-hsiang sees *hsing* as originally the songs sung collectively by workers lifting objects in their work. See *Chen Shih-hsiang wen-ts'un*, pp. 219-66. Also see Kuo Shao-yü 郭紹虞, "Liu-i shuo k'ao-pien" 六義說考辨, *Chung-hua wen-shih lun-ts'ung* 中華文史論叢 (Shanghai: Shanghai Ku-chi, 1978), VII, 207-38.

here as "using examples to create analogies" 引譬連類, which somewhat corresponds to a popular concept in China of poetry as "expressing oneself with the help of external objects" 托物言志. In both cases, social or rhetorical, *hsing* is conceived of as an indirect method of expression, different to a great extent from the direct presentation of discursive prose. It is, moreover, unique as a method of artistic expression in a wide variety of literary genres and possibly in other arts as well. The following pages are aimed at showing how *hsing* operates in ancient Chinese folk poems from *Shih ching* to the *yüeh-fu* ballads before T'ang, in the light of the combinational model of Roman Jakobson. Our purpose is to show how the surface structural, linguistic connections between the combined elements are suppressed. Yet through cultural and mythical readings the missing connections can be reconstructed. The study demonstrates, at the same time, the validity as well as the limitations of Jakobson's approach.

I

"The Great Preface" 詩大序 has this to say about the ingredients of poetry: "There are six elements in poetry: first, *feng*; second, *fu*; third, *pi*; fourth, *hsing*; fifth, *ya*; and sixth, *sung*" 詩有六義焉：一曰風、二曰賦、三曰比、四曰興、五曰雅、六曰頌. As we all know, *feng, ya* and *sung* refer generically to the three divisions of *Shih ching* on the basis of the different social origins of these 300-plus poems. *Fu, pi* and *hsing*, on the other hand, have to do with the different methods of composition. Traditional interpretations of these methods have been based mainly on *Shih ching*, without taking into consideration other folk songs from which *hsing* presumably originated, let alone elitist poetry or other media.[3] Such a practice clearly leaves something to be desired. The emphasis in the past has been placed, moreover, on the classificatory issue, and scholars ever since "The Great Preface" have been

---

[3] Evaluations have also been made of elitist poetry in terms of *pi* and *hsing*; yet the two terms are often used interchangeably, resulting more often in confusion. At times when *hsing* is used by itself, it denotes a poetic ideal of the so-called *ching chieh* 境界 (created world), without specific linguistic explanations being provided.

concerned mainly with the problem as to whether this or that poem goes rightfully under *fu, pi* or *hsing*. The true rhetorical nature of the three figures have not really been dealt with in depth.

To clarify the situation, some modern linguistic concepts will be used to describe not only the three static categories, but also the dynamic relationships among them. But first a much simplified description of the difference between the poetic language and the natural language is in order before one could see that *fu* is basically prose language and that it differs essentially from *pi* and *hsing*, around which the mysteries have centered over the centuries.

In a communicative event, ordinary and poetic alike, the following elements are involved: the addresser, the addressee, the message, the context (reference), the contact and the code. In very simple terms, the primary difference between prose and poetry lies in their respective emphases on the context and the message. In other words, whereas in prose one is more concerned with the referential meaning behind speech, in poetry one is more interested in the message, the way one's language is phrased.[4] Poetry, that is to say, is one of the cases in which language "celebrates" itself, as Roland Barthes puts it.

Fu, on the other hand, belongs basically to the prose language. K'ung Ying-ta 孔穎達 defines *fu* in a didactic vein as blunt political advice:

> *Fu* means presentations, straightforward presentations of the good and the evil in the present government's policies.
>
> 賦之言舖，直舖陳今之政教善惡。 （《毛詩正義》‧卷一之一）

Liu Hsieh 劉勰, in his *The Literary Mind and the Carving of Dragons* 文心雕龍, defines *fu* in a slightly more lyrical tone:

[4] Roman Jakobson, "Closing Statement: Linguistics and Poetics," *Style in Language*, ed. Thomas A. Sebeok (Cambridge, Mass: M.I.T. Pr., 1960), pp. 353-58.

> *Fu* means to arrange; it signifies arrangements of the
> patterns that give form to literature, and expresses the
> feelings that conform to objective things.[5]

賦者，鋪也，鋪采摛文，體物寫志也。 （「詮賦」）

Thus *fu* is capable of both describing the external world and
portraying the inner recess of the human mind. This can be accomplished through, for example, the devices of addition, ellipsis
and parallelism.[6]

Despite the fact that *fu* is not altogether different in kind
from prose, it is nonetheless artistic language, and hence is capable
of heart-felt lyricism, elaborate descriptions and detailed narra-
tions. It serves, moreover, as the basic substance of poetic language, even as *pi* and *hsing* are manipulated to the utmost extent to
foreground one effect or another. Specifically speaking, *pi*, which
I treat as primarily a metaphoric operation, is a rhetoric figure
whose internal relationship exists *in absentia*, with one term
present and the other absent. So far as their formats on the surface
level are concerned, *pi* and *fu* cannot really be distinguished. In
the same manner, it must be admitted that *hsing*, which I treat as
primarily a metonymical operation, is a relationship *in presentia*,
and it is this relationship that is of significance. But again on the
surface level, it is similar to *fu* in its elliptical operation—the only
difference being that with *hsing* the omitted element usually exists
beyond the bound of the sentence and needs to be reconstructed
on a cultural-mythical, rather than strictly linguistic, level.

II

While *fu* is a figure of speech sharing basically the same
features as ordinary prose, *pi* and *hsing* are figures of thought
which involve the transference of meaning. It is, however, no easy

[5]Translated by Vincent Yu-Chung Shih, *The Literary Mind and the
Craving of Dragons* (N.Y., 1959; rpt. Taipei: Chung-hwa, [new preface]
1970), p. 62.

[6]*Princeton Encyclopedia of Poetry and Poetics* (Princeton: Princeton
Univ. Pr., 1965), pp. 273-74.

task to distinguish between the latter two figures. Su Ch'eh 蘇轍 cautions precisely against this when he says: "In one's study of poetry, one must first of all not confuse *hsing* with *pi*; nor must one force one's interpretations" 欲觀於詩，必先知乎興之不可與比同，而無強爲說（《詩論》）.

 Pi is clearly a metaphoric operation which involves, in I. A. Richards' terms, tenor and vehicle, replacing, complementing and even competing against, each other. It is, as a result, a much more indirect and subtle mode of expression than *fu*. In line with the didactic tradition, K'ung Yin-ta defines *pi* as a subtle method of expressing oneself: "Seeing the wrongs in the government, one dares not expose them explicitly and thus resorts to analogies by using *pi*" 比，見今之失，不敢斥言，取比類以言之（《毛詩正義》·卷一之一）. To give a very simple example from the folk tradition, "Hsien-ti ch'u Ching-tu t'ung-yao" 獻帝初京都童謠（《古謠諺》卷六）expresses people's discontentment with a warlord, notorious for his cruelty and his total lack of loyalty:

> A thousand *li* of grass,
> Green beyond green.
> Ten days' forecast:
> Death will be seen.

千里草，何青青，十日卜，不得生。

At first look, the poem is a perfectly harmless ditty. Its true message is, nonetheless, hidden metaphorically behind a series of word games. We are told in the "Wu-hsing chih" 五行志 of *Hou Han shu* 後漢書（卷二三）that characters in lines 1 and 3 are treated as radicals. Thus "ch'ien li ts'ao" are combined into the character "tung" 董 and "shih jih p'u" into "cho" 卓, respectively the warlord's family and first names. There is, however, something unusual in the procedure. Ordinarily, radicals are assembled vertically downward from the top. In this particular case the procedure is reversed, by going upward from the bottom. The violation against the usual orthographic procedure suggests that, in both his name and his deed, Tung Cho acts against nature. Therefore, notwithstanding his miraculous rise like grass enjoying its luxuriant growth, he is doomed to a quick demise. *Pi* is employed in a rather devious way here to enable one to voice one's moral indictment by indirectly singing an innocent song about grass. We might also note by saying that the supernatural power vested in the song, as often is the case with children's songs in Han, seems to come from this riddling process in which the real and the unreal go through a reversal process.

There is in traditional scholarship no shortage of information on this figure. In fact, one needs only to look through a *lei shu* 類書 (a kind of encyclopedia) to see that practically all objects and names with their metaphoric representations are listed, presumably for the easy reference of students and practioners of poetry (a convenience which cannot be provided in the area of *hsing*). Of course, this does not mean that *pi* is used merely as a rhetorical convenience. Quite the contrary, *pi* is actually capable of expressing subtle nuances and, in some cases, even the so-called extra-verbal meaning (言外意). This is especially true in the couplet structure of Chinese poetry where two metaphors are combined to create a totally different effect. In other words, when the metaphoric operations are combined with the metonymic operations, meaning beyond the sheer linguistic level can be generated. The two contiguous lines by Ma Chai 馬載, as recorded in *Leng-tsai yeh-hua* 冷齋夜話, for instance, paint a picture which is at the same time real and unreal:

> The twilight sun setting beyond the tall trees;
> The distant fire entering the autumn mountain.

> 微陽下喬木，遠燒入秋山。 （「落日悵望」）

The exact parallelism here demands that the two lines be read together, as contrasting or similar units. In one's syntagmatic reading process, the sun in line 1 is substituted by the fire in line 2; and yet because of the similarity of the two images they are not intended to be purely metaphorical. In our mind's eye, the two images are juxtaposed against each other and are combined to create a visual picture with a strong sense of uncertainty. We shall come back to the combinational effect of the metaphoric operation later in our discussion of *hsing*.

III

Despite the fact that *hsing* seems to defy any effort to define it, one thing is clear: it has invariably been treated as the exact opposite of *pi*. In the didactic tradition again, K'ung Ying-ta defines *hsing* as the opposite of *pi* in a rather arbitrary way: "Seeing the merits in the government, one does not want to be flattering and thus lists all the good deeds as encouragement" 興，見今之美，嫌於媚諛，取善事以勸之 （《毛詩正義》·卷一之一）. A demarcation like his—*pi* for bad deeds and *hsing* for good deeds—is not satisfactory. What we need are definitions which are linguistically accountable and culturally relevant. Chu Hsi's 朱熹 formulation of *hsing* is, for instance, more concrete on the one hand and more flexible on the other. One could thus proceed from the linguistic description and move on to an explanation of the cultural patterns behind *hsing*. Chu's account is much more lucid and verifiable: "In *hsing*, one starts by mentioning something else which serves to provoke what one wants to sing about" 興者，先言他物，以引起所詠之詞也（《詩集傳》）. *Hsing*, in other words, is seen as preceding syntagmatically whatever follows. Semantically, it also refers to external objects as prelude before one enters the essentially lyrical core of the poem. Perceptive as his account is, it nevertheless leaves two major questions unanswered: how does one linguistic element manage to give rise to another; and how does something which is outside of the poet serve as prelude to the main text in which one expresses oneself? What exactly are the relationships between the two parts of the discourse?

Before taking up questions of this type, it is useful to put *hsing* into its historical perspective. As we are all aware, *hsing* exists mainly in *Shih ching* and *yüeh-fu* poems before the sixth century A.D. Strictly speaking, its popularity has been on a downward path since Han. Huang K'an's 黃侃 annotation on Liu Hsieh's didactic account of the decline of *hsing*—"The Han dynasty may have prospered generally, but the poets were weak. The principle of remonstrance was forgotten, and the meaning of *hsing* lost"[7] 炎漢雖盛，而辭人夸毗，詩刺道喪，故興義銷亡——makes pretty good historical sense. He says:

> Poets seldom employ *hsing* after the Han dynasty, the reason being that poetry has since declined. Yet it is also due to the fact that literature communicates by providing pleasure and if the reader cannot get the message, the impact on him is not likely to be obvious. It is only natural that *pi* is employed while *hsing* is forgotten.
>
> 自漢以來，詞人鮮用興義，固緣詩道下衰，亦由文詞之作，趣以喻人，苟覽者恍惚難明，則感動之功不顯，用比忘興，勢使之然。（《文心雕龍札記》‧「比興」）

What, one might ask, is the cause behind the difficulty in grasping the meaning conveyed through a rhetorical figure whose fundamental function is, after all, communication? To put it in a slightly different way, is the meaning of *hsing* in any way different from other kinds of meaning? And if so, how is its meaning created, syntagmatically or paradigmatically, or both, and in what order?

A study of *hsing* may well start with its linguistic aspect. To begin with, language—and by extension literature which is a kind of language—is a system in which rules dictate as to how linguistic elements are selected from, say, the preverbal *Gestalt*, and combined into units that bear meaning. These two primary functions of selection (substitution) and combination (contiguity) are present on almost all linguistic levels. According to Roman Jakobson, they are in fact present in other cultural activities, such as literature, film, painting, etc.[8] Though the two functions are inseparable and neither one is able to operate on its own without the other, it is, however, quite possible to put emphasis on one function or the other, depending on different historical periods, cultural patterns, personal styles, etc. Thus, for instance,

[7] See Shih, pp. 277-78.

[8] Roman Jakobson and Morris Halle, *Fundamentals of Language* (The Hague: Mouton, 1956), pp. 77-78.

while Romantic poetry stresses selection, "realist" novels rely
heavily on combination; and while Surrealism foregrounds selection, Cubism emphasizes combination. If these functions are as
pervasive and significant in the overall cultural phenomena as
Jakobson claims them to be, might it not be possible that certain
basic cultural concepts in China can also be re-examined in this
two-fold division? And, specifically, while we often hear of
Chinese literature being described as fundamentally lyrical,[9] what
is the possibility of scrutinizing this tradition—or the beginning
of this tradition, in our case—on technical and cultural levels?

   To begin with the technical-linguistic level, the distinction
of a contemporary critic serves as a convenient point of departure
in our discussion. According to Wang Ching-chih 王靜芝, pi is
"analogous association" [類似的聯想][10] which can very well be
seen as a metaphoric operation in which one term substitutes for
a similar term. *The Literary Mind and the Carving of Dragons* also
defines pi in more or less the same vein:

> What do we really mean by pi? A description of things
> used to stand for ideas, and the use of figures of speech
> to intimate the nature of certain facts.

   且何謂為比？蓋寫物以附意，颺言以切事者也。　（「比興」）

Examples of this kind are not lacking, and Liu Hsieh goes on to
give some well-known pi images from the classics:

> Thus gold and pewter are used to stand for illustrious
> virtue, a jade tally signifies an outstanding man, a
> caterpillar means education, cicadas and grasshoppers
> denote howling and shouting, washing clothes sym-

[9]Especially Chen Shih-hsiang, "On Chinese Lyrical Tradition," *Tamkang Review*, 2, No. 2 & 3, No. 1 (October 1971-April 1972), 17-24. Also see Kao Yu-kung 高友工, "Wen-shüeh yen-chiu ti mei-shüeh wen-t'i" 文學研究的美學問題, *Chung-wai wen-hsüeh* 中外文學, 7, No. 12 (May 1979), 44-50.

[10]Wang Ching-chih, *Shih Ching t'ung-shih* 詩經通釋 (Taipei: Fu-jen, 1968), as quoted in Pei P'u-hsien 裴普賢 *Shih Ching yen-tu chih-tao* 詩經研讀指導 (Taipei: Tung-ta, 1977), p. 300.

bolizes sadness of heart, and the rolling up of a mat is
used as a figure for firmness of will: these illustrate the
meaning of the *pi*.[11]

故金錫以喻明德，珪璋以譬秀民，螟蛉以類敎誨，蜩螗以寫呼
號，澣衣以擬心憂，席卷以方志固，凡斯切象，皆比義也。
(「比興」)

In a sense, *pi* is a metaphoric operation in which one term substitutes for another. Yet one must also note by saying that aside
from creating a sense of physical immediacy with the use of metaphors, *pi* is characterized by two facts. It is primarily used to yoke
together the internal and the external worlds, an act which finds
its philosophical justifications in the Chinese concept of the in-
distinctness between subject and object (主客不分). Second, in the
highly refined Regulated Verse 律詩, parallelism reigns supreme.
Semantically the coupling device (對仗) aligns the two contiguous
lines (聯) to such an extent that one metaphor in the first line is
paralleled by another in the next line. As a result, when coupled
by another metaphor, its metaphoric qualities are paradoxically
played down, and the reader—as all trained readers do—certainly
becomes more aware of the combinational effect. This perhaps
accounts for the fact that some of the more strictly regulated
poems in China are less metaphorically burdened, for its metaphors are often examined in relation to their respective counterparts, and the reader's attention is often diverted from the metaphors themselves to their inter-relationships. E. R. Hughes sees
this as a perfect example of the Chinese "double harness thinking," in which one phenomenon is usually examined from double
angles.[12] Provocative as it is, the point is well beyond the scope of
this study. We will say, however, that when Chinese poetry was at

[11] Shih, p. 277.

[12] See "Epistemological Methods in Chinese Philosophy," *The Chinese
Mind*, ed. Charles A. Moore (Honolulu: The Univ. Pr. of Hawaii, 1974), pp.
88-92. E.R. Hughes sees this vision as an outgrowth of *yin/yang* and the Five
Elements in Former Han. Linguistically, this vision is concretized in a highly
sophisticated language in which semantic fields are rich enough to allow for
great variations amidst conformity to parallelism.

its height, even *pi* seems to take on certain superficial qualities of *hsing*, and selection shows a tendency to project itself into combination. But upon closer look, it is actually the opposite of *hsing*. *Hsing* strikes us at first look as being purely metonymical, relying mostly on combinations. Yet due to its special kind of combinations, with gaps between the two terms, we as readers try to postulate some relationships by reading them in a metaphoric light. As a result, the metaphoric effect of *hsing* is greatly increased.

By contrast, *hsing* is "contiguous association" (接近的聯想), again in Wang's words. Here *hsing* will be treated as a metonymic operation in the Jakobsonian sense. Thus, instead of one term substituting for another, we have two terms placed next to each other. There is, however, something unusual about this kind of combination. Normally in natural language the ways two terms are combined are rule-governed. From the combination of distinctive features into phonemes to the arrangements of syntactic units into sentences, there are explicit rules governing our linguistic behaviors regardless of whether we are aware of them or not. In poetry, however, deviation plays as vital a role as conformity to convention and, of course, its concomitant rules. As a consequence, not all combinations are predictable, and the relationships between the combined elements are not exactly grammatical, much less logical. They are in this case more often determined by cultural orientations of the age. Take one typical *hsing* from *Shih ching*:

> *Kwan-kwan* go the ospreys,
> On the islet in the river.
> The modest, retiring, virtuous, young lady:—
> For our prince a good mate she.[13]

關關雎鳩，在河之洲，
窈窕淑女，君子好逑。 （「關雎」）

The first two lines as *hsing* (興句) are juxtaposed against the last

---

[13] Legge, IV, 1.

two lines as response (應句).[14] And it would be a mistake to treat the avian world as being replaced by the human world. Their connections are, nonetheless, absent—on the surface level, at least. One would have to base one's interpretation on one's cultural training. Thus "The Little Preface" (小序) gives the well-known interpretation, objected to by some critics as being overtly didactic. It sees the poem as a celebration of "the virtue of the queen":

> Therefore in the *Kwan ts'eu* ['Kuan chi'] we have joy in obtaining virtuous ladies to be mates to her lord; anxiety to be introducing ladies of worth; no excessive desire to have her lord to herself; sorrow about modest retiring ladies [not being found for the harem], and thought about getting ladies of worth and ability,—all without any envy of their excellence:—this is what we have in the *Kwan ts'eu*.[15]

關雎樂得淑女，以配君子，憂在進賢，不淫其色，哀窈窕，思賢才，而無傷善之心焉，是關雎之義也。

The remark comes as no surprise from that particular didactic tradition, but to criticize it as being morally biased does not really solve any problem. One ought to, instead, reconstruct the original stage in which the two worlds of the birds and men are connected by a common-denominator concept. This undifferentiated concept looms large above the two terms, thus making it possible for us to move from one to the other. This movement is precisely the same as the semantic operation of metonymy in which one's association starts from the part to the whole and then

---

[14] Shih's translation of *hsing che, ch'i ye* 興者，起也 is "*hsing* responds to a stimulus." The stimulus/response formula seems to reduce complex poetic and philosophical problems to a simple and mechanistic psychological phenomenon. We will therefore use the *hsing*/response format to stress the unpredictable verbal qualities of *hsing* without altogether losing sight of the homologous relationships between the two parts. See Shih, p. 276.

[15] Legge, IV, 37.

to another part.[16] Using "Kuan chi" as an example again, we may begin first from the birds in their mating environment to an undifferentiated, primordial world (in which the natural rhythm of life moves unobstructed and in which the mating of the male and the female plays a vital role) and finally to the human world where proper courtship is stressed as a natural and indispensable procedure. To be even more specific, we slide from the birds singing on the islet to a larger, but more abstract, concept (made up of vitality, love, cosmic harmony, etc.) and lastly to a human world which is geographically located next to the birds' sanctuary, for the speaker is picking plants in the river where the birds are. This linguistic movement may also be seen as a mythical movement, taking place mainly in the communal mind of the primary reader who relies on this movement to account for what happens in nature and to put himself in the overall context of nature.[17] In this mythical light, we move first from the birds' desperate need for procreation to a vague view of life as a process of perennial continuity, and finally to a solution of some sort in which man goes about his courtship methodically to procure his mate. The connections between the two worlds of birds and man are vague at first look, though, thus causing all kinds of ambiguities.

It must be stressed, however, that such ambiguities, or such uncertainties of meaning, are an intrinsic part of literature, and likewise an inalienable part of one's reading process. In other words, while Jakobson and Lévi-Strauss claim some degree of explicitness and exhaustiveness of their analysis on the basis of their equivalence principle, it is perhaps more appropriate to restrict the strictly linguistic analysis within a certain limit and leave room for another phase of the reading process where one's

[16] See Jonathan Culler, *The Structuralist Poetics* (Ithaca: Cornell Univ. Pr., 1975), pp. 180-81.

[17] The term "mythical" here is used mainly for lack of a better term. It is used in its special sense of man—and in this case the reader—with his mythical outlook toward life. It is a symbolic reading of life, aimed at solving the apparent discrepancies and problems confronting man. See Claude Lévi-Strauss, "The Structural Study of Myth," *Structural Anthropology* (New York: Basic Books, 1963), pp. 206-12.

cultural or even archetypal knowledge seems to be more useful. There is, of course, in this view a certain lack of explicitness which can normally be expected of a purely linguistic analysis; yet in a literature which relies heavily on the associational habit of the mind, explicitness derived from models imported from abroad without considerable modifications may actually sacrifice its nuances.

Aside from the problem of ambiguities, the position of *hsing* is equally baffling. In addition to the intial position in a poem (as in "Kuan chi"), *hsing* may also occur almost anywhere else. Since almost all *hsing* lines are objective descriptions of the external world (in contrast with the response part which deals with human affairs), *hsing* may very well be treated as a technique which enables a poet to make transitions back and forth between the subjective and the objective worlds. In its initial position, for example, *hsing* is undoubtedly used by the poet in his lived world as a convenient poetic opening into a created world.[18] We have often heard of the saying that "folk songs are easy to sing, but difficult to begin" 山歌好唱口難開. As a solution, *hsing* is used to allow the poet to begin by mentioning objects or scenes nearby which are conducive to the poet's subsequent self-expression. For all that, *hsing* lines in folk songs tend to be trite (due presumably to their communal nature), causing critics such as Cheng Ch'iao 鄭樵 and some modern folk literature scholars to conclude that *hsing* lines contain hardly any semantic meaning. *Hsing*, in other words, is functional only in so far as it provides a final syllable, to be rhymed with in subsequent lines. The device reminds one of the second line of a traditional English ballad stanza with an A-B-C-B rhyming scheme, in which the second line is not narratively functional. However, to really understand the intricate operations of *hsing*, one ought to move beyond this mechanistic—

---

[18] James Liu sees literature as the created world of the author which is different from his lived world *(lebenswelt)*. It is an extension of reality, but it is not unreality. Once it is created, it exists as a potential for the reader to recreate that imaginary world from. See "Toward a Synthesis of Chinese and Western Theories of Literature," *Journal of Chinese Philosophy*, 4 (1977), 7-8.

linguistic level to a mythical-cultural level where connections between *hsing* and response of a profounder kind can usually be found. Even in the simple forms of folk songs, such examples are not lacking. A modern Wu song 吳歌 makes this point perfectly clear:

> The bamboo leaves on top of Yang Hill appear green.
> New daughters-in-law behave like Kuan Yin.

> 陽山頭上竹葉青，
> 新做媳婦像觀音。 （《歌謠週刊》，九四〔一九二五〕）

Aside from the pararhyme (a linguistic connection), other, and profounder, connections are also present. In terms of similarities, the bamboo leaves of the human world perhaps represent metonymically the Purple Bamboo Grove 紫竹林, Kuan Yin's residence. In terms of oppositions, the bride is in sharp contrast to the goddess—while the latter is in full command of the world and is in charge of universal salvation, the former faces an uncertain future in her husband's household in which her role is at best marginal. These connections are what is meant here as mythical-cultural connections.[19]

An initial *hsing* (首興) serves as a stepping stone, as it were, into the created world which is the emotional core of the poem. Thus it can very well be seen as a mediation between the poet anchored in his lived world and his created world. In "Kuan chi," for instance, the birds are a first step from the poet's world toward his fabricated, imaginary world in which birds and men are at one with each other. When positioned in the middle of a poem—or, for that matter, at the end of a poem—*hsing* can in the same way be seen as operating in an opposite direction by referring back toward the presumably real world where the poet is firmly grounded. According to Hsü Fu-kuan 徐復觀, "Chün-tzu yü yü" 君子于役 from the "Wang feng" 王風 section of *Shih ching* talks about the speaker's longing for the return of her husband from service. She

---

[19]Interpretations may vary from reader to reader, but what is important is that any reader with certain cultural competence can easily move from the purely linguistic to the cultural-mythical level.

begins by saying she does not know when he will return. *Hsing* is then introduced at this juncture as a transition from her subjective wish into an objective description. We are told specifically that the fowls are roosting, the sun is setting and the cattle are coming home from the field for the night. After being so reinforced, as it were, by nature, the speaker is finally prepared to go back to her world of pure self-expression. And, indeed, she deduces from the normal rhythm of life that prolonged separation is against nature and that her wish for his return is perfectly justifiable.

When *hsing* occurs at the final position, it serves effectively as a poetic closure by bringing the poetic flight back to earth and placing it next to the poet's real world. The last few lines of "Southeast Fly the Peacocks" 孔雀東南飛 serve precisely this purpose when they pick up from where the narrative has left off and put the poem in a physically immediate context again. Earlier in the poem we are told at great length of the tragic relationship between Lan Chih 蘭芝 and her husband, which ends in their double love suicide, and their bodies buried next to each other. At this point, the final *hsing* (尾興) thrusts a vivid picture in front of our eyes. From their graves grow two trees whose branches are eventually joined to form a canopy. In this canopy two mandarin ducks perch together, neck to neck, singing to each other into the dead of the night. As a *tour de force*, this final *hsing* specifically brings the poem—and, for that matter, the reader as well—from an imaginary world back to a real world in which widows are said to be "roused and stirred" by the touching sight.

In terms of their positions, the initial *hsing* opens a poem into an imaginary world. The medial *hsing* (中興) provides a transition halfway through a poem by referring back to a world closer to us. And the final *hsing* closes a poem by bringing it back next to a human reality. Because of the fact that *hsing* occurs almost anywhere in a poem, position itself clearly does not account for its quintessential nature. We should instead see it as a description of external events or objects which have at the same time direct bearings on human life, and which lend themselves to poetic self-expression. In other words, *hsing* should be seen in two lights. By itself, *hsing* is a description of a world which is an extension of our lived reality. In context, however, the true meaning of *hsing* lies in its relationships with the core of the poetic world. In either light, *hsing* plays the role of a mediating factor, existing between our lived reality and an imaginary world of poetry. So, in a way, *hsing* is an artistic sleight of hand which allows a poet and his readers to move back and forth among man, nature and art with a great deal of freedom. The freedom, as mentioned before, is mythically and culturally endorsed. In the folk poetry in question, there is at the outset a primitive outlook which enables man to see himself as part of nature, not above nature. There is also at this time an undifferentiated view which does not see art as reified or treat it as distinct from other human activities. As such, barriers have not yet been established to mar the harmony at this stage. In the elitist tradition, the situation can no longer be said to be the same. Nonetheless, *hsing* persists after Han. It exists now in a different format, perhaps as a result of the Taoist insistence on the emptying of self, objects being all equal, and life as a process toward art in which subject and object are interfused. Linguistically, the frequent deletion of subject, the rejection of the first person pronoun as a privileged category and the omission of grammatical connectives also provide a nice ground for *hsing* to grow in.

In its development from a primitive form to a cultural product, something important persists in *hsing*. We have earlier mentioned that the combined elements in their interrelationships are different from daily speech. In Chinese poetry, the combined elements are syntagmatically contiguous and there is nothing unusual about this. Normally the fact that verbal elements are combined and contiguous almost necessarily implies that they are related. But in Chinese poetry, connectives are very often deleted or absent. The reader is forced initially to read the two parts separately, with the result that their imagistic effects are greatly highlighted, at the expense of their contextual meanings. This stage of reading is, however, only temporary, for an experienced reader of poetry is soon tempted to treat the two parts as if they were equal. In Jakobson's words, this is precisely "the projection of the equivalence principle from the axis of selection to the axis of combination."[20] Some tension is as a result created between the two stages of reading; between reading the two parts on their own and aligning the two parts into paradigms. The situation is also circular in the sense that in the absense of connections, the two parts take on the semblance of total independence, and this total independence in turn makes it even more difficult to have them connected. Under this condition, ambiguities seem to be self-perpetuating.

Hsing has traditionally been treated as a semantically ambiguous operation. Liu Hsieh is quite explicit about it:

> the *pi*, or metaphor, is obvious, but the *hsing* alone is obscure.[21]

比顯興隱。 （《文心雕龍》・「比興」）

The obscurities are caused, according to some critics, by the unique associational method of *hsing*.[22] Cheng Ch'iao, for instance, believes that *hsing* "cannot be grasped through analogies or arrived at by reasoning" 不可以事類推，不可以義理求（《六經奧義》・《詩辨妄》）. Its true essence lies thus in its rhyming function. There is yet another school that sees *hsing* as a process of emotional arousal. Hsü Fu-kuan, for instance, argues convincingly that *hsing* connects on a spontaneous basis without going through a rational process.[23] Hsü's view is in line with *The Literary Mind and the Carving of Dragons*, which sees *hsing* in a stimulus/response pattern:

> *Pi* involves reasoning by analogy, and *hsing* responds

[20] "Closing Statement: Linguistics and Poetics," p. 358.

[21] Shih, p. 276.

[22] P'ei P'u-hsien classifies critics on *hsing* into four schools which believe respectively that: (1) *hsing* is a didactic vehicle; (2) *hsing* is merely sound without meaning; (3) *hsing* arouses emotionally, not rationally; and (4) *hsing* is a variety of combinations of the three cardinal rhetorical devices. See *Shih Ching yen-tu chih-tao*, pp. 309-31.

[23] *Chung-kuo wen-hsüeh lun-chi* 中國文學論集 (Taipei: Hsüeh-sheng, 1974), p. 102.

to a stimulus. When we reason by analogy, we group things by comparing their general characteristics; and when we respond to stimuli, we formulate our ideas according to the subtle influences we receive.[24]

故比者，附也；興者，起也。附理者切類以指事，起情者依微
以擬議。 (「比興」)

In the interpretation of Chung Hung 鍾嶸, *hsing* has even taken on some mystical qualities: "When words are finished, their meanings linger on. That's *hsing*" 文已盡而意有餘，興也 (「詩品序」). The spectrum of *hsing* thus ranges from total absence of meaning, to emotive meaning, to meaning lying apparently beyond the linguistic code. In all three cases, we find meaning being produced in an unusual manner. Unlike the normal communication in which meaning is generated from the message, here we have the message so artistically manipulated that its normal function is disrupted in the first place. Jakobson argues that poetic function stresses message itself and that message creates poetic meaning by following the equivalence principle. Chinese poetry, however, seems to take a more radical approach by disrupting the message itself at the outset as a means of stressing the message. This is done by fragmenting the message. From the communication point of view, the reader in receiving the fragmented message is forced to focus his attention on the fragments, while at the same time trying to organize the fragments into an integrated, meaningful message. In a situation like this, lineal narrative reconstruction is of very little help, while a spatial reading seems to be more suitable. In other words, the projection of one fragment on to another fragment is the only solution to ensure the maintenance of the communication between the addresser and the addressee. What is involved is thus not only a poetic reading process but also a very realistic communicational need.

Jacques Lacan sees the difference between metaphor and metonymy as corresponding to substitution and displacement in psychoanalytic theory. Metaphor thus moves from the signifier

[24] Shih, p. 276.

to the signified. Its strength lies in saying one thing which signifies something else. That is, it is what is not said that gives poetry its provocative power. Nevertheless, there is definitely something specifically referred to, no matter how indirectly expressed. Metonymy, by contrast, operates by sliding from signifer to signifer. In this sliding process, one term after another is called up, but these terms are only contiguous to the original term. They are not the original term, which all along remains hidden.[25] This inscrutable original term is perhaps what traditional critics mean by the ambiguity of *hsing*, whose meaning is either missing, emotive or extra-linguistic. One thing, however, is clear: the sliding process definitely creates a gap between *hsing* and response, a gap which can best be filled through mythical-cultural readings.

IV

If the projection of the equivalence principle from the axis of selection to the axis of combination is not only a poetic habit —or poetic function, in Jakobson's terms—but also a communicational necessity, the equivalence principle also needs to be scrutinized. Equivalence seems to imply mechanistic equations which are, of course, not the case with *hsing*. Chu Hsi in his annotation of *Shih ching* often uses the model: "Whereas that . . . is (does) . . . this . . . is (does). . . ." 言彼…則… ; 此…則 (或「以」). . . . Obviously, this discontinuous analogy forces the reader to look for homologous, rather than mechanically equivalent, relationships between the two parts. So if we could combine Jakobson's projection concept (which is mainly linguistic) with the homologous model (which we treat on a cultural-mythical level), then we might be able to come to a better understanding of this unique aspect of Chinese poetry.

In the *yüeh-fu* poems in question, bird motifs are extensively used as *hsing* to hint at different human situations that follow. Normally it does not matter what kinds of birds are involved, as is often the case in *Ch'u tz'u*, for instance.[26] Here in this corpus,

[25] *The Language of the Self* (New York: Dell Pub. Co., 1968), pp. 240-43.

[26] See C.H. Wang, "The Bird as Messenger of Love in Allegorical Poetry,"

what really matters are the behaviors of the birds and, specifically, whether they are flying or perching. Through collocations of various examples we will see that lone birds in flight as *hsing* almost always give rise to a response in which human relations are marred by disharmony. By contrast, paired birds on their perch invariably foreshadow a harmonious human relationship. These two connection patterns, though discovered in a study of empirical facts, can be accounted for in the mythical implications behind the different behaviors of the birds.

The relationship between *hsing* and response can generally be interpreted on two levels. On the concrete level, *hsing* must be seen as descriptions of actual scenes or events which exist side by side with the human world. The birds singing to each other in "Kuan chi" of *Shih ching* is one obvious example. The scene constitutes part of the overall landscape on the concrete level, and the birds' singing takes place right beside human courtship. The enigmatic opening of "Southeast Fly the Peacocks" is another example:

Southeast fly the peacocks,
Every five miles he flits back and forth.

孔雀東南飛，五里一徘徊。

On the concrete level, it can be seen as part of the activities which follow. Immediately after this *hsing* opening, we are told, "At thirteen I could weave silk" 十三能織素. Thus, according to Wang Yün-hsi 王運熙, the flying birds are a motif on the heroine's needle work.[27] Concretely speaking, the bird motif happens to be something close to the speaker, which allows her to proceed with her story. Such a connection between *hsing* and response is, in the true sense of the word, metonymical, for the birds here are related

New Asia Academic Bulletin, I (1978), 69-76.

[27] See "Lun *k'ung-ch'üeh tung-nan fei* te ch'an-sheng shih-tai ssu-hsiang i-shu chi ch'i-t'a wen-t'i" 論孔雀東南飛的產生時代思想藝術及其他問題, *Yüeh-fu yen-chiu lun-wen chi* 樂府研究論文集 (Hong Kong: Lung-men, 1970), II, 120-23.

to man's world on a physical basis. However, it must be pointed
out that such a realistic, physical connection does not do full
justice to *hsing* as a poetic device. On yet another level, one ought
to see how the two parts stand in a metaphoric relationship with
each other. This secondary metaphoric relationship (in contradistinction to the primary metaphoric relationships before projection) is, however, difficult to decipher, unless one adopts an
extra-linguistic perspective.

In "Southeast Fly the Peacocks" the initial bird motif is
followed by a numerical series:

> At thirteen I could weave silk,
> At fourteen I knew how to tailor clothes,
> At fifteen I played the harp,
> At sixteen I could recite the *Classic of Songs* and the
> > *Classic of Documents*,
> At seventeen I became your wife.

> 十三能織素，十四學裁衣，
> 十五彈箜篌，十六誦詩書，
> 十七爲君婦。

Her entire education culminates in marriage, and her training
prepares her to be a member in her husband's household (including her husband, her mother-in-law and her sister-in-law). Briefly
speaking, the poem as a whole is about her double role as wife and
a new member of the household. It is, moreover, about the con-
flict between her two roles. Enough has already been said about
her mother-in-law's displeasure with her. (The mother-in-law says,
"This wife has neither manners nor morals,/She does only what
suits her fancy./Long have I resented her" 此婦無禮節，舉動自專由，
吾意久懷忿. On the other hand, the couple's mutual attachment
is one of the most touching stories in Chinese literature. We ought
to, however, give attention to the mediating factor of these two
relationships in Lan Chih's role as a sexually productive member
of the household. After all, her husband is the only male member,
and the continuity of the entire family depends solely on him.
It seems that Lan Chih has been married for years, but remained

childless and, of course, that constitutes grounds for a married woman to be divorced and expelled. Though we are not told about this, the reasons are not far to seek. No mention has been made whatsoever about her child in her elaborate leave-taking to members of her family. Her husband pleads for her by pointing out that she has been married less than two or three years and there has not been enough time. Later on, immediately before her ex-husband commits suicide for the sake of their love, he says to his mother:

> Your son's day is now darkening.
> I am causing Mother to stay behind alone.
> This is my own evil design,
> Do not blame ghosts and spirits.

> 兒今日冥冥，今母在後單，
> 故作不良計，勿復怨鬼神。

The confession clearly implies that once he is gone, his mother will be left behind helpless, without an heir to take care of her. Seen in a cultural-mythical light, the lone bird in flight thus corresponds with the situation of the couple whose married life is ruined because they could not produce offspring. This *hsing* opening has actually been traced back to another *yüeh-fu* ballad:

> Two white swans come flying
> From the northwest,
> In fives and tens, flying
> In tidy formations.
> Now the wife is sick,
> And cannot follow.
> He looks backward every five *li*,
> And flits back and forth every six *li*.

> 飛來雙白鵠，乃從西北來，
> 十十五五，羅列成行，
> 妻卒被病，行不能相隨，
> 五里一返顧，六里一徘徊。　（「豔歌何嘗行」）

Here in this prototype the wife becomes so sick that she cannot keep up with the flock in their southward migration, forcing her husband to go without her. Their relationship is no longer sound and, as happens later, the wife feels jealous over the prospect of her husband taking another mate. The fully developed situation certainly underlines the mythical meaning behind the male/female relationships in "Southeast Fly the Peacocks."

One might wonder why poets put so much weight on the behavior of birds. The answer lies in the seasonal changes which play a very important role in people's daily life. Migratory birds symbolize with their flight the inviolable rhythm of life in which procreation is all-important—birds, as we all know, mate in their migration or on reaching their destination. Because of this trait, birds are often taken as a symbol of matrimonial harmony in the overall cosmic scheme. *Pai-hu t'ung-i* 白虎通義（卷四）, for example, lists the symbolic meaning behind the practice of using migratory geese in the courtship formalities:

> Because they go southward and northward in accordance with the progress of the seasons, without violating the rhythm of life; and also because they do not waste women's prime.
>
> 取隨時南北，不失其節，明不奪女人之時也。

The sexual implications behind the migration of the birds are even more explicit as we examine some entries of folk beliefs. *Ku Yao-yen*, for instance, tells us that herons become pregnant merely by chasing each other. Other birds are also believed to become pregnant by singing to each other, by having the shadow of one bird fall on that of his mate, or simply by gazing at each other. In other words, people tend to interpret the behavior of birds in sexual terms. It is thus only natural for poets to initiate their poems about matrimonial and sexual troubles by employing opening *hsing* about a bird being forced to leave behind its mate because the latter cannot keep up with the rhythm of life, nor fulfill its sexual role.

While lone birds in flight initiate human situations with

domestic troubles, paired birds on their perch usually lead off a world of domestic harmony. "Southeast Fly the Peacocks" begins with the birds separated from each other, resulting, metaphorically, in the tragic fate of Lan Chih and her husband. The story reaches its denouement in the double suicide of the two lovers. The poet, however, has not yet said his last word, for he needs to sublimate the couple's death. At this point, the poem leads away from its imaginary narrative back to a world which is much more immediate to us. The events after their death go like this:

> The two families asked for a joint burial.
> Jointly they were buried by the side of Mount Hua.
> East and west were planted pines and cypresses,
> Left and right were set *wu-t'ung* trees,
> The branches covered each other,
> The leaves crossed each other.
> In the trees there was a pair of flying birds
> Called mandarin ducks,
> Raising their heads they called to each other
> Every night until the fifth watch.

> 兩家求合葬，合葬華山傍，
> 東西植松柏，左右種梧桐，
> 枝枝相覆蓋，葉葉相交通，
> 中有雙飛鳥，自名爲鴛鴦，
> 仰頭相向鳴，夜夜達五更。

It is not altogether impossible that dead lovers have been transformed into the birds. Elsewhere in a similar case from *Lieh i chi* 列異記 we are told:

> Han P'in and his wife are buried by Lord K'ang of Sung. That night two mandarin ducks were born in the trees, one male and one female. They perch in the trees all the time, neck to neck, all day long. Their songs are quite touching.

> 宋康王埋韓憑夫婦，宿夕文梓生有鴛鴦，雌雄各一，恒栖樹上

，晨夕交頸，聲音感人。（《淵鑑類函》・卷四二六）

Singing occurs in both cases and, of course, it lends itself to mythical, sexual interpretations mentioned earlier. In the latter case,
the birds cross their necks, an act which, according to Yang Shen
楊慎, also causes pregnancy.

  Mandarin ducks have all along been used as a symbol of
eternal love. There is very little doubt about this, but two points
are of special interest to us: firstly, mandarin ducks perch in trees
or on ponds; and, secondly, they stay in pairs, never alone. (Mandarin ducks are mated for life; once one of them is dead, the
surviving mate is believed to die soon afterward.) In both "Chi
ming" 鷄鳴 and "Hsiang feng hsing" 相逢行, we are told of three
brothers serving in the imperial court. On their return for regular
leave, they are seen to walk through the yard where seventy-two
mandarin ducks are swimming two by two, on the pond. In Han
belief, the number signifies cosmic completion.[28] And in the two
poems here, the ducks symbolize not only husbands and wives
enjoying conjugal bliss, but also domestic harmony among all the
members of their big family.

  Even though it is impossible to demonstrate it here in a brief
space, on the basis of the *yüeh-fu* ballads of the period, we can
safely say that flying or perching birds signify not only marital
relationships, but also relationships among brothers and even
members of a community. And as in the case of married couples,
flying signifies disruptions of order and perching symbolizes the
presence of harmony.

  Hsing, in other words, appears on the surface as a metonymical device, placing one natural object or event next to a human
situation. Yet through careful cultural-mythical readings, one finds
beneath the surface linguistic phenomena the metaphoric relationships which place the natural world and the human world on top
of each other. This two-fold rhetorical operation is different from
a primary, unprojected metaphor in which only one term is pre-

---

[28]Yang Hsi-mei 楊希枚, "Lun shen-mi shu-tzu ch'i-shih-erh" 論神秘數字七
十二, *Kuo-li Taiwan ta-hsüeh k'ao-ku jen-lei hsüeh-k'an* 國立台灣大學攷古人
類學刊, 35-36 (Oct. 1970), 12-47.

sent while the other is absent. Here in this *hsing* type of metaphoric relationship, certain mythical patterns actually run through
the two terms, turning one into a foreshadowing of the other—
one being homologous with the other. The relationship is therefore an inevitable one, dictated by the overall cultural code, or
to use a different term, the subconscious communal mind. It is
no longer adequate to say such an expression is simply a poet's
manipulation of a linguistic operation.

V

We have tried in this study to clarify the different aspects
of an important rhetorical figure as well as a central esthetic
concept in Chinese literature in its initial stage. In terms of scope,
we have placed *hsing* in the overall context of the three-fold
compositional methods of *fu, pi* and *hsing*. *Hsing*, as we have
ascertained, involves a special transference of meaning in which
two terms are combined, but with a semantic gap interposed between them. As a result, a special kind of two-fold set is involved:
(1) primary metonymic combinations of *hsing* with response, and
(2) secondary metaphoric substitution, or complementing, of one
term with another. Methodologically, in demonstrating the
secondary metaphoric operation, it is necessary to put *hsing* in an
overall cultural context and view the homologous relationships
in a cultural-mythical light in order to reconstruct paradigmatic
connections between the two phases of perception which are
supposed to be viewed on a simultaneous basis. In terms of the
relevancy of this study to a comprehensive understanding of
Chinese poetry, possibilities exist to expand this initial attempt
by including an account of the characteristic interfusing of subject
and object in Chinese poetry in sufficiently rigorous terms. Of
course, due to the limitations of relative autonomy of any critical
approach, a perspective or a method is only as good as the material
from which it is derived. Thus our linguistic and cultural-mythical
reading of *hsing* may have to be modified before it can be used
in T'ang poetry, for instance, with its totally different linguistic
requirements, poetic conventions, esthetic outlook, cultural
orientations, etc. What is proposed here should be seen merely

as a working model, aimed at contributing to a better understanding of the beginning of the Chinese lyrical tradition.

METHODOLOGICAL IMPLICATION OF THE PHILOSOPHY OF JACQUES DERRIDA FOR COMPARATIVE LITERATURE: THE OPPOSITION EAST-WEST AND SEVERAL OTHER OPPOSITIONS

Donald Wesling

An able modern interpreter of Taoism has described Taoism's effort of thought as a "decreative-creative dialectic," wherein a seeming renunciation of the world "is not negation, but a new way of repossessing this concrete world by dispossessing the partial and reduced forms the process of abstract thinking has so far heaped upon us."[1] Since Jacques Derrida remains and glories in the decreative moment, calling all perception and interpretation into question and leaving them there unrescued, we may perhaps begin by calling his philosophy an incomplete Taoism.

To open with an aphorism and call this writer half a Taoist is very Derridian, for as we shall see, he likes the concisions, extravagances and play of language. Indeed, this play of language is the central subject of Derrida's philosophical work. But such will be my only Derridian gesture. This paper will not adhere to Derrida in aim, method or style. It will finally call in question the fierce narrowness of the limitations he has set upon the act of interpretation. I intend a summary and evaluation of this body of thinking, in order to establish Derrida's contribution as a methodologist. Pursing Derrida's commentary on the implications of binary oppositions in logic, his most productive methodological insight may be used to inspect the argument of a few recent studies in East-West comparative literature. And last, since Derrida comments on the West's reception and study of the Chinese language, in his book *De la grammatologie* (1967; English trans-

---

[1] Wai-lim Yip, "The Taoist Aesthetic: *Wu-yen tu-hua*, the Unspeaking, Self-generating, Self-conditioning, Self-transforming, Self-complete Nature," *New Asia Academic Bulletin*, 1 (1978), 24.

lation *Of Grammatology*, 1976), some accounting of his own relation to the East seems to be in order.

Derrida is as interesting in his limitations as in his merits. His brilliant formalist theory is set up in such a way that most cultural and historical questions, or literary questions such as those concerning genre or the practice of translation, cannot be adequately posed. In this crucial respect his philosophy is more a warning than a model to be emulated. Nevertheless, Paul de Man is correct when he says that "Derrida's work is one of the places where the future possibility of literary criticism is being decided . . ."[2] and thus I should say our task is to sort out what is productive from what is extreme. There are reasons—in Derrida's own discussion of Europe's collective hallucination concerning the Chinese language, in his professed hatred of ethnocentrism— why East-West literary studies could be a worthy context for such analysis.

Necessarily sceptical summary, then, and a tentative application of the notion of oppositions to recent essays to see what might be clarified, is my intent. In France and America much is being claimed for Derrida's method of deconstruction as a way to restructure the discipline of literary studies, but here let us say only that this body of work gives East-West studies some admirable definitions and reminders. Especially since Edward W. Said's devastating account of Oriental studies as a discourse (1978), Western scholarship is under the imperative of abolishing its ethnocentrism—that strategy of a "flexible *positional* superiority, which puts the Westerner in a whole series of possible relationships with the Orient without ever losing him the relative upper hand."[3] In our dealings with language and thought, we need to avoid (if we can) those presuppositions of orientalism which made it, in Said's words, an "enormously systematic discipline by which European culture was able to manage—and even produce—the

[2] Paul de Man, "The Rhetoric of Blindness: Jacques Derrida's Reading of Rousseau," in *Blindness and Insight: Essays in the Rhetoric of Contemporary Criticism* (New York: Oxford Univ. Pr., 1971), p. 111.

[3] Edward W. Said, *Orientalism* (New York: Pantheon Books, 1978), see pp. 7, 3 for quotations in this paragraph.

Orient politically, sociologically, militarily, ideologically, scientifically and imaginatively during the post-Enlightenment period."
Derrida perhaps provides some of the lucidities with which we
may analyze certain all-too-easy oppositions of the discourse of
orientalism; but then, as I will show, his own account of the issues
is not sufficient. The opposition East-West is the most pervasive
of all those needing to be undone by understanding, but the undoing will not be accomplished merely by bringing French
fashions to the Far East.

I

Jacques Derrida is the foremost post-Structuralist philosopher in France. He is read, there, by students and young university
teachers in philosophy, linguistics and literature, and also by
psychoanalysts, by writers interested in questioning the very
meaning of writing, by scientists and persons who work in drama,
painting, music. His iconoclastic work is also resisted by the more
quietly empirical sector of the French university establishment.
His influence is perhaps more powerful in America than in Europe,
especially in centers such as Johns Hopkins and Yale—and his
work has been translated into several languages, including
Japanese. He and his followers publish in major French journals,
and, in America, in *New Literary History, Yale French Studies,
The Georgia Review, Glyph, Diacritics*. There have recently been
published books in English on Wordsworth and on William Carlos
Williams which explicitly credit their methodologies to the ideas
of Derrida.[4] His first book, edited in 1962, was *Introduction
à l'origine de la géométrie de Husserl* (P.U.F.), and thereafter
followed six fundamental works published three by three with a
five year interval, in 1967 and 1972. In 1967; *L'ecriture et la
différence* (Seuil; American translation, 1978), *De la grammatologie* (Minuit; American translation, 1975); *La voix et le phéno-*

[4] I refer to Frances Ferguson, *Wordsworth: Language as Counter-Spirit*
(New Haven and London: Yale Univ. Pr., 1977); and Joseph N. Riddel,
*The Inverted Bell: Modernism and the Counterpoetics of William Carlos
Williams* (Baton Rouge: Louisiana Univ. Pr., 1974).

mène (P.U.F.; American translation, 1973). In 1972; *La dissémina-tion* (Seuil); *Positions* (Minuit); *Marges* (Minuit; sections trans-lation in *New Literary History, Glyph*). In 1973 Derrida published his introduction to Condillac, *L'archéologie du frivole* (Galilée), and in 1974 his bizarre commentary on Hegel and Genet, *Glas* (Galilée).

Several works have appeared since, including introductions to psychoanalytic studies on language by Nicolas Abraham and Maria Torok. *Positions* consists of several interviews with Derrida which amplify and explain his writings, and there is also a volume (*Écarts*, edited by Finas et al., Fayard, 1973) which collects four essays about him by students of his work. The list is incomplete, but serves to show something of Derrida's range and abundance. Of all these, the best introduction to his theories and the book which has most direct bearing on East-West studies is *Of Gram-matology*.

In one way or another, all his books are readings of his pre-decessors in philosophy, and yet all the books are, as he says himself, "terribly autobiographical. Incorrigibly."[5] As the final, complicating gesture of personality in *Marges*, he even causes his own signature to be printed on the last page. The self-conscious peculiarity of the argumentation, the phrasing and the typography of *Glas*, a book whose intent and genre are not decidable, merely exaggerates a direction present in all his work. Derrida is a pro-fessional commentator upon earlier thinkers, albeit nearly always negative and demolishing in his corrections—but he also makes claims as a creator, an original. Philosophers are uneasy about Derrida; they complain about his metaphors and call him "liter-ary." Newton Garver, in the Preface to the American translation of *Speech and Phenomena* (1973), remarks that the "primacy of difference over identity is an eerie departure from common sense"; and speech-act philosopher John Searle, angrily disputing the final essay in *Marges*, says "Derrida has a distressing penchant

---

[5] Annexe II, Entretien de Lucette Finas avec Jacques Derrida, in Finas, et al., eds., *Écarts: Quatre essais à propos de Jacques Derrida* (Paris: Fayard, 1973), p. 309.

for saying things that are obviously false."[6] Increasingly Derrida
has found his audience among advanced students of literature who
seek a systematic theory. He offers to them a position from which
to criticize most of the existing forms of criticism as banal and
unrigorous; an emphasis on the figural tendency of literary
language; a special terminology and a method under the by-now-
famous banner of "deconstruction"; and some compelling arguments for breaking down partitions between creation and criticism, between literature and philosophy.

The difficulty of entering into dispute with Derrida, and also
of summarizing his leading ideas, follows from the scornful lucidity of his attack on common sense. Unless one is a disciple trying
to out-do him in radical rejections, there is always the chance that
an argument or metaphor in the exposition will reinstate a gambit
of thinking Derrida has already, somewhere, condemmed as
spurious. However, the literary critic who wishes to test the
method need not be intimidated. Usually there can be found
reasons why Derrida is allusive, emphatic or devious. Also, it is
entirely possible that Derrida is often wrong. It is possible, too,
that part of his project, consciously or not, is precisely to overstate the attack on commonsense empiricism and on historical
thinking and on accepted accounts of the human studies. Perhaps
his philosophy, like avant-garde manifestos in the arts, takes its
inner form through the explosion or exaggeration of what is
traditionally accepted; perhaps his philosophy defines its discipline
and very creativity by the degree to which it can re-structure the
situation, frustrate and provoke.

It is revealing that in the early journal versions of sections
later published in the *Grammatology*, Derrida described his
method by the explicitly avant-garde term "destruction." Only in
the later, book version of this text did he use the weaker but more
subtle' term "deconstruction." What will be deconstructed?
Derrida is bold. He will take apart nothing less than the conceptual

---

[6]Newton Garver, Preface to Jacques Derrida, *Speech and Phenomena*,
trans. David B. Allison (Evanston: Northwestern Univ. Pr., 1973), p. xxviii;
John R. Searle, "Reiterating the Differences: A Reply to Derrida," *Glyph*
I (Baltimore and London: Johns Hopkins Univ. Pr., 1977), p. 203.

edifice of Western philosophy from Plato to Hegel, from the pre-Socratics to Heidegger. The task is to show how Western thinking has been regulated by a cardinal opposition between *reality* and *the sign*. This reigning opposition has been diversified into an immense chain of other dichotomies which preserve the same structure, and which privilege the former term as the real, the substantial, the concrete, the valued, the original: presence/non-presence; thing/image; inside/outside; content/expression; substance/form; essence/appearance; depth/surface; before/after; more/less; original/derived; nature/culture, and a hundred others. Derrida continually refers to the "era of Western metaphysics" as if he might be able to think himself beyond the categories of 2500 years of philosophy. The thought-experiment requires that he undo the system of hierarchical oppositions between representation (in Saussurian linguistics: *the signifier*) and a pre-existing thing or sense (*the signified*). The written sign, to Derrida's regret, has a "metaphysical appurtenance," carries with it the belief that writing is the "trace" of the spoken word and its original thought or meaning. (*Vouloir dire* = the idea of anteriority.) This logic which exalts speech over writing Derrida calls *logocentrism*, a metaphysical myth of presence. Since the human voice is the subtlest expression of the *logos*, since speaking is the era of Western metaphysics privileged over writing, logocentrism in practice is *phonocentrism*. There was, for Derrida, no original moment of speaking; language was always writing.

Two implications may be noticed before we proceed. (1) The attack on the presuppositions of Western philosophy is also an attack on aesthetics and criticism since Plato, because literary interpretation has been an accomplice of the metaphysics of presence and accepted the logic of logo-phonocentrism. Accordingly, for Derrida, literary criticism must stop repressing the concepts and effects of writing. (2) The metaphysics of presence is in complicity with the alphabetic writing of the West, and this alphabetic or phonetic script is in process of trying to gain hegemony over the whole planet. Accordingly, for Derrida, the morphematic script of the Egyptians, the Mayans and the cultures of the Far East functions both as a victim of Western script and logic, and as the object of a "hieroglyphicist prejudice" in the form of a hyperbolical admiration.[7] Whether these other forms of writing are taken as victim or as primitivist alternative, it is unlikely the West will see them for what they are, or at any rate see them from the perspective of a native speaker, writer, or reader.

Derrida's contribution to an international symposium in 1966, "Structure, Sign, and Play in the Discourse of the Human Sciences," accompanied by a transcribed debate with Lucien Goldmann and others, has especially influenced American readers; it was one of the first of his texts available in English translation (1972). The impromptu question-period has some crucial remarks, such as Derrida's statements that "the risk of sterility . . . has always been the price of lucidity," and that he does not "believe that there is any perception," but the essay proper is a very substantial early summary of his central ideas. These sentences, especially, convey well the differences between classical thought and his own thought:

> There are thus two interpretations of interpretation, of structure, of sign, of freeplay. The one seeks to decipher, dreams of deciphering, a truth or an origin which is free from freeplay and from the order of the sign, and lives like an exile the necessity of interpretation. The other, which is no longer turned toward the origin, affirms freeplay and tries to pass beyond man and humanism, the name man being the name of that being who, throughout the history of metaphysics or of ontotheology—in other words, through the history of all his history—has dreamed of full presence, the reassuring foundation, the origin and the end of the game.[8]

[7] Jacques Derrida, *Of Grammatology*, trans. Gayatri Chakravorty Spivak (Baltimore and London: Johns Hopkins Univ. Pr., 1976), p. 90. Hereafter this book and translation will be abbreviated *Grammatology*.

[8] Jacques Derrida, "Structure, Sign, and Play in the Discourse of the Human Sciences," in R. Macksey and E. Donato, eds., *The Structuralist Controversy: The Languages of Criticism and the Sciences of Man* (Baltimore and London: Johns Hopkins Univ. Pr., 1970), pp. 264-65.

One interpretation faces backward, toward the origin; the other faces forwards toward a future "beyond man and humanism," a future of that freeplay which is the "disruption of presence."[9] One interpretation affirms a traditional moral and epistemological center and believes that texts have determinate meaning; the other looks to the play of signifiers in language and writing, looks to the act of writing as the conceptual space where "the as yet unnameable . . . is proclaiming itself."[10] Derrida finds these two interpretations of interpretation irreconcilable: "I do not believe that today there is any question of choosing . . . we must first try to conceive of the common ground, and of the *différance* of this irreducible difference."[11]

This single passage comprises many typical gestures. A major opposition is announced and declared undecidable, so that we remain mired within, yet straining beyond the metaphysics of presence; the diacritical difference between terms of the opposition is conceived as a postponement or putting-off of a solution, through a neologism Derrida makes upon the verb *différer*, to defer; ultimate decidability is reserved for the resolutions of a grammatology, a science of language which will come in the "ineluctable world of the future,"[12] but of which we have only glimpses now; until such resolution, perception and determinable meaning had better be called impossibilities. All the operations converge on the axiom that everything is in doubt. And in fact *aporia*, the Greek word for difficulty, question, problem, lack of resources, is a term often used by the deconstructionists. It is as if Descartes as methodologist called all in doubt and then halted his project of thought. But, by Derrida's account, Descartes was hostage to those metaphysical entities God, man, and meaning; Derrida abolishes these, and enters the porticos of language, where spiraling galaxies of signifiers play on each other down the vistas to infinity. Banished also, as a matter of course, are the

[9] Derrida, "Structure," p. 263.

[10] Derrida, "Structure," p. 265.

[11] Derrida, "Structure," p. 265.

[12] *Grammatology*, p. 4.

concepts of ordinary language, the referent, the human subject and history.

Perhaps "banished" is too strong a term. In *Positions*, when he is questioned about his deconstructions, Derrida denies that these concepts are being scrapped, and says, if I understand him, that while he subjects these notions to radical questioning, they still maintain a hold on his thinking. It may be that his conversational commentary on his philosophy is less boldly emphatic than the philosophy itself. Perhaps, too, his thought is here essentially in contradiction with itself, and must necessarily overstate its premises. There is the delicate calculus to be engaged between cutting away the traditional ground of philosophy, and having same ground left on which to stand, from which to write and analyze instances and solutions. One example: Part I of the *Grammatology* has a first section called "The End of the Book and the Beginning of Writing," a relentless criticism of the Western concept of language as primary writing, of *logos* as a lie from the start. But the third and last section of Part I treats "Of Grammatology as a Positive Science," and while this section is full of splendid commentary on the Western understanding of Chinese writing, it can find no hint of positive method beyond the mention of Champollion's decipherment of the Rosetta Stone and of Ezra Pound's "irreducibly graphic poetics" as derived on the model of the Chinese ideogram. Rarely, I have suggested, is Derridian deconstruction followed by construction. As a method, elaborated through specific analyses in many books, it remains deficient in rules of thumb for practical application. For this reason, to say nothing of the almost maniacal difficulty of Derrida's style, the prestige of this philosophy is something of a surprise, something which in itself calls for a sociology of scholarship.

Derrida is not the first but is perhaps the most severe thinker in the Western tradition to say that there is no such thing as the thing in itself. Unquestionably he has gained his influence as the initiator of a destructive discourse, as a critic of presuppositions and the idea of presuppositions. "I try," he says, "to hold myself at the limit of philosophical discourse."[13] He does this by imagin-

---

[13] Jacques Derrida, *Positions: Entretiens avec H. Ronse, J. Kristeva J.-L.*

ing a writing without prior speaking, a thinking without primal presuppositions. Derrida is, in fact, obsessed by prior states, can hardly begin an essay without either decapitating or extending the preliminaries, or commenting on the initiation of his utterance, or wondering where the opening ends and the real text starts.

The rejection of absolute beginnings and archetypes is the master theme, subject of his most powerful arguments. Related to it by reversal is the theme of the future. Ahead is the time when we escape not from history, but from the metaphysical concept of history; ahead is the time which is not only the closure of the era of metaphysics (for a closure can continue indefinitely), but the emphatic end. Never at length but in hints along the way, all the books foreshadow this future. At least twice Derrida uses the strange image of a welcome but monstrous birth:

> Perhaps patient meditation and painstaking investigation on and around what is still provisionally called writing, far from falling short of a science of writing or of hastily dismissing it by some obscurantist reaction, letting it rather develop its positivity as far as possible, are the wanderings of a way of thinking that is faithful and attentive to the ineluctable world of the future which proclaims itself at present, beyond the closure of knowledge. The future can only be anticipated in the form of an absolute danger. It is that which breaks absolutely with constituted normality and can only be proclaimed, *presented*, as a sort of monstrosity. For that future world and for that within it which will have put into question the values of sign, word, and writing, for that which guides our future anterior, there is as yet no exergue.[14]

Houdebine, G. Scarpetta (Paris: Minuit, 1972), p. 14. My translation. Hereafter abbreviated as *Positions*.

[14]*Grammatology*, Exergue, pp. 4-5. Another place Derrida uses the metaphor of monstrous birth: the end of the essay "Structure" (see note 8).

The philosophy of *écriture* is the philosophy of the future, when philosophy as such will perhaps no longer be necessary; when all thinking is purified to full lucidity. *Grammatology*, in such a chronology, is not a fully achieved science of writing, but a prospectus which considers the conditions of possibility for that science. (The trouble with ordinary philosophy, for Derrida, is that it cannot see, cannot thus extend, its own limits, its own borders with other disciplines.) There is, then, a positive moment in this philosophy, albeit a faint, rather ineffectual one. These rare hopeful passages do not weigh much against the prevailing tone. They do not convince, perhaps because there is no fully worked-out procedure in Derrida for getting from now to then, no stringent relationship shown between means and ends, no severe recognition of the mutual shaping of means and ends.

"Letting [writing] develop its positivity as far as possible": Derrida does search for ways to make a constructive science out of the subversion of logocentrism. I think he is most successful when he makes *undecidability* into a method in itself. The tendency of ordinary and literary language to be *figural*—the tendency for philosophers and even literary scholars to forget the way a connection between a sign and a thing is always shaken loose—is a continual emphasis. Derrida shows on many occasions that our belief in a magical presence has sedimented itself into the very metaphors and idioms of our language. But there is no other language to use, so we are guided by (as we guide) this twisted one with its deceptive figures, double-senses, ellipses, rhymes and puns. To gain some control over his own words and to dramatize the abominable exigencies of language, Derrida takes from Heidegger the practice of the "sous rature," a habit of writing a word, crossing it out, and then printing both word and deletion. There is the instance from the *Grammatology* already used by his translator Gayatri Chakravorty Spivak in her excellent summary of writing "under erasure:" Derrida writes "the sign~~is~~ that ill-named ~~thing~~, the only one, that escapes the instituting question of philosophy."[15] Says Spivak: "It is the strategy of using

[15] *Grammatology*, p. 19; and see Spivak's Preface to *Grammatology*, pp. xivff. Apparently now (1979) Derrida has given up his notion of the "sous

the only available language while not subscribing to its premises."[16] Of course, when you have crossed out a few chosen
words here and there, why not, if you are thoroughly sceptical
about communication, put the whole book under erasure? Derrida
seems to have thought of this objection himself, in his idea of "the
end of the book and the beginning of writing." But perhaps reservations can be conveyed economically, and without undue distraction, if a few crucial terms are taken for dramatic bracketing.

The most useful of all forms of undecidability in Derrida is
the method of problematizing oppositions. On the negative side
Derrida shows how metaphysical oppositions like space/time,
diachronic/synchronic, passive/active, covertly subordinate "the
movement of difference to the presence of a value or of a sense
which would be anterior to difference, more original than difference, exceeding and commanding it in the last instance."[17] As
a student of the language of classical philosophers in the essay
"White Mythology," Derrida deciphers in metaphors their
metaphysical "blind spot or deaf point."[18] The working tools of
philosophy—"*eidos, arche, telos, energia, ousia* (essence, existence, substance, subject), *alethia*, transcendentality, consciousness,
or conscience, God, man, and so forth"[19]—are all, for Derrida,
not devices for unlocking the problem but constitute the problem.

To avoid the snares of language when he develops his own
working concepts, he refuses to permit any hierarchy between
the oppositions they subsume. For example, *gramme* is neither
signifier nor signified, neither sign nor thing, neither absence nor
presence; *dissemination* is neither a single meaning nor its disper-
sion and multiplication; *pharmakon* is neither the poison nor the
remedy; *hymen* is neither consummation nor virginity. The intent

---

rature" as imprecise.

[16] Spivak, Preface to *Grammatology*, p. xviii.

[17] *Positions*, p. 41. My translation.

[18] Jacques Derrida, "White Mythology: Metaphor in the Text of Philosophy" (1971), *New Literary History* 6, No. 1 (Autumn 1974), 28. The
essay originally appeared in *Marges (de la philosophie)* (Paris: Minuit, 1972).

[19] The list is Derrida's, from "Structure," p. 249.

is that philosophical terms should themselves evoke an interminable chain of differences.

The master-terms are *écriture, différance, dissemination*, deconstruction, freeplay; but there are many others. A typical sentence reads: "Dominated by the so-called 'civilisation of writing' that we inhabit, a civilisation of so-called phonetic writing, that is to say of the logos where the sense of being is, in its telos, determined as parousia."[20] Through repetition and the special emphasis of italics, the grammatological terms become ontological terms. Beyond this special use of key terms, the larger style is of an extreme complexity, with a whole range of rhetorical effects including aphorism, sentence-fragment, modernist typography and a willingness to follow almost anywhere the lure of the language-derangement of the pun. Another, slightly longer passage will hint the texture of this writing about writing:

> writing as the possibility of the road and of difference, the history of writing and the history of the road, of the rupture, of the *via rupta*, of the path that is broken, beaten, *fracta*, of the space of reversibility and of repetition traced by the opening, the divergence from, and the violent spacing, of nature, of the natural, savage, salvage, forest. The *silva* is savage, the *via rupta* is written, discerned, and inscribed violently as difference, as form imposed on the *hylè*, in the forest, in wood as matter; it is difficult to imagine that access to the possibility of a road-map is not at the same time access to writing.[21]

It is as if Derrida had determined to illustrate his theory by defying translation. He employs style consciously as one expression of the infinite play of figural language. In metaphor and pun, several meanings co-exist in the same textual space; when signifier reverberates against signifier, the speaking subject tends to fade

[20]*Grammatology*, p. 52.

[21]*Grammatology*, p. 108.

away. Language speaks Derrida.

This extravagance of style foregrounds language. As Geoffrey H. Hartman remarks: "To transfer to one's prose these puns, equivocations, catachreses and abusive etymologies, these double-entendres and double-takes, these ellipses and purely speculative chains of words and associations, has a desacralizing and levelling effect which the generic neutrality of the word *écriture* reinforces."[22] The desacralizing fever is catching, and may be seen in the language of Derrida's French and American commentators. Paul de Man on the television comedy with a character named Archie Bunker: "But suppose that it is a de-bunker rather than a 'Bunker,' and a de-bunker of the arche (or origin), an archie Debunker such as Nietzsche or Jacques Derrida for instance, who asks the question 'What is the Difference.' "[23] Gayatri Spivak: "As the father's phallus works in the mother's hymen, between two legs, so *Glas* works at origins, between two columns, between Hegel and Genet. This work will mime the graphic that the father (n)ever inseminates and by which the mother is (n)ever ravished."[24] Another American, Andrew Warminsky, concludes an article by not concluding it, with the words "But if" not followed by a period. Such playfulness does emphasize the identity-deferring nature of words. "He shows," says Hartman, "how much metaphor remains and must remain, how much equivocation and palimpsest-residue. He does not advocate a more literary philosophy but he doubts that philosophy can get beyond being a form of language."[25] Derrida does not ·just complicate, enormously, the relation between language and the practical world of things and actions, he writes as if there is no relation whatsoever.

The style is deliberate, and as such, fully aware of the risks

---

[22] Geoffrey H. Hartman, "Monsieur Texte: On Jacques Derrida, His *Glas*," *The Georgia Review* (Winter 1975), p. 781.

[23] Paul de Man, "Semiology and Rhetoric," *Diacritics*, 3, No. 3 (Fall 1973), 29.

[24] Gayatri Spivak, "Glas-Pieces: A *Compte Rendu*," *Diacritics*, 7, No. 3 (September 1977), 23.

[25] Hartman, p. 782.

of sterility. The problem, as Hartman says, "is the persistence, the seriousness, with which an intelligence of this order employs devices that may seem to be at best witty and at worst trivial."[26] Are these devices necessary to deconstruction's acts of lucidity, or will they serve to turn it into a minor sect, a criticism which vies with the most extreme of modernist literature in the creation of language permutations, joycing (Hartman's verb) its own list of master-terms?

The ultimate justification of deconstructive criticism will be that it works, it reveals structures of intention in texts. The pyrotechnic style, so I judge, will eventually seem only a minor obstacle. The attraction of this work to Anglo-American critics, who have been by tradition empirical and somewhat anecdotal, is that it has ideas, it has speculative reach and daring. Deconstruction is the opposite of a patient mimetic criticism. It sets out to make mimetic assumptions (such as the very idea of realism, or the notion of a continuity between natural language and literary rhetoric) so difficult that they destroy themselves in contradiction. For deconstruction, literary criticism exists because texts are undecidable. Setting out to undo the illusion of presence, till now it has preferred to analyze texts which are already self-conscious about language and point of view. The best work has concerned Rousseau (Derrida, de Man), Wordsworth's views on language (Ferguson), Coleridge's startling invention of a letter from a "friend" in Chapter XIII of *Biographia Literaria* (Spivak), Lautréamont's *Maldoror* (Derrida, Gasché), Mallarmé (Derrida), Husserl (Derrida), and William Carlos Williams and American modernism's criticism of origins (Riddel).[27] These studies take as typical subjects for analysis texts where there is already evident the textuality of consciousness and character; or the contradictory

---

[26] Hartman, p. 781.

[27] Derrida reads Rousseau in *Grammatology*; Ferguson reads Wordsworth in the book cited in note 4; Spivak reads Coleridge in "The Letter as Cutting Edge," *Yale French Studies*, 55/56 (1977); Derrida reads Lautréamont in *La dissemination*; Gasché reads Lautréamont in *Genre* 11, No. 4 (Winter, 1978); Derrida reads Mallarmé in *La dissemination* and Husserl in *La voix et le phénomène*; Riddel reads Williams in the book cited in note 4.

situation of the reader; or the fracturing play of poetic language, "language as the undoing of its own illusion of bridging a gap between word and world" (Riddel). So far, deconstruction has found only certain texts available to its methods, but plainly the hope is for an "open system" (Derrida), a new rhetoric of all the undecidable functions of texts.

Must this criticism get its intensity and preserve its challenge precisely by seeing itself as a denial of common sense? Does this exclusionary insistence on the figurative nature of literary and philosophical texts amount to a new formalism, thus opening Derrida to the argument that he emphasizes only a narrow part of the whole task of interpretation?

Let us measure deconstruction against the idea of an adequate literary criticism embodied in two demands:
(1) Interpretation must show the specific nature of literary discourse within the field of possible discourses, while giving an account of the internal structures of literary texts.
(2) Interpretation must give an account of the relation of texts to the society and history of which they are a part, of which they are the final articulation.

While literariness and historicity have increasingly been concerns for Derrida, it does seem impossible for him and his followers to meet either of these demands without retracting the system as a whole. (Deconstruction finds indispensable the dismantling of traditional distinctions between natural and literary language, literature and other writing, author and reader, intrinsic and extrinsic.) The demands are not unreasonable if they are understood as ideals at which criticism might aim. But deconstruction strictly construed would not recognize these as pertinent requirements of a theory—would consider that the terms of the demands reinstate the metaphysics of presence.

But what is this metaphysics and this presence? Are they synonymous? Are they both accurately diagnosed as disasters for thought? Can they be separated, with presence retained—if not as a value, at least as an unavoidable necessity of human subjects as they communicate with one another about themselves and about everyday life?

To answer, we can reverse the inquiry and evaluate Derrida

from the point of view of the system he claims to have overturned. Up to this point I have made a common sense review of a position violently antagonistic to common sense. (This may have been unfair, but it has been determined by my own beliefs and limitations, as influenced by the methodological scare of deconstruction.) There is, of course, "no such thing" as common sense if we join Derrida in understanding this as untutored intuition. But that the term retains force may be illustrated by an earlier quotation in this paper, from a professional philosopher who writes that Derrida's notion of difference is an "eerie departure from common sense."

Derrida is right when he condemns a naive-reflectionist poetics of representation. And yet to condemn as "metaphysical" or "transcendental" any poetics which takes an interest in person, voice, communication and the human subject in history, does seem a peculiarly private use of the terms, and an avoidance of some major tasks of criticism. Again, as I shall argue in the next section, to say that the representativist conception of writing is linked to the practice of a phonetic-alphabetic writing[28] corresponds not to what we know about Chinese ideograms but to what Ernest Fenollosa and Ezra Pound chose to believe about them; for the Chinese conception of writing, ancient and modern, is arguably as representativist, and soaked in presence, as the West's conception of writing.[29]

To evaluate Derrida's philsosophy from the vantage point of a chastened common sense, we may say that this philosophy comprises an attack on the referent, on the subject, and on history. Let us question whether or not Derrida has been too hasty in announcing the death of the referent, and of the human subject, and of history.

[28]For Derrida's comments on representativism and its linkage to a phonetic-alphabetic writing, see *Grammatology*, passim; and *Positions*, p. 36.

[29]The point receives corroboration in a non-Derridian context in Hugh Kenner, "The Poetics of Error" (on Ezra Pound's ideas about Chinese language and poetry), *Tamkang Review*, 6, No. 2 and 7, No. 1 (October 1975-April 1976), 89 ff.

(1) Lack of an Adequate Theory of the Referent

In a paper on "Deconstruction and the Social Text," John Brenkman speaks of Derrida's interest in the "infinite referral from signifier to signifier, from text to text," and Brenkman wonders why deconstructive reading could not be opened to "the problematic initiated by Freud and Marx." To understand literary figuration "as a function akin to fantasy in the psychoanalytic sense or utopian thought in the political realm" would "precisely require that the figurative swerve be read against its referent—that is, against the social reality out of which it emerges and to which it responds."[30] Deconstructionist critics are defiantly anti-dialectical critics, and do not set the literary text over against culture, society, history, myth or language. The oddity, then, is that while they are anti-dogmatic materialist critics, they do not possess the correspondence theory of knowledge that materialism seems to require. As one student of materialist theories of knowledge has written, "If the theory of knowledge does not preserve the contingency of the relationship between known objects and the knower, the credibility of materialism is undercut, since no known object could then be essentially independent of mind. There may be such objects, but they would be unknowable."[31] Another philosopher writes with Derrida specifically in view: "the worry is that [he] may not have left himself any ground on which to stand and may be enticing us along a path to nowhere."[32] The Derridian lexicographical habit of thought, which juxtaposes all the "senses" of a word, takes language out of the sentence and out of the larger context: Henry Meschonnic remarks that rather than being a surpassing of structuralism, these formulations are epistemologically anterior to Saussure, and constitute a regression: "Une *idolâtrie* substantialiste du langage est ainsi

---

[30] John Brenkman, "Deconstruction and the Social Text," *Social Text*, 1 (Winter 1979), 186-187. Hereafter cited as Brenkman.

[31] David-Hillel Ruben, *Marxism and Materialism: A Study in Marxist Theory of Knowledge* (Hassocks, Sussex: Harvester Press, 1977), p. 3.

[32] Newton Garver, Preface to *Speech and Phenomena* (see note 6), p. xxviii.

compensatoire par rapport à l'idéologie scientiste du structural-isme."[33]

This attack on the referent—summarized in the headnote de Man takes from Proust, "Cette perpétuelle erreur qui est précisément la 'vie' "—has led deconstructionists to coy statements which call doubtful the very possibility of reading, interpretation, translation, literature itself, and criticism (de Man: "interpretation is nothing but the possibility of error"). Very likely this worry is unnecessary, because there exists a satisfactory theory of the relation of language to its object. The literary referent is not "the inert, unsignifying. . . realm of the *thing-in-itself*," because, as Thomas E. Lewis has argued, "the nature of semiosis makes the interpretant, and not the referent as *thing*, the proper object of cultural studies."[34] Lewis sets his own materialism against that of Derrida when he argues that the literary text possesses multiple referents, and that the literary referent "ultimately cannot be defined in purely historicist terms." Representation "is by definition 'imperfect,'. . . it is neither simply nor objectively a deceptive 'myth of presence' but, rather, constitutively a dialectic of signification between present and absent cultural units." Lewis would agree with Derrida that a naive empiricism must be rejected, but finds that the ideas of the interpretant and the cultural unit help us to show how the literary referent both constitutes and deforms its historical reality —how the referent is the result of a continuous production process which includes the possibility of interpretants in other times and cultures.

(2) Lack of an Adequate Theory of the Subject

One can see why there might be overstated metaphysical accounts of the spoken human voice. The spoken word implies the existence of the human or divine other, and implies that the

[33] Henri Meschonnic, *Pour la poétique V: poésie sans réponse* (Paris: Gallimard, 1978), pp. 282-283.

[34] Thomas E. Lewis, "Notes Toward a Theory of the Referent," *PMLA* 94, No. 3 (May 1979), 463; other quotations in this paragraph come from the same article, from pp. 463, 465.

speaker has a kind of otherness in himself. Voice forces man to enter into others and is "the least exterior of sensible phenomena because it emanates not only from the physical but also from the divided psychological interior of man and penetrates to another physical and psychological interior where . . . it must be re-created in the imagination in order to live. Unlike a picture, it lives by contact with these interiors—when they are gone, it is gone."[35] The world of voice, so considered by literary theory or by a modern linguistics which has turned from study of the written word to direct analysis of spoken language, involves the impalpable relation of language to the human person. There are openings to theological meanings in this account, if we but take God as the other, and there are openings too for a theory of the moving or persuading offices of literature. The study of the world of voice has been especially engaged by religious writers like Gabriel Marcel, Louis Lavalle and Walter J. Ong; even if we follow Derrida and cut away from their thought every obviously theological dimension, there remains much that is valuable, in the vein of the passage just quoted from Father Ong.

In viewing the literary work as separate from voice and from natural language systems, deconstructionists would deny the relation between literary features and the social sources they imply or derive from. Literature considered as a self-contained language must omit the category of the speaking subject. Derrida performs the excision very consciously and boldly. The omission, as his first premise, gives him the luxury of avoiding not only the weaker theological concepts of voice, but also the powerful formulations on the unconscious from Freud through to Lacan. At issue, as John Brenkman has argued, "are the effects of speech on the human subject, for whom any utterance contains a constitutive gap whereby it communicates more or less something other than what it says; for Lacan, this always unbalanced relation of the subject to the signifier results from the fact that every human being enters into language—the symbolic network of

[35]Walter J. Ong, S. J., "Voice as Summons for Belief," in *The Barbarian Within* (New York: Macmillan, 1962), p. 60.

intersubjecticity—before he or she can speak."[36] Derrida's various debates with Lacan in his writings, and his more recent introductions to the work on magic words and "anasemic" figures of speech done by Nicolas Abraham and Maria Torok,[37] do not serve to dispel our sense that he is interested only *in the way words use us*—not, correlatively, in the way we use words within a language community, a literary community. It is true, of course, that cases of aberration and breakdown say something important about the usual case; but it does not follow that an adequate approach to language and the human subject should for this reason abandon the usual case as an explicit part of theory. Here again common sense withdraws from wilful extremity.

(3) The Lack of an Adequate Theory of History

To a questioner in *Positions* who wonders whether he has "refused history," Derrida replies that he finds the allegation a little comic; he responds at length and with great caution, stating that he is not against history but against the metaphysical character of the concept of history. This concept is, he says, linked not only to an idea of linearity, but to a whole system of implications (teleology, eschatology, a certain type of traditionalism, a certain concept of continuity, of truth, etc.).[38] But his response does not really dispose of the question.

Derrida makes constant reference, in *Positions* and elsewhere, to the need to surpass the "era of Western metaphysics." He refers in this phrase to a system of fundamental oppositions and constructs by which idealist philosophy since Plato has organized itself. Thus, as Brenkman says, the deconstructed system "remains a purely philosophical one" (and, one might add, a purely Western one), and "this indefinite broadening of history into the era of

[36]Brenkman, p. 186.

[37]See Jacques Derrida, "Fors: The Anglish Words of Nicolas Abraham and Maria Torok," *The Georgia Reivew*, 31 (1977), 64-116; and "Me-Psychoanalysis: An Introduction to the Translation of 'The Shell and the Kernel' by Nicolas Abraham," *Diacritics*, 9, No. 1 (Spring 1979), 4-12.

[38]See *Positions*, pp. 76 ff.

metaphysics . . . hides the evasion of all historical specificity."[39]
It seems appropriate that Derrida takes for study, in Rousseau,
not one of the great social texts but an essay on the origin of
languages. Gayatri Spivak, in the Preface to her *Grammatology*
translation, points out that Derrida often engages in very fine
historical scholarship, but only by contradicting his own injunc-
tions against such work as secondary, inessential, and anyway
impossible. The fascination with the physical fact of writing,
especially with writing in the form of the Chinese ideogram or
the graphic poetics of Mallarmé's "Un coup de dés," suggests
that Derrida's is essentially a spatializing intelligence of the sort
which, in the twentieth century, has always accompanied an
aversion to historical modes of thought. Apparently the attack
on the referent and the subject are really aspects of this larger
aversion to history.

Among deconstructionists, the most neglected areas of
literary scholarship are genre-study and literary history proper,
because the theory itself has no critical norms for explaining how
conventions arise and disappear, no period-construction beyond
the "era of Western metaphysics" and the imagined moment of
its surpassing by a science of writing. Thus the infinite deferral
from figure to referent is matched, in the theory, by the infinite
deferral from the avant-garde destructive discourse to the actual
conditions of literary knowledge. Once again Brenkman is
accurate: "the subject who deconstructs is strangely at peace with
the work of criticism and negation" because "the subject's own
entanglement" in the heritage being dismantled is "hardly felt.
We must ask where, for this philosophy of the future, the risks,
the adventure, the submission to chance can lead if everything is
in question except ourselves."[40] I think the deconstructing reader
is so at peace because of the peculiar logic of the infinite deferral.
The heritage of presuppositions from the past is cleared, the
solution of all difficulties is projected into the future, and thereby
is created a fully armored philosophy.

[39] Brenkman, p. 188.

[40] Brenkman, p. 188.

Our opponents, after learning the vocabulary of indecision and disembarrassing themselves of illusions of presence, before they can talk to us, are taken onto ground where nobody can raise any more issues for dispute. We become impregnable in the unreachable future.

The declared present enemy of deconstruction is hermeneutic theory, as it has come down from Biblical-exegetical, legal and German tradition to American scholars like Richard E. Palmer, E. D. Hirsch, Jr. and Cyrus Hamlin. Palmer is especially good on hermeneutical experience as historical encounter, and Hamlin in two articles has reaffirmed the role of dialogue between author and reader in literature and the central place of literature in education.[41] Hirsch in particular has argued strenuously for objective interpretation and the need for stable meaning in texts, in opposition to notions of infinite deferral. For the issue as between hermeneutics and deconstruction is *determinable meaning*.

In *The Aims of Interpretation* (1976), Hirsch's chapter on "Stylistics and Synonymity" is an implicit criticism of "difference," for it emphasizes shared knowledge and the value of paraphrase. In his Introduction, Hirsch uses the term "cognitive atheists" for dogmatic relativists, like Derrida, "who deny the possibility of hermeneutical knowledge;" at another point Hirsch goes on to make a judgment: "It is ethically inconsistent to batten on institutions whose very foundations one attacks. It is logically inconsistent to write scholarly books which argue that there is no point in writing scholarly books."[42] In response, Derrida would very likely begin by noticing the biblical and theological presuppositions which are sedimented in hermeneutical theory. For Derrida often asserts that a philosophy based on a notion of the sign is profoundly theological; "sign and deity have the same place and same time of birth." Derrida would willingly accept

[41] See, for example, Richard E. Palmer, *Hermeneutics* (1969); Cyrus Hamlin, "The Limits of Understanding: Hermeneutics and the Study of Literature," *Arion* (Boston Univ.), N.S. 3/4.

[42] E. D. Hirsch, Jr., *The Aims of Interpretation* (Chicago: University of Chicago Pr. 1976), pp. 3, 13.

"atheist," then, if not the accompanying adjective "cognitive." This exposes the theological roots of such a modern confrontation, as does Don E. Wayne's statement from another perspective than hermeneutics. Wayne questions: while we may share the post-structuralist distrust of origins and of absolutes, "must we therefore accept the solipsistic and in some instances nihilistic conclusions to which some of these critics have been led? . . . To an intellectual culture like ours, with its faith in 'facts,' the concept of absence has an important descriptive and polemical purpose. But to hypostasize this structural or functional concept of 'absence' into a sort of ontological 'presence' in its own right, a metaphysical nothingness which is said to be the grounding of reality is . . . a religious act rather than a critical one."[43] Essentially both Hirsch and Wayne are asking that deconstruction reform its negative and speculative tendencies by accepted, or at least shareable, canons of evidence and definitions of literary knowledge.

Let me predict that the eventual enemy, the enemy which will conquer deconstruction by absorption and refinement, will be Anglo-American empirical-moral criticism itself, or at any rate an internationalist or comparative literature which by and large adheres to accepted canons and definitions. Common sense, Derrida's current victim, will in some form or other be his eventual master, but common sense will in the process be given a methodological chastening. After twenty years, grammatology as a positive science will have disappeared, will be known as a professional deformation of writers who overpraised the act of writing at a certain moment in history. (Why this crucial element in any criticism has been taken as the whole task of criticism in the 1970s cannot be answered here.) The severe reminders about figural language, and about the logical deceptions in our oppositions, will sift out as the genuine heritage of this methodology.

[43]Don E. Wayne, "Absence makes the heart grow fonder—faster: Dialectical Criticism and the Problem of Ideology," p. 5 of discussion-paper delivered to the Philological Association of the Pacific Coast, 1977 (typescript). A revised version of this article will be published in the journal *Helios*.

Accordingly, the more unstartling assumptions of criticism will come once again to be accepted as workable: neither writing nor speaking can be privileged, but each has a significant role and must be seen in relation to the other; language "is not window-glass, but rather a system of lenses which focus and refract the rays of an hypothetical unmediated vision,"[44] but nonetheless through and by means of its language-medium literature is related to the human person and to things in the world; the force of genre must be described; history exists and is in vivid relation to literary production. It seems likely, then, that man and humanism will not disappear, only that imaginary Derridian man who served temporarily as a remembrance of the role of doubt in the human sciences.

II

Jacques Derrida's points about the dissociative and divestive function of language throw a brilliant light on an idea we have always recognized but have never, until now, pursued to its final hiding place. Modernist literary texts performed Derrida's entire theory of language in advance in the years 1910-1930, but it has taken half a century for modernism to drive itself fully into critical theory, by means of this philosophy which specializes in finding ways to say the unsayable.

However, Derrida's other major contribution, his unfolding of a philosophy of oppositions, does not so much face literary critics with something in their own materials they have repressed, as import into their studies a relatively new clarification from a related discipline.[45] It is especially here, I think, that deconstruction best fulfills the claims of its supporters to be nothing more nor less than analytic criticism as such. As I have suggested, the

---

[44]The phrasing is from Sigurd Burckhardt, "The Poet as Fool and Priest," in his *Shakespearean Meanings* (Princeton, N.J.: Princeton Univ. Pr., 1968).

[45]R. G. Collingwood has said that nothing in thought is absolutely new, there is no new word needed for an absolutely new thing, "But we do constantly need relatively new words for relatively new things": *Philosophical Method* (Oxford: Oxford Univ. Pr., 1933), p. 205. Collingwood's book will be found to anticipate, and to refute in advance, much that is in Derrida.

method asserts that some opposed pairs of terms, such as speech/writing, lack meaning in the one side and thus require to be dismantled, reversed, understood not as a hierarchy but as a rapport-of-difference. Supporters say that the method involves an undoing at the same time as a doing, but on the face of it the method seems to reveal much more about the incompetence of any given theory than about the competence.

The general strategy of deconstruction, for Derrida, requires that we "make a double move according to a unity at once systematic and as if set apart from itself."[46] The first phase of this "double science" is a phase of reversal:

> in a classic philosophical opposition, we do not find the peaceful coexistence of two opposite sides, there is rather a violent hierarchy. One of the two terms commands the other (axiologically, logically, etc.), and takes the dominant position. To deconstruct the opposition is first, at a given moment, to reverse the hierarchy. . . . The importance of this phase is structural, and it is part of an interminable analysis: the hierarchy of the dual opposition is always reconstituting itself.

This is what Derrida himself does when he substitutes writing for speech as a commanding concept, but simply to do this is, as he says, "still to operate on the deconstructed terrain." So it becomes necessary to move on to a second phase, that of the irruptive emergence of a new concept "that never was understood in the previous system."

All Derrida's accounts of this exploratory second phase seem vague, perhaps necessarily so. But the point appears to be that one must avoid the Hegelian type of dialectic, which resolves a contradiction in a third term "that produces *Aufheben*, that negates through sublation, while idealizing and sublimating in a

---

[46]The following two paragraphs quote and summarize from Derrida's account of oppositions in *Positions*, pp. 58-61. My translation. Compare also Lao-tzu: "Reversal is the movement of Tao."

recollecting *(Erinnerung)* interiority, and that confines the difference in a presence of its own." To elude the idealism of this third term, with its easy synthesis, we have to disorganize the opposition by making it undecidable. Undecidables are "the unities of illusions, of 'false' verbal characteristics, nominal or semantic, that can no longer be understood in the philosophic (binary) oppositions and that all the same are present in it, that resist, disorganise it but *without ever* constituting a third term, without ever forming a solution according to [Hegelian] speculative dialectics." So, for example, the *gramme*, Greek for writing, is neither a signifier nor a signified; "neither/nor is at the same time or else *or else.*" The ancient opposition reconstitutes itself, then requires undoing, endlessly, as we show how the one side is locked with the other in a system, and then disorganize the reversal itself by demonstrating how each side is contained in the other.

Delimiting his subject in the Introduction to a book on *The Art and Architecture of Japan*, a Western scholar writes:

> In China landscape art expresses the ideal relation of man to nature. In Japan nature, as the creation of the Gods, was too divine to be viewed idealistically. In the field of bird and flower paintings, too, where the Chinese mind sought frequently for a symbolic or intellectual representation, the Japanese was satisfied with a simple statement close to life itself.[47]

The opposition ideal (China) vs. real (Japan), which privileges Japanese art as the author's subject, immediately breaks down because of the polemical reductions implicit in this writer's idea of "life itself." To deconstruct the statement would be to show the different relation of nature to divinity in these cultures, and then to show the different ways in which both Chinese and Japanese landscape art are "real" and "ideal." Structurally, the procedure would be similar to what occurs in these sentences on

[47] Robert Treat Paine, *Introduction to The Art and Architecture of Japan* (Harmondsworth, Middlesex: Penguin Books, 1955, 2nd ed. 1974), p. 2.

the attitudes of the young toward the old:

> There is much in our treatment of the old and our
> attitudes toward them reminiscent of those that domin-
> ated thinking about the "intractable" problem of the
> poor in the nineteenth century. They are not *us*, is what
> we are often saying (politely and humanely, of course),
> and there are so many of them! Such a situation can
> change only when it becomes natural to say that the old
> *are* us—and to believe it.[48]

That seems definitive. The first of these pertinent examples privileges the idea of "life itself" or "reality" which is the most
prevalent of all ideas in false hierarchical oppositions. The second
example not only performs an undoing concisely, but admirably
pushes beyond, and beyond Derrida, to see results in belief and
action.

In looking at these examples and the few which follow, we
do not strictly require Derrida's two-phase program. Derrida
serves to make us more alert to the difficulties involved, and
perhaps on occasion gives a precise term. In East-West comparative
literature, the role of deconstruction may take the general form
of a policing of logics of argumentation, with special emphasis
on the use of oppositions. My literary examples come from
two recent publications which contain the most excellent work
in the field: *Tamkang Review* [hereafter *TR*], October 1975-
April 1976, which has the Proceedings from The Second International Comparative Literature Conference, held in Taipei, 1975;
and *New Asia Academic Bulletin* I [hereafter *NAAB*], (Hong
Kong, 1978), published by the Hong Kong Comparative Literature
Association. The discussion of these examples is intended to begin
a dialogue on methodological issues in work which I consider of
the first order of quality.

One of the most interesting of these logical phenomena
comes when a writer dismisses one side of an opposition and then

[48] Ronald Blythe, "Living to Be Old," *Harpers Magazine* (July 1979),
p. 37.

reinstates it by going against the grain of the argument. This occurs in a structural analysis of the Yang Lin story series, which speaks of avoiding a "tumble into the pitfall of diachronic study," but at one or two points (e.g., *NAAB*, p. 213) moves away from formalist-structuralist operations to discuss social history. Thus does the paper recognize the limitations of a chosen method. The reverse of this would appear to come when oppositions, which have been scrupulously dismantled throughout a paper, will be put into hierarchy again when the paper rises to its conclusion. A careful dialectical paper on "Conservatism and Originality in Chinese Literature" may thus close on the idea that "In the future, conservatism will become weaker and weaker. And creativism will be encouraged under favorable conditions" (*TR*, p. 108). A paper which discusses the Chinese imitations of Carolyn Kizer conducts the comparison and then, surprisingly, ventures in a final sentence the claim that "her works . . . on occasion, exceed even the Chinese poems themselves," thus privileging the version over the original; this may well be the case, but the unexpected new hierarchy requires further argumentation (*NAAB*, p. 84).

Derrida's critique of the metaphysics of presence, his attempt to restore the materiality of the sign which is systematically repressed in "Western discourse," may sometimes be directly relevant. Derrida: "At the point where the concept of difference intervenes, with the chain [of signifiers] which it brings along with it, all the conceptual oppositions of metaphysics, insofar as they have for ultimate reference the presence of a present, . . . become non-pertinent."[49] Sometimes when scholars compare post-Romantic English and American poetry with Ancient Chinese poetry, a vocabulary of ideal/real (*TR*, p. 185), or of idea/feeling (*TR*, p. 181), or of abstract/concrete (*NAAB*, p. 32), or of artifice/nature (*NAAB*, pp. 17ff), tends to give all presence to the Chinese texts, thus making the comparison asymmetrical through the use of what Derrida calls transcendental signifiers. It is fascinating that the hierarchized opposition, a supposed defect of "Western discourse," should lead these writers into their state-

[49] *Positions*, p. 41. My translation.

ments about the limitations of Western poetry.[50]

In East-West comparative literature, "nature," "reality" and their many analogues such as "Phenomenon," are perhaps the most frequently used terms which imply a hierarchical opposition. A paper on literature as a mediating process, which uses the Han folk ballad, "Lord, Do Not Cross the River," as its focus, brings together formal and social-cultural approaches in a convincing demonstration that comparative literature may be at once structural and historical. The paper describes the several stages between a presumed actual event, a drowning in a river, and the literary account of the event in an ancient oral ballad; and describes, too, the several stages between the poem as "oral" and as "literary" text. Derrida would perhaps worry that the structuralist method derived from Lévi-Strauss, which assumes that mythic thought "progresses from the awareness of oppositions toward their solution" (quoting Lévi-Strauss, NAAB, p. 111), takes the "fullfledged reality" (NAAB, p. 116) of the actual event, and the original oral version of the poem, as absolute presences. Are actual event and the oral version here taken as "solutions" or givens rather than as difficulties in themselves, myths of origin? The paper quotes the poem, choosing one variant over several others, while continuing to call this written version an "oral ballad." Is there a privileging of the imagined actual event over its textual version in the ballad, a privileging of the imagined orality of the text over its written version?

These examples are taken from Chinese scholars writing on Chinese literature. It is likely that these writers are trained in the "Western discourse" whose tradition Derrida must draw upon even as he disorganizes it. It is also possible that Derrida's understanding of "Western discourse" in the "era of Western metaphysics" is itself at fault. This paper concludes by taking up the second of these possibilities, and by attempting to deconstruct Derrida with cultural and linguistic models from beyond the boundaries

---

[50] In partial confirmation: a very similar "deconstruction" is made without Derridian terminology by Pauline Yu in "The Poetics of Discontinuity: East-West Correspondences in Lyric Poetry," PMLA, 94, No. 2 (March 1979), especially p. 272, left-hand column.

of the West.

Along with Hebrew, Chinese writing was just coming to be known in the West in the eighteenth century. In the first half of the *Grammatology*, Derrida studies among other things the reception of Chinese script in Descartes, Leibniz and others. Then in the second half of his book, he performs an immense exegesis of Rousseau's "Essay on the Origin of Languages," a text where Chinese is called a language which does not, like modern western languages, surrender expressiveness to gain exactitude. Limited understanding of Chinese in Rousseau's century permitted the language to stand as one example of a universal script. For Leibniz, according to Derrida, "what liberates Chinese script from the voice is also that which, arbitrarily and by the artifice of invention, wrenches it from history and gives it to philosophy."[51] For Hegel, who subscribed to the Leibnizian praise of non-phonetic writing, hieroglyphic writing was suited well to "the exegeticism of Chinese spiritual culture" (Hegel as quoted by Derrida);[52] but non-phonetic writing was not the way of the West, and writing itself, says Derrida summarizing Hegel, "is to speech what China is to Europe."[53] So, beginning in the eighteenth century, "the concept of Chinese writing . . . functioned as a sort of European hallucination," a "hieroglyphicist prejudice" from which Fenollosa, Pound and others in the twentieth century are not free.[54] Derrida argues that these assumptions, which turn Chinese into something of a perfect language, free of the fallacies of phonetics, have their value in reversing the phonocentrism and logocentrism of the West; that value is not any less for being based on a mistake.

Hence the logocentrism of the West is also an ethnocentrism. There is no purely phonetic writing, but nonetheless alphabetic writing in the West wrongly claims to be like speech; and thus to the practice of a phonetic-alphabetic writing there is linked a

[51]*Grammatology*, p. 76.

[52]In *Grammatology*, p. 25.

[53]*Grammatology*, p. 25.

[54]*Grammatology*, pp. 80-81.

representativist concept of writing. Leibniz, Hegel, Champollion, Mallarmé, Fenollosa and Pound represent movements against this logocentrism, a testing of its limits by the challenge of hiero- glyphic script. And yet: "each time that ethnocentrism is pre- cipitately and ostentatiously reversed, some effort silently hides behind all the spectacular effects to consolidate an inside and to draw from it some domestic [i.e. Western] benefit."[55] Naturally Derrida considers that his own text is the most thoroughgoing reversal of ethnocentrism. But Derrida is described by the law of silent effort he has himself propounded. Gayatri Spivak notes a geographical pattern in the *Grammatology*:

> The relationship between logocentrism and ethnocen- trism is indirectly invoked in the very first sentence of the "Exergue." Yet, paradoxically, and almost by a reverse ethnocentrism, Derrida insists that logocen- trism is a property of the *West*. He does this so frequent- ly that a quotation would be superfluous. Although something of the Chinese prejudice of the West is dis- cussed in Part I, the *East* is never seriously studied or deconstructed in the Derridian text. Why then must it remain . . . as the name of the limits of the text's knowledge?[56]

One way of eluding the presuppositions of the West is to bring on the East, as Derrida does in the *Grammatology* and in the final pages of his "White Mythology" *(Marges)*. But his East, while modest and positive in its force, is no less an ideological fiction than the East of Flaubert and Ernest Renan. Fortunately we now have a correction of Derrida's geographical fiction in Edward W. Said's extensive historical analysis of a discourse where "in all cases the orient is *for* the European observer."[57] Further correction of specifics in Derrida would involve a demonstration

[55] *Grammatology*, p. 80.

[56] Spivak, Preface to *Grammatology*, p. lxxxii.

[57] Edward W. Said, *Orientalism* (1978), p. 158.

(1) that the Chinese written character has a strong phonetic component which is forgotten or de-emphasized by Fenollosa, Pound and Derrida; (2) that the Chinese philosophical and literary tradition, for instance in such works as Lu Chi's *Essay on Literature* and Liu Hsieh's *Literary Mind and the Carving of Dragons*, is to the same extent as the Western tradition subject to the myths of origin and presence.[58]

If Derrida is correct in his assumptions about figurativity and infinite deferral of sense, then perhaps nothing, certainly not Chinese, is suitable for use as a language. But he is not correct. Surely he over-emphasizes the degree of ambiguity of the internal relations of language, for any language as infinitely difficult as he proposes would not be learned by children or read or written by philosophers and critics, or anyone else for that matter. Yet Derrida's limitations need not hide from us his usefulness as a commentator on the way we think. In its special power and weakness, Derrida's extreme critique of the metaphysics of presence may be pertinent to comparative genre-study and terminology, translation studies, and inquiry into the native strengths of different languages.

[58] On Fenollosa and Pound and the ideogram, see the superb account of Girolamo Mancuso, *Pound e la Cina* (Milano: Feltrinelli, 1974), especially ch. 1.2, "L'ideogramma cinese come mezzo di poesia," pp. 17-26.

STRENGTH AND WEAKNESS OF THE MARXIST THEORY OF LITERATURE WITH REFERENCE TO MARXIST CRITICISM IN THE PEOPLE'S REPUBLIC OF CHINA

Douwe Fokkema

At the explicit request of the organizers of this conference, I shall deal with Marxist literary theory as it has been reflected in Chinese criticism in the People's Republic. The limitation of my topic to the Marxist theory of literature in China implies that in general I will not deal with the diverse critical ideas expressed by neo-Marxist authors such as Adorno, Benjamin and Fischer, as so far these have hardly played any role in China. I have to restrict myself to the Marxism of Marx, Engels, Lenin and Mao Tse-tung, but even in spite of this restriction, our presentation must focus on the main points only in view of the limited time that has been set aside for this topic. As to Marxist criticism, various attitudes are possible, such as the attitude of total neglect or, its very opposite, uncritical acceptance. But if one brushes these two extremes aside, there are still the following problems: (a) the methodological problem of how to study Marxist criticism, (b) the problem of the presentation of the main tenets of Marxist criticism, and (c) the problem of how to estimate their value for the study of literature. I have dealt with the first question elsewhere,[1] but for the sake of coherence of my exposition I must briefly summarize the methodological justification of my approach. The solution of the second problem requires a certain systematization which must be imposed on the scattered pronouncements on literature in Marxist writings. The third problem belongs to the domain of evaluation; as it is hazardous to hope

---

[1] D.W. Fokkema and Elrud Ibsch, *Theories of Literature in the Twentieth Century: Structuralism, Marxism, Aesthetics of Reception, Semiotics* (London: C. Hurst and New York: St. Martin's Pr., 1977), ch. 4.

for a satisfying degree of certainty in matters of evaluation, I will restrict myself to a review of the degree of coherence in Marxist literary theory and some personal observations.

1. A Method for Studying Marxist Criticism

Our discussion of methodological problems in the examination of Marxist criticism presupposes agreement on a certain standard of scientific research. In the scientific study of literature, we claim a greater degree of precision and reliability than in casual conversation. In the course of a long tradition, several instruments have been developed which bring us closer to the greater precision and explicitness we are aiming at. Among these instruments I would consider the technical language or metalanguage, which has been shaped for describing the phenomena of literature, to be of paramount importance. At present we have a considerable set of technical terms at our disposal to distinguish between the various genres, subgenres, stylistic devices, narratological modes, metres, rhyme patterns, etc. The technical language the scholar uses consists of well-defined terms which enable him to make more precise distinctions than the layman, and which enable others to check and possibly criticize his observations. Whatever concept of truth one may have, scientific truth is to be shared by a number of experts. It aims to be intersubjective. The researcher will always try to persuade others in a straightforward manner to accept his point of view. Therefore he will present his findings in a clear-cut way so that they can be either accepted or refuted. Any of his scientific results must be worded in such a way that, in principle, they can be falsified.[2] In the study of literature the concept of metalanguage is an indispensable instrument to reach that goal.

The researcher distinguishes himself from the politician, who also aims at persuasion, but who tries to make himself immune to criticism by shrouding himself in vagueness and contradictory promises. The scientific researcher, who ideally is not personally

[2] Karl R. Popper, *The Logic of Scientific Discovery*, rev. ed. (London: Hutchinson, 1972). This is a revised translation of *Logik der Forschung* (Vienna, 1934).

involved in the results of his research but committed only to truth, is open to criticism of his findings as this may further the approximation of truth. The student of literature, for instance, will avoid identification with his object or part of his object, such as the hero in a novel or the emotional tone of a poem. He will respect a certain distance to his object in order to enhance the possibility of correcting his own views under the influence of criticism by himself or others. Of course, usually the researcher is reader at the same time; yet his response to a text as a reader differs from his scientific attempt at observations of general validity. The aim of intersubjective agreement implies a fundamental distinction between the role of reader and that of researcher, although we admit that all researchers at some time have been readers. The distinction between scientific research and the adventure of reading produces the distinction between the technical language of the researcher (metalanguage) and the language of the literary text (object language). These distinctions are generated by the larger dichotomies between the approximation of truth and the participation in action (e.g. attempts to change the world), or between theory and practice.

This methodological position runs counter to the Maoist axiom of the "unity of theory and practice," which even does not permit the hypothetical separation of the approximation of truth and social practice, as "practice is the criterion of truth."[3] Here we meet with one of the most crucial epistemological issues which separate Marxist and critical rationalist theories.

Apart from the instrument of a well-defined terminology or metalanguage, tradition has produced the desirability of a scholarly attitude. The scholar is not a politician aiming at power, nor a mystic indulging in hermetic language. Critical portraits of the lives of scholars in fiction confirm rather than deny the conventional conception of the scholar as a man who searches for truth and who is modest enough to accept justified criticism. Through his attempt to suppress his subjective bias he contributes to the tradition of open-minded discussion, which is the only

[3]Mao Tse-tung, "On Practice," in *Selected Works*, I (Peking: Foreign Languages Pr., 1967), pp. 295-309. The quotations are from pp. 308 and 305.

guarantee of increasing objectivity of scientific results. The aim of objectivity has a psychological and a social aspect. It would be a fine thing if all scholars were honest, fair, humble etc., but if the truth is that many of them are vain, arrogant and influence seeking, one can do little about it except by way of open and free critical discussion.[4] Here the possibility of scientific progress is closely connected with democratic institutions, such as the possibility of free discussion in a free press, the possibility of competition between various schools and scholarly journals, the respect for differing opinions, and of course the absence of censorship. If many scholars morally fail to live up to the ideal of the perfect scholar, a free and democratic society will provide an opportunity for correcting the individual failure and criticizing the scientific results which could have been tested more severely by the scholars who found them. These observations, largely inspired by Karl Popper, give a rough impression of the position of the scholar in a democratic society.

If on the basis of this concept of scientific research we envisage to study Marxist criticism, it immediately strikes us that we are applying criteria of scientific behaviour which are alien to Marxism. However, there is no reason to be discouraged by this. There are many phenomena in the world which are objects of scientific study but have themselves very little in common with the principles of scientific exploration such as precision, explicitness, falsifiability, free criticism and open-minded discussion. Animal behaviour as an object of biology, or the sick mind as an object of psychoanalytic research have little in common with the rational approach of the scientist. Just as it is possible—and rewarding—to study the dream from a rational, psychological point of view, it is possible to study Marxist criticism in terms of critical rationalism, as long as this intention is explained. We propose then to study Marxist criticism as a phenomenon in which we, as students of literature, are not involved. We shall briefly describe its main tenets from a position that lies outside Marxism.

---

[4] Karl R. Popper, "Die Logik der Sozialwissenschaften," in Theodor W. Adorno et al., Der Positivismusstreit in der deutschen Soziologie, 3rd ed. (Darmstadt und Neuwied: Luchterhand, 1974), pp. 103-125.

Only in that way can we heed the fundamental distinction between object and subject, and will we be able to present our findings in terms that admit critical discussion without interference by dogmatic views.

2. Basic Tenets of Marxist Criticism

Any discussion of Marxist criticism must be preceded by the preliminary remark that Marx and Engels have never produced a book and hardly a single study about problems of literature. This fact has been acknowledged by non-Marxist as well as Marxist scholars.[5] Marx and Engels were not primarily interested in matters of literature. Moreover they believed that literature cannot be dealt with as an isolated phenomenon. This brings us to the most fundamental Marxist thesis, which in a different wording was phrased by Friedrich Engels in 1894.[6]

(1) Literature is part of the superstructure, which ultimately is determined by the economic basis.

As this thesis is not applicable under all circumstances, attempts have been made to qualify it by a number of complementary theses, which in various respects are seemingly or indeed contradictory. However, in the Marxist system contradictions are not mutually exclusive due to the application of the dialectical method which tries to reconcile contradictions by accepting a certain tension between opposite notions. In fact, the

---

[5] Cf. the opinion of the Marxist philosopher Georg Lukács in his *Probleme der Ästhetik, Werke X* (Neuwied: Luchterhand, 1969), pp. 205-233.

[6] In a letter to W. Borgius of January 25, 1894, Engels wrote: "We consider the economic conditions as determining the historical development in the last instance. . . . The political, legal, philosophical, religious, literary, artistic etc. development is based on the economic development. But they all also react to each other and to the economic basis. It is not so, that the economic condition is a *cause, active alone*, whereas the rest has a passive role. But there is interaction on the basis of the *in the last instance* determining economic necessity" (Karl Marx and Friedrich Engels, *Werke*, XXXIX [Berlin: Dietz, 1968], 206). The basis for this view had been laid by Marx in his famous "Foreword" (1859) to *Zur Kritik der Politischen Ökonomie*. See Karl Marx and Friedrich Engels, *Über Kunst und Literatur*, I (Berlin: Dietz, 1967), 74-75.

dialectical method relies on the concept of dynamic evolution, i.e. on the principle that a thesis calls for an antithesis which next is superseded by a synthesis. Marxism studies thought, nature and history as if these always are in motion, with projections into an unknown but postulated future. The following qualifying theses can be formulated, although we must be aware of the fact that the explicitness of our wording cannot easily be found in Marxist writings, which as a rule defy explicitness and falsifiability.

(2) The relation between literature and the economic basis is of a dialectical nature.[7]

This means that on the one hand literature will reflect certain developments in society, whereas on the other hand it can influence the developments in society. The relation between literature and society, therefore, can be presented in two different theses—(3) and (4):

(3) Certain texts represent advanced developments and other texts regressive developments in the socio-economic basis.

The latter thesis is based on the presupposition that:

(3a) Literature aims at verisimilitude.[8]

In the practice of Marxist criticism, the judgment whether, in a particular work, a truthful representation had been given, was increasingly based on preconceived cognitive notions. Therefore, thesis (3a) can be elaborated as follows:

(3b) The criterion of verisimilitude attributes priority to knowledge of society over the creative power of the writer.

In a later stage of Marxist criticism it appeared that it is political authorities which have a unique access to knowledge of society:

(3c) The distinction between advanced and regressive developments in society is made by authorities outside literature, such as Marx and Engels, and their political heirs, including the Com-

[7] See the preceding note, in particular the phrase "But they all also react to each other and to the economic basis" and the term "interaction" *(Wechselwirkung)* in the last sentence.

[8] The aim of verisimilitude was defended most clearly by Engels in his letters to Minna Kautsky (1885) and Margaret Harkness (1888). See Marx and Engels, *Über Kunst und Literatur*, I, 155-159.

munist Party as the infallible interpreter of the writings of Marx,
Engels, Lenin, Stalin and Mao Tse-tung.
(4) Certain texts strengthen advanced developments in society,
other texts strengthen regressive developments in the socio-
economic basis. Yet, as a consequence of thesis (1), it is the
economic basis which ultimately determines the nature and course
of literature.
    This can be elaborated as follows:
(4a) Advanced literature, by a careful selection of truthful
representation, has a positive effect on the development of society.
    This thesis accounts for the method of Socialist Realism
which in 1934 was defined as the "truthful, historically concrete
representation of reality in its revolutionary development." The
definition was slightly modified at the Second Congress of the
Soviet Writers' Union in 1954.[9] Verisimilitude remains the aim
of Marxist writers and a crucial standard for Marxist critics, but
the truth should be represented only in a selective way. Only those
elements of social reality should be highlighted which would point
to the communist future.
(4b) The criterion of *selective* truthful representation attributes
priority to political conviction over the intuitive knowledge of
the writer.
(4c) The selection of those elements of social reality which are
held to be progressive is made by political authorities, in communist countries by the Communist Party, who have or believe
to have foreknowledge of the future development of society.[10]
(5) Like their authority in general, the literary taste of Marx and
Engels should be respected. Their preference for Goethe, Shakespeare, Aeschylus and other classical writers (which was in accord-

[9]Harold Swayze, *Political Control of Literature in the USSR, 1946-1959*
(Cambridge, Mass.: Harvard Univ. Pr., 1962), pp. 113-14.

[10]The basis of this thesis can be traced down to Marx's criticism of Las-
salle's play *Franz von Sickingen* (1859). Marx cannot accept Sickingen as a
tragic hero, as he considers him a reactionary who failed "because he as a
knight and representative of a disappearing class rebelled against the existing
order" (Marx and Engels, *Über Kunst und Literatur*, I, 180).

ance with the literary canon of their time), should be assimilated.
(6) The relation between historical facts, including the facts of
literary history, and their significance in the light of present and
future political conditions is of a dialectical nature.

This thesis has produced the concept of "critical inherit-
ance."[11] The value attributed to historical facts may shift with
the change of the political situation. The more, or less, historicist
explanation of the facts of literary history depends on political
expedience.

The concurrence of theses (3), (4), (5) and (6) have led to the
following more specific theses:
(7) Periods of great artistic momentum do not necessarily cor-
respond to a high development of the material basis. The art of
an archaic society, such as ancient Greece, can radiate "eternal
charm."[12]

This thesis is commonly known as the "theory of the unbalanced development of artistic and material production."
(8) Fidelity to historical truth may lead to literary texts which
contradict the political opinions of the writer.

Balzac is the standard example of a writer who, despite his
sympathy for the nobility, wrote with admiration about men,
who according to Engels in the 1830s, represented the masses
of the people and were his own political opponents. Engels called
this "one of the greatest triumphs of Realism."[13] In discussions
of Chinese literary history, Ts'ao Hsüeh-ch'in 曹雪芹 has been held
to be a writer who, through the faithful description of real life,
has overcome his own class sympathy and political prejudice.[14]

---

[11] The concept was worded by Mao Tse-tung in his *Yenan Talks* and
repeated over and over again, e.g. by Chou En-lai in speeches held in 1961.
Cf. "Zhou Enlai on Questions Related to Art and Literature," *Chinese
Literature*, No. 6 (1979), pp. 83-95, in particular: "Chairman Mao urges us to
take over the fine things in our cultural legacy and absorb critically whatever
is beneficial" (p. 94).

[12] This position was worded by Marx in 1857, but published only in 1903.
See Marx and Engels, *Über Kunst und Literatur*, I, 125.

[13] Marx and Engels, *Über Kunst und Literatur*, I, 125.

[14] *Wen-i pao* 文藝報, No. 18 (1954), p. 32.

This thesis is known as "the theory of a possible discrepancy between the political views of the writer and the meaning of his work." It presupposes the possibility that the writer relies more on artistic intuition than on conscious observation and interpretation. The effect of the theory is that the work of classical writers has been assimilated into the corpus of permitted reading matter. The theory prevents a quick judgment of literary work on the basis of the author's biography. The thesis, however, is restricted to older writers, living before the October Revolution or, in the case of China, before 1949, and applies only to a discrepancy between the progressive significance of the work and the overt reactionary views of the author, and not the other way round, to reactionary work by progressive authors.

3. Coherence and Incompatibility of the Main Theses of the Marxist Theory of Literature

As far as I can see, these eight theses and their derivations provide the core of Marxist criticism. They are defended in the Soviet Union and in the People's Republic, as well as by Marxist critics outside the communist world. The strength of the Marxist theory of literature obviously is its appearance of coherence. A theory of literature which itself is part of an overall theory of nature, thought and history, and which on superficial examination appears to be a consistent whole, evidently has a great appeal to many critics and readers of literature. In a world where one easily loses one's direction due to the recent decline of support for the great philosophies and religions, a comprehensive theory of human life and culture, such as Marxism, is likely to find response, if only because it presents the world as a whole and attributes a neat place to the individual in the great mechanism of historical development. Marxism has the message that human beings, wherever they live, may play a useful role. The sense of purpose that Marxism conveys can largely explain its success. Its appeal has been strong, the more so as its holistic philosophy misleadingly has been called scientific.

This brings us to a second aspect of Marxism, which in my view is rather a weakness. Although Marxism presents the materialist interpretation of the world as scientific, its basic tenets are immune to criticism. Historical materialism relies on the primacy of changes in the material conditions, which, sooner or later are believed to transform the entire superstructure; cf. thesis (1).[15] As was suggested by the Russian Formalist Eikhenbaum, in his polemics with Marxist critics, fifty years ago, the primacy of material conditions must be considered a dogma, rather than scientific statement.[16] At best it can be a hypothesis, but Marxist scholars are not interested in testing their most fundamental thesis, which they consider to be unshakable truth and not merely a hypothesis. In agreement with Eikhenbaum, as well as Popper, I would subscribe to the view that all scientific assertions are in principle open to criticism. One can see here the dividing line between religion and scientific research, between superstition and rational discussion, between dogma and hypothesis. By making its basic tenets immune to criticism, Marxism, according to my conception of scientific exploration, cannot be called scientific. By ignoring all rational criticism, Marxism may have acquired a great capacity for proselytizing, but at the same time it has become a belief, rather than a scientific conception.

From the point of view of critical rationalism, the intellectual invulnerability of Marxism is not an asset, but a liability. The very basis of Marxism is not falsifiable, but also the various theses of the Marxist theory of literature can hardly be refuted as they are worded in such a way that counter examples are easily assimilated, or relegated to the realm of another, complementary or even contradictory thesis.

Thesis (2), stipulating that there is a dialectical relationship between literature and the economic basis, means that in some cases literary texts may influence the economic basis, that in the same and other cases the economic basis may influence the literary text, and that in some or all of these cases there may be an interaction between the two. As long as it has not been specified which

---

[15]Marx in his "Foreword" (1859) to *Zur Kritik der politischen Ökonomie*. See Marx and Engels, *Über Kunst und Literatur*, I, 74-75.

[16]Boris M. Eikhenbaum, "Literary Environment," in Ladislav Matejka and Krystyna Pomorska, ed., *Readings in Russian Poetics: Formalist and Structuralist Views* (Cambridge, Mass.: MIT Pr., 1971), pp. 56-66.

case one has at hand, this thesis is too vague to make refutation at all possible. The impossibility to refute it is of the same order as with the assertion that "yesterday it may have rained somewhere in the world."

Some theses of Marxist criticism are applicable only to a certain period of history, which partly accounts for their mutual incompatibility. One may observe a certain tension between theses (3a) and (4a). Thesis (3a) primarily applies to pre-revolutionary texts—roughly the kind of literature which has been called Critical Realism—and thesis (4a) to post-revolutionary literature, or Socialist Realism. This draws our attention to the fact that several of the theses we have mentioned have only restricted validity. However, in practice, there is no clear watershed between the two areas where theses (3a) and (4a) are valid. In the last instance, their applicability will be decided by ideological and political contingency. Here we touch on one of the causes of the various fluctuations which can be observed in the practical application of the Marxist theory of literature.[17]

Whereas theses (3a) and (4a) can be held to be roughly complementary, the tension between, on the one hand, theses (3b) and (4b) and, on the other hand, thesis (8) is less easy to explain. Theses (3b) and (4b) emphasize the priority of a political analysis of society; thesis (8) stresses the power of artistic intuition. This contradiction was dealt with by Mao Tse-tung in the Yenan Talks, in a rather unclear passage on the relation between the political and the artistic criterion.[18] In general, theses (3b) and (4b) must be held to have priority over thesis (8). The latter thesis has been made rather less damaging by making it applicable only to writers who have lived long ago, or who can be considered to belong to pre-revolutionary times. Again, thesis (8) has restricted validity

---

[17] See, e.g. the difference between the vehement criticism of Lao She 老舍 in "On Lau Shaw's 'City of the Cat People' " by the Revolutionary Criticism Group of Peking Normal College in Chinese Literature, No. 4 (1970), pp. 98-109, and the positive judgment of his work by Kuo Mo-jo 郭沫若 in the belated obituary in Chinese Literature, No. 10 (1978), pp. 3-9.

[18] Mao Tse-tung, Selected Works, III (Peking: Foreign Languages Pr., 1967), 89.

only, but is extremely important as it opens the way to the literary heritage.

Thesis (6) fully reveals the predominance of political considerations in Marxist criticism. At the same time, this thesis provides some margin of freedom of interpretation to Marxist critics, which nowadays again is fully exploited in the People's Republic. At present, discussions of literary history do not have immediate repercussions on the cultural policies of the day. In fact, the pendulum has swung again in the direction of a more historicist approach,[19] although complete historicism remains incompatible with Marxism, which always will project its nineteenth-century philosophy of history backwards to the earliest times.

Thesis (7) plainly contradicts the very foundation of Marxism as expressed in theses (1) and (6), but has not been removed from the Marxist system, although under certain circumstances, such as during the Cultural Revolution, it was almost never mentioned. One must recall here that Mao Tse-tung in his *Yenan Talks* seemed to be critical of "eternal values," when he denied that "there is an abstract and absolutely unchangeable artistic criterion" and added that "each class in every class society has its own political and artistic criteria."[20] Nevertheless, thesis (7), like (5) and (8), provides a justification for reading the great classics of literature.

Also thesis (8) seems to be at odds, not only with theses (3b) and (4b), but with the major body of Marxist concepts. Here artistic integrity is to play a mysterious role. The artist is believed to have adequate knowledge of social life, by means of his artistic intuition, without the intermediary of a political (Marxist) analysis. In that way, artistic intuition is on equal footing with Marxist analytical knowledge. During the Cultural Revolution, several

---

[19] See the matter-of-fact introductions to classical writers in recent issues of the journal *Chinese Literature*, which lack almost all Marxist verbiage, e.g. Qiao Xiangzhong and Wu Gengshun, "Tang Dynasty Poets (1)," and Wu Gengshun, "Tang Dynasty Poets (2)," in *Chinese Literature*, No. 5 (1979), pp. 86-93 and No. 7 (1979), pp. 73-79.

[20] Mao Tse-tung, *Selected Works*, III (Peking: Foreign Languages Pr., 1967), 89.

young theoreticians have seen this anomaly, and they have expressed their views in criticism of Chou Yang 周揚 and his Russian
sources, who had defended the idea that literature "reflects life
and reality through images."[21] Indeed, the concept of artistic
intuition, which originates in idealist theories of the early nineteenth century, is hard to reconcile with Marxist economic deter-
minism. Yet, neither the Soviet authorities, nor those in Peking
seem inclined to do away with the anomaly, for which, in the
final instance, Friedrich Engels is accountable. In spite of the fact
that Hua Kuo-feng has declared that one should not cling
dogmatically to the writings of Marx, Lenin and Mao Tse-tung,[22]
I know of no statement by Marx or Engels or Lenin which openly
has been criticized by the Chinese Communist Party.

Of course, the Chinese communist leaders may fear that the
open criticism of any part of the official Marxist doctrine will
weaken the authority of Marx and Engels, as well as their own
authority. But the explanation is possible as well that they badly
need theses (7) and (8) in order to maintain the possibility of
printing and reading the older writers, which is a cultural necessity
as well as politically harmless, or at least less harmful than the
suppression of the literary heritage.

Another explanation for maintaining the anomalous theses
(7) and (8) may be that the cultural authorities in China are not
bothered at all by logical contradictions. First, so far it has not
been one of their aims to further logical thinking in ideological
matters among the people. Second, they probably hold that the
anomalies can easily be explained away by way of dialectics.
Third, they may in fact welcome contradictory theories, as these
will give them the leeway to change their policies by emphasizing
at one time or in one case theory A, at another time or in another
case, theory B. They may find it an advantage to adjust their

[21] Cf. D.W. Fokkema, "The Concept of Typicalness in Russian and Recent
Chinese Literary Theory," *Proceedings of the VIth Congress of the Inter-
national Comparative Literature Association* (1970) (Stuttgart: Kunst und
Wissen, 1975), pp. 707-711.

[22] "Chairman Hua Guofeng on May 4th Movement," *Peking Review*, No.
19 (1979), pp. 9-11.

policies in view of changing conditions by referring now to this, then to another element of the Marxist doctrine. From the point of view of practical politics, logical anomalies seem to be an asset, at least within the framework of the dictatorship by the Communist Party. Here we see how precisely those elements which, from a rational and scientific point of view, we would consider weaknesses of the Marxist doctrine, can be considered strong points in the practice of the communist regime.

The mutual incompatibility of the various theses appears to be considerable. The superficial impression of coherence of the Marxist theory of literature derives from its being embedded in a larger philosophy of nature, thought and history, rather than from the compatibility of its constituent elements. On close analysis one must conclude that the holistic appearance of the Marxist theory of literature shows many cracks, whereas, as we have seen, the scientific basis it claims to have, can be denied.

4. Conclusion

An estimate of the value of Marxist criticism for the study of literature, like all value judgments, necessarily must have a subjective character. Due to the fact that I do not share the Marxist belief in the decisive function of material conditions and would rather adhere to the view that under specific conditions it is as well possible that the *mind*, and not matter, determines historical events, I tend to be rather critical of various aspects of the Marxist theory of literature. At this point our exposition would acquire a very broad scope, if we would point to the role of the *mental* effort of elaborating and spreading the ideology of Marxism, which—perhaps more than the so-called objective material conditions—has been decisive in changing the course of modern Chinese history. Let us restrict ourselves, therefore, to Marxist criticism of literature.

My main criticism would pertain to the vagueness of the basic tenets of Marxist literary theory. If indeed literature, as part of the superstructure, is ultimately determined by the economic basis in the sense that changes in the economic basis sooner or later will cause changes in the production of literature, it almost never has been explained what precisely the relation between the changes in the economic basis and in literature is. Are these economic changes, for instance, to affect rhyme? Or do they, for instance, cause first person narration, or rather third person narration? Or in general, in what way do they affect literary *form*?

One of the few Marxist critics who has seen that these questions should be at the center of interest of Marxist criticism is Lucien Goldmann, who has suggested that there is a parallelism between the structure of the novel and the structure of exchange in the free market economy. He has observed that the French *nouveau roman* is characterized by dissolution of the character and, consequently, by increase in the autonomy of objects. He explains this development as the result of reification *(Verdinglichung)* which, in his view, is the product of the unrestricted growth of the free market economy, its trusts and monopolies, capital investment and government intervention.[23]

One should appreciate that Goldmann has attempted to become more specific than many other Marxist critics, including those in China, but his explanation can quite easily be refuted, since the kind of literature he has in mind, i.e. literature with almost no interference by the narrator and very little scope for the individual characters, is by far not the only sort of literature that has been produced in the industrial countries in the second half of this century. How would he explain the extremely subjectivist fiction of Cortázar, Borges and John Barth, or the fiction of Malamud or Saul Bellow, who do respect the individual inclinations of both narrator and characters?

Even Lucien Goldmann—whose influence in China has been small to non-existent—has not been explicit enough to produce a plausible theory, and the Marxist critics who have been less explicit have had little to say about the development and explanation of literary history. Indeed, most Marxist critics have restricted themselves to very general, unfalsifiable expositions. The number of monographs on a Marxist basis about one text and its relation to the socio-economic basis, is extremely small. Marxism *seems* to provide a comprehensive theory of literature,

[23] See Lucien Goldmann, *Pour une sociologie du roman* (Paris: Gallimard, 1964).

but, in fact, does not. The scientific status of the Marxist theory of literature is, to say the least, questionable. Its holistic appeal has no basis in the various tenets of the Marxist theory, several of which are contradictory.

Our conclusion must be that the persuasive power of Marxism is largely based on the fact that it provides an answer, though largely an irrational answer, to the general human need for direction in a chaotic world. As Hua Kuo-feng said last May: "If we deviate from the basic principles of Marxism-Leninism-Mao Zedong Thought, we will lose our bearings and will be led astray."[24] The human inclination to accept a makeshift answer originates in a failing intellectual self-confidence. If we take our responsibility as intellectuals seriously, we should be suspicious of all holistic solutions, comprehensive theories and totalistic systems, as they are hard to test and tend to restrict the possibility of criticism by the individual researcher.

[24]"Chairman Hua Guofeng on May 4th Movement," *Peking Review*, No. 19 (1979), p. 11.

FRAGMENTARY NEGATION: A REAPPRAISAL
OF EZRA POUND'S IDEOGRAMMIC METHOD

William Tay

In his well-known essay on James Joyce's *Ulysses*, T.S. Eliot suggests that the narrative method of realist fiction is no longer capable "of ordering, of giving a shape and a significance" to what he describes as "the immense panorama of futility and anarchy which is contemporary history."[1] Facing the atomization and irrationality of the modern experience, the modern artist, according to Eliot, can no longer present a coherent picture of the new reality in the traditional method. Eliot goes on to praise Joyce's adoption of "the mythical method"—"the manipulation [of] a continuous parallel between contemporaneity and antiquity"—as a "step toward making the modern world possible for art."[2] Indeed, the mythical method, at least on the surface, has provided the unifying frame and device capable of totalizing the disintegrated fragments into a seeming whole. However, what the method has been able to totalize is but an experience trivial, empty, peripheral in character and in want of meaningful action.

Writing about some of her fellow artists, Virginia Woolf describes them as "great egoists," writing "about themselves honestly."[3] But for writers struggling against the monadization of reality, such solipsism is clearly the only guarantee of their artistic integrity. Writing for an audience that may be merely imaginative,

---

[1] T. S. Eliot, "Myth and Literary Criticism," in *The Modern Tradition: Backgrounds of Modern Literature*, ed. Richard Ellmann and Charles Feidelson, Jr. (New York: Oxford Univ. Pr., 1965), p. 681. This is a reprint of the 1923 essay "Ulysses, Order, and Myth" with a new note by Eliot.

[2] Eliot, p. 681.

[3] *Collected Essays*, II (New York: HarBrace J., 1967), 177.

and with the immediate need to communicate forever dwindling, the only assurance they can confidently embrace is the material being of their linguistic tool, which is now painfully and endlessly forged into a meditative purity. When language is no longer a way to discover and share some ultimate "truth," it merely becomes the appropriate means to release the self in a last but futile effort to make the phenomenal world once again possible for purposeful action.

Ezra Pound has always been more rebellious and vocal than his friends. By comparison, his reaction to the affirmative dominance of the cultural tradition and the suffocating void of contemporary reality is also the most radical. He condemns capitalism early in his career, for, in his opinion, it has become the greatest obstacle for artistic creation. He thinks that all modern artists have been forced to perform certain "mental hygiene" before they can even properly produce their works. This, of course, is an assertion of a close and organic connection between the economic base and cultural production. The health and growth of art, from architecture to poetry, can then be gauged by the tolerance and intolerance of usury. The early Pound, however, still retains some hope for a cultural revival to be promoted by the good will and direct action of the liberal-bourgeois government. Writing in 1912, after his visit to America in 1910-11, he had hoped for an American Renaissance: "Art was lifted into Alexander by subsidy, and by no other means will it be established in the United States."[4] Apparently he then still had some faith in the validity of the system. By limiting himself to such rear-guard criticism and occasional public appeals, he was still capable of devoting most of his attention to esthetic issues in the next several years.

Pound's evolution from esthete to reactionary propagandist is tentative and gradual. The descent into Hades which is the Pisa camp is the culmination of decades of disappointment, indoctrination and self-questioning. Pound's opinion and bigotry can be isolated to establish a political profile, which may serve as a guide

---

[4] "Patria Mia," published in *New Age* from September 5 to November 14, 1912, is perhaps the best introduction to Pound's early view of the relation between art and society.

to his poetry. Since the content of the poem sometimes appears to be far more paraphrasable from the prose, such an effort is indeed justifiable. But in so doing, one runs the risk of dichotomizing form and content, and creating the impression of form or style as ideologically neutral.

In the modern world, the avant-garde artist usually subsists meagerly and parasitically at the fringe of society. More often than not, his works, either subtly or vociferously, condemn, indict and refute that society. This is because the practice of artistic production, like the general mode of production overdetermining the nature of all other social practices, is predominantly capitalistic. The goal of all the practices is then the generation of profit through the continuous and avaricious consumption of commodities. A product that is not profitably marketable and massively consumed is doomed to be ignored or buried. In this context the reaction of the avant-garde artist is quite understandable. But such a reaction is by no means limited to the provocative opinions or paraphrasable content; often the art form is in itself a stylistic reaction, at once negative and negating. A style or form which is not only shocking to the consuming taste but esthetically refuses to commodify itself so as to be pleasing and marketable, is a subversion of the dominant mode of production, a negation of the consumptive practice.

Theorizing about the development of modern music, Theodor W. Adorno sees the production and dominance of melody in musical composition as consumption oriented, catering to the bourgeois taste, reducing the audience's active participation to a passive listening.[5] Clearly such a practice is very much in conformity with the prevailing mode of production. Schoenberg's twelve-tone system, in contradistinction to the mechanical production and passive consumption of familiar melody, and facing

---

[5] See Theodor W. Adorno, *Philosophy of Modern Music*, tr. Anne G. Mitchell and W. V. Blomster (New York: Seabury, 1973). The obvious problem with Adorno's thesis is the outright dismissal of Stravinsky without any evaluation of his later works. As we are only interested in the concept of inert consumption versus active re-creation, we will not indulge in this controversy.

the increasing refusal of the public to accept new and unfamiliar music, achieves a shocking effect and refuses to comply with the familiar hearing pattern. Schoenberg's music, which demands a total participation and new awareness of the audience, is interpreted by Adorno as a more deserving heir to the music of the high bourgeois period. A piece of music is no longer a commodified object to be easily consumed, but remains always a compositional process to be actively realized through the listener. Unlike the early Stravinsky who flattens and harmonizes the opposites and provides his audience with rhythmic jolts, Schoenberg's counterpoint offers no false reconciliation of the contradictions which Adorno believes to be inherent in the bourgeois society. The sophistication, individualization, and the defiance of the popular taste of the avant-garde form constitute, in Adorno's view, a denial of the bourgeois society and its dominant social practice.

It is from this perspective that Pound's early poetics should be examined. This poetics, by denouncing the excessive Victorian rhetoric through a linguistic virtuosity of imagistic concreteness, tends to shock the imagination which has grown accustomed to a William Watson or even a Kipling.[6] By demanding the active participation of the reader through its method of precise suggestion, this poetics helps to demolish the numbing habit of passive, detached and easy consumption; and the seemingly "philosophical" thoughts or explanatory, adjectival, cliché-ridden descriptions masquerading as poetry are thus put to task. Early in his career, Pound had harshly criticized this consumption mentality of the vast majority of the reading public. In 1912 he made the appeal that the modern artist should not "play up to the law of supply and demand."[7] In a 1913 letter to Harriet Monroe, he observed that the "people who cared were puzzled"

[6] Watson and Kipling were then probably the most widely-read poets and this fact clearly reflects the situation faced by the young poets at that period. For an elaborate discussion, see C. K. Stead, *The New Poetic: Yeats to Eliot* (Middlesex, England: Penguin, 1967), ch. 2.

[7] *Selected Prose*, ed. William Cockson (New York: New Directions, 1973), p. 110. Hereafter this work is abbreviated as *SP* and all further references appear in the text.

by the acclamation for Masefield. Pound even repeated the opinion of one anonymous gentleman with whom he clearly agreed: "[Masefield] will appeal to lots of people who don't like poetry but who like to think they like poetry." Pound commented in italics: "If one is going to print opinions that the public already agrees with, what is the use of printing 'em at all?"[8] But obviously what the passive, unthinking readers would appreciate are works that conform to their habits and familiar patterns. And for artists who manage to produce the reassurance in an agreeable way, they are duly rewarded. Almost at the same time, Harriet Monroe found some of Pound's contributions "offensive" to the public taste (most likely a reference to Pound's bold use of language). Pound refused to budge, politely asked her to discard them, and proclaimed that "the public can go to the devil" (*SP*, p. 13). A much fuller exposition of his stance at this time on the relation between art and the reading public can also be found in the essay "The Serious Artist." Once again he promotes the idea that good art or accurate art does not "make false reports." The serious artist does not "falsify" for financial benefits, nor does he do so in order to "conform to the taste of his time . . . , to the conveniences of a preconceived code of ethics." And once the artist "lies," whether it is done out of carelessness, laziness, cowardice or negligence, he "nevertheless lies" and "should be punished or despised in proportion to the seriousness of his offence."[9]

Despite such pungent language, Pound knows that in the bourgeois society there is not much breathing space for the artist. He sees some individual artist preserving his integrity by quietly doing some fine work with the hope of being discovered after his death. He sees some other "good enough poet" corrupted by writing "stuff as vendible as bath-tubs." Then some others simply abandon writing and prepare themselves for university careers. Great art, in Pound's opinion, does not necessarily "depend upon

[8] *The Letters of Ezra Pound*, ed. D. D. Paige (New York: Harcourt, 1950), p. 12.

[9] *Literary Essays of Ezra Pound*, ed. T. S. Eliot (New York: New Directions, 1954), pp. 43-44. Hereafter cited as *Literary Essays*.

the support of riches, but without such aid, it remains individual,
separate, and spasmodic; it will not group and become a great
period."[10]

With the arrival of the mechanical age, modern man is finally
liberated from the direct combat with nature for his survival, and
the accumulation of wealth in the form of capital is rapidly increasing. Then there should be "living conditions for artists; not
merely for illustrators and magazine writers, not merely for
commercial producers, catering to what they think 'the public'
or their readers' desire."[11] To those who believe that the function
of art, such as the writing of "The Seafarer," is merely to enter-
tain, Pound refuted in "The Constant Preaching of the Mob"
(1916) by saying that this poem or even the more uneven "The
Wanderer" was written "not for after-dinner speakers," but
because "a man believing in silence found himself unable to
withhold himself from speaking."[12] Whatever meaning Pound
might have intended originally, the implication is that poetry is
to be taken seriously, and the reader could learn something or
enhance his appreciative power by paying close attention. The
refusal to be consumed easily is once again echoed. This resistance
to pander to the bourgeois taste by providing an art that is com-
forting, non-provocative and consumption-oriented persists
throughout Pound's career, and similar statements are scattered
about in the immense prose output of the next three decades.
But the link between the art work as commodity and hence its
inherent nature to conform is perhaps most succinctly expressed
in this statement made in 1917: "Art that sells on production is
bad art, essentially. It is art that is made to demand. It suits the
public. . . . The taste of the public is always bad. It is bad because
it is not an individual expression, but merely a mania for assent,
a mania to be 'in on it.' "[13] Despite these incisive declarations,
the realization of a poetics and a poetic form which, besides

[10] *Literary Essays*, p. 221.

[11] *Literary Essays*, p. 221.

[12] *Literary Essays*, p. 65.

[13] "Imaginary Letters, IV," *The Little Review*, (Sept. 1917), p. 20. This is

being non-conformative, can also demand the strong, active and creative participation of the reader in the reading process so as to negate the inert consumption habit, is a slow and gradual evolution.

As early as 1908, Pound told William Carlos Williams that the kind of poetry he was then writing, the "so-called dramatic lyric," "is the poetic part of a drama the rest of which (to me the prose part) is left to the reader's imagination or implied or set in a short note." And a character only interests him in "a moment of song, self-analysis, or sudden understanding or revelation."[14] While the first statement reveals that the quest for non-explanatory suggestiveness has not been a sudden move, the second reminds us of a technique practiced by a fellow artist who later became a friend—the "epiphany" of James Joyce's *Dubliners*. In the same letter to Williams, Pound also mentions the necessity to be free from didacticism and "to paint the thing as I see it." These two rules appear to be the prefigurations of the first two tenets of the 1913 "Imagisme" manifesto: "1. Direct treatment of the 'thing,' whether subjective or objective. 2. To use absolutely no word that did not contribute to the presentation."[15] That suggestion or suggestiveness can be an effective weapon in combating the non-participational, consuming mentality of the reader lies in its ability to stimulate the imagination into creative activity. The incompleteness or indefiniteness demands the reader to leap the gap, to make the necessary links and to re-create the meaning in its entirety. In short, the reader in his active involvement in the quest for meaning is now in a small way also a creator.

But by so saying one runs the risk of being accused of both hypostatizing a process and endangering the ontological status of

reprinted in *Imaginary Letters* (Paris, 1930), but instead has become the opening letter.

[14] *Letters*, pp. 3-4.

[15] F. S. Flint and Ezra Pound, "Imagisme," *Poetry*, I (1913). Since Pound's contribution is reprinted with alterations in *Literary Essays*, I am quoting from a reprint of the original piece now collected in *Ezra Pound*, ed. J. P. Sullivan (Middlesex, England: Penguin, 1970), p. 41.

the art work. At this point the distinction made by Jan Mukarovsky, the Prague structuralist, between the "artefact" and "the
aesthetic object" may be of some help. Mukarovský identifies the
text in print as the "artefact" and opposes it to the coming-into-
being of the artefact via the reader's imagination. It is then possible to assume that one "artefact"—a printed text is no longer a
hypostatization—embodies potentially various "aesthetic objects" to be realized through the reading processes of readers
living in a specific social formation at a certain historical moment.[16] Following this argument, one can claim that for the
passive, unthinking reader, the smooth consumption of the printed
text or the "artefact" by no means signifies the realization of the
"aesthetic object," which can only come into being through active
reconstruction.[17]

In *The Spirit of Romance*, his first book of prose, Pound
enthusiastically praises Dante for his "objectivity and again
objectivity, and expression." He also observes that "language is

[16]See Jan Mukarovsky, *Structure, Sign, and Function*, tr. and ed. John
Burbank and Peter Steiner (New Haven: Yale Univ. Press, 1977), pp. 49-69.
Earl Miner, in an essay on the cognitive process, has actually gone one step
further by saying that even the format and the print of the book, and the
time and place of reading may also determine the outcome of the reading
experience (or the re-creation). See his "That Literature Is a Kind of Knowledge," *Critical Inquiry*, 2 (1976), 492.

[17]Pound's relation with Whitman's poetry has been studied in detail by
some critics. Sam Haynes, however, has bought our attention to some affinities shared by Pound and Whitman in their poetic goals. See his "Whitman, Pound, and the Prose Tradition," in *The Presence of Whitman*, ed.
R.W.B. Lewis (New York: AMS Pr., 1962). Cf. also Roy Harvey Pearce, *The
Continuity of American Poetry* (Princeton: Princeton Univ. Pr., 1965),
pp. 83-88. In light of the discussion on suggestiveness here, I would like to
quote a passage from the preface to the 1888 edition of *Leaves of Grass*
("A Backward Glance O'er Travel'd Roads") which may be of some interest
for the purpose of comparison: "I round and finish little, if anything; and
could not consistently with my scheme. The reader will always have his or
her part to do, just as much as I have had mine. I seek less to state or display
any theme or thought, and more to bring you, reader, into the atmosphere
of the theme or thought—there to pursue your own flight."

made of concrete things." Interestingly enough, these are exactly
the same words he used to describe the "proper" way of writing
modern poetry to Harriet Monroe.[18] This is written after the
Imagist/Vorticist movements and in the context of the so-called
"French prose tradition." The search for concreteness clearly
had begun in 1910. But what further distinguishes Dante is that
he "wrote his poems to MAKE PEOPLE THINK."[19] And elsewhere Pound also expresses his own wish of writing a literature
which can compel "the reader to think."[20]

Dante is quoted quite extensively by Pound in his discussion
of Arnaut Daniel in *The Spirit of Romance*. Several of Daniel's
poems are cited by Dante in *De Vulgari Eloquentia*, and in the
Purgatorio Daniel is referred to as "the better craftsman in the
mother tongue." Pound's interest in Daniel apparently has much
to do with Dante's high estimation of him.[21] In the fourth essay
of the series called "I Gather the Limbs of Osiris" (1911), the
"accuracy" of Daniel's description is noted, and Dante's "precision of observation and reference," according to Pound, is
probably indebted to Daniel too.[22] Although Pound thinks that
the main contribution of the Provençal is the art of "rhyme and
rhyme-blending," in another occasion he also speaks of a classical
virtue shared by both Dante and the troubadours: "One might
learn from Dante himself all that one could learn from Arnaut:

[18] *Letters*, p. 48.

[19] *Literary Essays*, p. 204.

[20] "Pastiche. The Regional. XIV," *New Age*, No. 25 (October 23, 1919),
p. 432.

[21] See *Literary Essays*, p. 102: "If we are to understand that part of our
civilization which is the art of verse, we must begin at the root, and that root
is medieval. The poetic art of Provence paved the way for the poetic art of
Tuscany; and to this Dante bears sufficient witness in the *De Vulgari
Eloquio*" (1913). For an excellent study of this subject, see Stuart Y. Mc-
Dougal's *Ezra Pound and the Troubadour Tradition* (Princeton: Princeton
Univ. Pr., 1972).

[22] "I Gather the Limbs of Osiris, IV," *New Age*, No. 10 (December 21,
1911), p. 79. This series in twelve parts is now included with some omissions
in *Selected Prose*.

precision of statement, particularization."[23] That these pronouncements bear some resemblances to the Imagistic tenets really needs
no further belaboring.

   The entire "Osiris" series actually begins in a way which can
be interpreted as a practice of the suggestiveness concept. With
only a "philological" note at the end explaining the condition of
the text, the first installment of the series is simply a new translation of "The Seafarer." There is no explication of any kind
provided by the poet. Old English poetry has always been known
as a poetry of nouns. Metrically it even stresses the nouns rather
than the verbs. And the kennings can be seen as some kind of
compound noun images. This prominence of concrete noun
quality, to a student of classical Chinese poetry as exemplified by
the T'ang poets, is certainly not unfamiliar. Pound's translation
and study of both Chinese poetry and the ideogram have prompt-
ed some similar thoughts too. First he sees a certain resemblance
between the kenning and the ideogram: "I once got a man to
start translating the *Seafarer* into Chinese. It came out almost
directly into Chinese verse, with two solid ideograms in each half-
line." Then for the purpose of comparison he praises a poem
about war and warriors by Li Po: "Apart from the *Seafarer* I know
no other European poems of the period that you can hang up with
the 'Exile's Letter' by Li Po, displaying the West on a par with the
Orient."[24] Earlier in another essay, Pound has lauded a similar war-
lamenting poem by Li Po for its directness, restraint from "mel-
liflous circumlocution" and abstention from "sentimentalizing."[25]
In other words, the weaknesses often identified by Pound with
late Victorian poetry cannot be found here. If the omission of
discursive explication in the first of a series of essays can be
viewed as a gesture of suggestiveness, then the concrete quality
exuberant in the translation itself is an indication of another
poetic goal of Pound's.

   Despite the silence on Pound's part, A. R. Orage, the editor

[23]*Literary Essays*, p. 215.

[24]*ABC of Reading* (New York, 1960), p. 51.

[25]"Chinese Poetry," *To-Day*, No. 3 (April, 1918), p. 57.

of *New Age*, points out at the beginning of the "Osiris" series that under this heading, "expositions and translations" would be made by Pound "in illustration of 'The New Method' in scholarship." In the essay immediately following the "Seafarer" translation, Pound finally explains this "new method of scholarship" as "the method of Luminous Detail, a method most vigorously hostile to the prevailing mode of today—that is, the method of multitudinous detail, and to the method of yesterday, the method of sentiment and generalisation. The latter is too inexact and the former too cumbersome" (*SP*, p. 21). If these ideas are to be applied to the writing of poetry, they can easily be translated into some other Poundian tenets such as: "no sentimentalizing"; "no decorative frill adjective"; "general expressions in non-concrete terms are a laziness"; and "the only escape from [clichés and set phrases] is by precision." Hence in claiming to write about a new method of scholarship, Pound is again proselytizing his poetic ideals and continuing the battle. In the same essay there is also an echo of his 1908 "epiphanic" concept: "Any fact may be 'symptomatic,' but certain facts give one a *sudden insight* into circumjacent conditions, into their causes, their effects, into sequence, and law" (*SP*, p. 22, my italics). But the most important trait of this new method is that it does not "state," it "presents." The artist's duty is to "seek out the luminous detail," the "symptomatic fact" that reveals intuitively in a sudden flash, and then "presents it. He does not comment" (*SP*, p. 23). The aim of suggestiveness is embodied again in this restraint from commentary and explanation.

In the last of the "Osiris" series, Pound argues that modern poetry should be "closer to the thing," and that the "beauty of the thing" should replace "rhetoric and frilled paper decoration" (*SP*, p. 41). In another essay written around the same time, imagistic concreteness is again elaborated as the goal of modern poetry. Besides the usual assault against "emotional slither," rhetoric din" and "painted adjectives impeding the shock,"[26] for the first time he uses some terms with sculptural implications— such as "harder," "nearer the bone" and "like granite"—to

[26] *Literary Essays*, p. 12.

express his expectation of the new poetic language. In the closing of the "Osiris" essays, apart from the condemnation and prognosis, there is also a prescription for actual practice: the use of language is to be direct and simple, but these two qualities should come in a different way from that of daily speech. Since "florid adjectives" and "elaborate hyperbole" will not create this difference, it has to come from elsewhere, notably "the art of verse structure" (*SP*, p. 41). This "verse structure," nonetheless, remains unspecified and undemonstrated. It is not until the appearance of the "Vorticism" manifesto that the technique of "imagistic juxtaposition" is finally realized and fully explained.

At this point, it is necessary to distinguish the Poundian suggestiveness from the kind generally associated with the Symbolists. In *The Spirit of Romance*, Yeats as an example of "vague" and "atmospheric suggestion" is contrasted with Dante's imagistic precision. And in 1913, Pound was very much in favor of Ford Madox Hueffer's anti-Symbolist stance. He made it quite clear that "in today's London," he would rather discuss poetry with novelist Hueffer than with many other poets. As for Hueffer's views on art, Pound believes that they "run in diametric opposition to those of Mr. Yeats. Mr. Yeats has been suggestive; believes in the glamour and associations which hang near the words. . . . He has much in common with the French Symbolists. Mr. Hueffer believes in an exact rendering of things. He would strip words of all 'associations' for the sake of getting a precise meaning."[27] The attitude expressed here is consistent with a subsequent pronouncement in the "blast" of Vorticism that Imagism has no relation with Symbolism: Imagism "does not use images *as ornaments*. The image is itself the speech."[28] Pound's goal is to present vividly and objectively and not to be transcendental, metaphysical and allegorical.

What Hueffer has taught Pound is the so-called "prose tradition" represented by Stendhal and Flaubert. Influenced by

[27] "Status Rerum," *Poetry*, No. 1 (1913), p. 125.

[28] *Gaudier-Brzeska: A Memoir* (New York: New Directions, 1970), p. 88.

Hueffer's interpretation of this tradition,[29] Pound admires the two
novelists for their "clear presentation": "[The prose tradition]
means constatation of fact. It presents. It does not comment. It
does not present a personal predilection for any particular fraction
of the truth. . . ."[30] The correspondence between the "method of
luminous detail" and that of the "prose tradition" is quite
obvious: both are for suggestiveness and objectivity, and against
analysis and discursiveness. The poet is supposed to concentrate
on concrete, precise images and present them objectively. But one
legitimate question to ask is how the poet is expected to express
the "internal emotions." Pound's answer, however, is still the
same. He insists upon a reflection through the same precise,
concrete images and warns against the use of explanatory statements or abstract, rhetorical descriptions. According to his own
explication, the metro poem which deals with a "lovely" "sudden
emotion" is meant "to record the precise instant when a thing
outward and objective transforms itself, or darts into a thing
inward and subjective."[31] A similar answer defining the Imagistic
presentation has also been provided by Richard Aldington: "We
convey an emotion by presenting the object and circumstance of
that emotion without comment. For example, we do not say 'O
how I admire that exquisite, that beautiful, that—25 more
adjectives—woman' . . . but we present that woman, we make an
'Image' of her, we make the scene convey the emotion."[32]

No matter how much promotion Aldington and Pound can
give in explanatory prose, in order to be convincing their method
has to be demonstrated in actual practice. For this matter the best
illustration is perhaps Pound's adaptation or imitation of a Chinese
poem rendered into English by Herbert Giles. The original translation and Pound's version are as follows:

[29] The best discussion on Pound and the prose tradition is the first chapter
of Herbert Schneidau's *The Image and the Real* (Baton Rouge: Louisiana
State Univ. Pr., 1969).

[30] "The Approach to Paris," *New Age*, No. 13 (October 2, 1913), p. 662.

[31] *Gaudier-Brzeska*, p. 89.

[32] "Modern Poetry and the Imagists," *Egoist*, No. 1 (1914), p. 202.

The sound of rustling silk is stilled,
With dust the marble courtyard filled;
No footfalls echo on the floor,
Fallen leaves in heaps block up the door . . .
For she, my pride, my lovely one is lost
And I am left, in hopeless anguish tossed.

—Giles[33]

The rustling of the silk is discontinued,
Dust drifts over the courtyard,
There is no sound of footfall, and the leaves
Scurry into heaps and lie still,
And she the rejoicer of the heart is beneath them:

A wet leaf that clings to the threshold.

—Pound[34]

Comparing Giles' ending with Pound's, we can see that Pound has indeed realized his own program. Contrary to Giles' abstract, discursive ending, Pound has come up with a concrete, imagistic, self-contained line of his own. The pathos of the loss and the bleakness of solitude are implicitly suggested and not explicitly stated. Indeed a scene, as Aldington has mentioned, is created to intimate the inner emotion. While Pound allows the self-contained images to present and to speak for themselves, Giles merely explains and reports. More significantly, Pound's ending displays a specific "verse structure," which is the juxtaposition of images. Notice that between the statement of the penultimate line and the "presentation" of the last line, there is no metaphorical or linguistic connection. The relationship, shown by a colon, remains a subtle hint, inviting the reader to leap the gap. In this case, the reader is no longer informed of an experience; he is required to participate, to act out that process of perceiving the interplay between the two lines, to re-create that moment when the "outward and objective" is transformed into the "inward and sub-

[33] Herbert Giles, *A History of Chinese Literature* (London: Heineman, 1901), p. 100.

[34] *Personae* (New York: New Directions, 1971), p. 108.

jective."[35]

In the "Vorticism" article, Pound has called this imagistic juxtaposition a "form of super-position" (this term subsequently is replaced by juxtaposition).[36] But the explanations he gives there indicate that he then considers juxtaposition to be a *haiku* technique. First he cites this Japanese *haiku* as an example: "The footsteps of the cat upon the snow/(are like) plum-blossoms." He hastens to add that in the original there would not be any explanatory connectives ("are like"), for they are inserted by him "for clarity." Clearly the metro poem uses the same structure. Despite his praise for the merit of condensation in Japanese poetry, Pound has not yet realized that this technique is also prevalent in classical Chinese poetry.

In his discussion of Chinese syntax and its effect on poetry, Wai-lim Yip has cited a line by Li Po to demonstrate what he calls the "unique mode of presentation" of Chinese poetry. The line in gloss reads like this: "floating/cloud(s)/wanderer('s)/mood." Between "floating cloud(s)" and "wanderer('s) mood" there are various possible connectives that one can insert, but which are absent in the original—such as "are," "are like," "is," "is like"; and the syntactic order of the two images may also be reversed in one's contemplation. The ephemeral and fugacious quality associating the clouds with the traveler's feeling and situation, as Yip has aptly observed, is not all that obscure for the reader to perceive. But once the correspondence is explicitly linked by transforming the line into a metaphor or a simile, the "flash of interest" created by the syntactic disconnection will be ruined.[37]

---

[35] For an illuminating study of Pound's translation of Chinese poetry, see Wai-lim Yip's *Ezra Pound's Cathay* (Princeton: Princeton Univ. Pr., 1969).

[36] *Gaudier-Brzeska*, p. 89.

[37] *Gaudier-Brzeska*, p. 21. Juxtaposition, however, is not limited to two discontinuous images within one line; as some examples of T'ang Poetry have indicated, it can also extend to two separate lines. Quite surprisingly, a T'ang poet-monk has actually analyzed this technique in his "poetry talks." See my book *Ao-fei-erh-shih ti pien-tsou* 奧菲爾斯的變奏 (Hong Kong: Su-yeh, 1979), pp. 71-72.

Yip's analysis undoubtedly can serve as an annotation to Pound's experiment. More relevant to our immediate concern is the participational nature of this mode of presentation, which challenges the reader's consciousness and demands a more active reading process. In effect it resists the habit of inert consumption of the text. After more than half a century of exposure to modern poetry, "suggestiveness" through unconnected juxtaposition of concrete images may not be all that surprising and invaluable to us. In Pound's time, however, even some of the Imagist poets did not have a clear grasp of the reasons and intentions behind his experiment. In an essay on modern poetry, for instance, John G. Fletcher considered Pound's metro poem a failure because the relationship between some beautiful faces and the "petals on a wet, black bough" "is not absolutely clear."[38] Fletcher's opinion is indubitably wide off the mark and totally ignorant of the Poundian method. Such confounding jumble, when seen beside some of Amy Lowell's muddling and failures,[39] indeed seems to substantiate the claim that the so-called Imagist movement is in essence a one-man revolution.

Borrowing a term from Eisenstein, Wai-lim Yip has described this mode of presentation as a kind of montage, which originally refers to the non-lineal juxtaposition of cinematic images. The development of this cinematographic technique in the 1920s, according to one film theorist, had much to do with the idea of "stimuli" or "shocks." The montage theory had also merged "with two other currents: the extremist assault on the spectator and the demands of political agitation."[40] What Eisenstein himself has actually said about the power and possibility of the montage is

[38] John G. Fletcher, "The Orient and Contemporary Poetry," in *The Asian Legacy and American Life*, ed. Arthur E. Christy (New York: John Day, 1945), p. 158.

[39] As for Amy Lowell's indebtedness to Pound and Japanese poetry and her subsequent failure, see my article "*Ukiyo-e*: Waka, Haiku, and Amy Lowell," *American Studies*, No. 5 (1975), pp. 55-72.

[40] Peter Wollen, *Signs and Meaning in the Cinema* (Bloomington: Indiana Univ. Pr., 1969), pp. 36-37. Cf. Eisenstein's "The Cinematographic Principle and the Ideogram," in his *Film Form* (New York: HarBrace J., 1949).

highly complementary of the line of argument we have been pursuing here. "The strength of montage," he explains in *Film Sense*, "resides in this, that it includes in the creative process the emotions and mind of the spectator. The spectator is compelled to proceed along the selfsame creative road that the spectator not only sees the represented elements of the finished work, but also experiences the dynamic process of the emergence and assembly of the image just as it was experienced by the author."[41] Furthermore, to Eisenstein, works of art can be divided into two categories: the "lifeless" and the "vital." While a "vital" art pulls the audience "into the process as it occurs," in the "lifeless" case the audience merely "receives the represented result of a given consummated process of creation."[42]

In the "Vorticist" manifesto, Pound has repeatedly proclaimed that "vorticism is an intensive art." After explaining the deletion or suppression of the linguistic connectives in *haiku* and his own poem, the poet ventures into a criticism of the pictorial art, which also bears some relevance to our discussion. The impressionist art is derided by him as "the toy of circumstance, as the plastic substance *receiving* impressions." This is contrasted with vorticist art—defined by Pound as "expressionism, neo-cubism, and imagism gathered together in one camp"—which directs "a certain fluid force against circumstance, as *conceiving* instead of merely reflecting and observing."[43] Despite his earlier claim that the two directions only reflect "a diversity of temperament," Pound makes it quite clear that "one desires the most intense," the "more dynamic."[44] Arnold Hauser, in the last volume of his *The Social History of Art*, also sees the impressionist method as a "reduction," a resignation of the viewer's role as an active, meditative subject; and if the spectator assumes an attitude of non-involvement, it is actually reciprocated by that "fundamentally passive outlook on life" expressed on the impressionist

[41] *Film Sense* (New York: HarBrace J., 1970), p. 32.

[42] *Film Sense*, p. 17.

[43] *Gaudier-Brzeska*, pp. 89-90.

[44] *Gandier-Brzeska*, p. 90.

canvas.[45] It is obvious that whether the object to be consumed is a printed text or a visual artefact actually makes very little difference to the consumer consciousness, which characteristically remains non-participational, insensitive, uninventive and hostile to the unfamiliar. At this point, however, Pound still believes that the artist can change all this on the level of culture, not of the socio-economic determinants; hence the advocacy to "make people think," "to preach constantly to the mob."

This necessity to educate the public, as indicated by a re-trospective essay, is the aim of Pound's translation of classical Chinese poetry. He takes pains to do so not only because of the availability of the Fenollosa manuscripts, but because of certain qualities he finds in this poetry—the "vivid presentation" and the abstinence from "moralizing" and "comment." Since these qualities Pound championed are rather familiar to anyone who has followed closely his unrelenting proselytizing, perhaps the most interesting observation made in the article is this: "The first great distinction between Chinese taste and our own is that the Chinese *like* poetry that they have to think about, and even poetry that they have to puzzle over." Although "the latter taste has occasionally broken out in Europe," he immediately adds, "it has regretfully never held its own for very long."[46] This provoca-tive acclaim for the Chinese should be more correctly read as a lament over the numbness of the contemporary reading public. He moves on to quote an early translation of his, Li Po's "The Jewel-stairs Grievance," to exemplify the concept of "suggestion." In order to prove his point, he provides half-a-page of discursive explanation on the implicit meanings of the images.[47] Throughout his early London years, as this brief article has implied, Pound continuously has to wage his war against both the bourgeois reading habit and the products which satisfy and prolong that

[45] Arnold Hauser, *The Social History of Art* (New York: Random House, 1962), IV, 169-170.

[46] "Chinese Poetry," pp. 54-55.

[47] "Chinese Poetry," pp. 55-56. Both Pound's translation and a more literal rendition by Yip can be found in the appendix of *Ezra Pound's Cathay*.

addiction. "Literature is not a commodity," he declared two months earlier, "literature emphatically does not lie on the counter where it can be snatched up at once by a straw-hatted young man in a hurry."[48]

The vicissitude of Pound's battle can be illustrated by the delayed appearance of Fenollosa's essay on the Chinese ideogram. Although the manuscript was ready soon after its transference to Pound in 1913, it was not published until 1919. The Fenollosa essay clearly had played a very significant role in the formation of Pound's poetics and practice.[49] One of Fenollosa's arguments is that the Chinese language is the closest to nature since its construction is based on pictorial representation. Anyone with some knowledge of the Chinese language surely knows that this is a most misleading half-truth. To the advocate of a new poetry promoting concreteness in language, this discovery is, of course, happily adopted. The Fenollosa essay, with its investigation of an entirely foreign language and culture, evidently affords a resounding, shocking effect which, hitherto, Pound could not possibly get from Dante, the Greek epigram or the Anglo-Saxon poem. In so saying, I am not trying to discredit some of Fenollosa's insights and contribution, but to draw the attention to Pound's urgent need to instigate and stimulate.

Another assertion by Fenollosa is that the radicals of many Chinese words are actually "short-hand pictures" of action or process of actions. The ideogram of "to speak" 言, for instance, "is a mouth with two words and a flame coming out of it" (言).[50] More complicated or abstract ideas can be expressed by the combinations of these short-hand pictures. The concept of "east" is denoted by the "sun" pictogram being overlapped or "entangled" with that of the "tree" (日 or ☉ + 木 or 朮 = 東). Chinese

[48] "Three Views of H. L. Mencken," *The Little Review*, 4 (January, 1918), 11.

[49] For a discussion of Fenollosa's theory of poetic syntax and its influence on Pound, see Donald Davie's *Articulate Energy* (London: Routledge & Kegan Paul, 1955), ch. 4.

[50] Ernest Fenollosa, *The Chinese Written Character as a Medium for Poetry* (San Francisco: City Lights, 1936), p. 10.

poetry, Fenollosa then concludes, speaks not only "with the vividness of painting," but is "more objective" and "more dramatic," for "in reading Chinese we do not seem to be juggling mental counters, but to be watching *things* work out their own fate."[51] Hence the theory of the ideogrammic construction embodies both the concrete quality and the ability to hint at abstractions without being discursive. It is not surprising that the term "juxtaposition" is eventually replaced by that of the all-inclusive "ideogrammic method."

Apparently, by combining several pictorial elements to intimate an idea, the ideogram as Fenollosa sees it demands a conscious involvement in the reconstruction of the whole process. If the method is compared with rhetorical techniques, it can be described as, in Fenollosa's words, "a more compressed or elliptical expression of metaphorical perception." In an ideogram, one certainly does not find any linguistic connectives; but in poetry, the compression and ellipsis will result in Pound's juxtaposition experiments or the so-called "unique mode of presentation" of some Chinese poems. Linguistically speaking, this phenomenon can be more accurately described as the "metonymic mode of expression." Roman Jakobson, in his pioneering "Two Aspects of Language and Two Types of Aphasic Disturbances," has suggested that prose tends to be metonymic and poetry metaphoric. The metonymic is identified with contiguity and the metaphoric with similarity. Although "language in its various aspects deals with both modes of relation," "under the influence of a cultural pattern, personality, and verbal style, preference is given to one of the two processes over the other." He goes on to suggest that the "sign systems" of some arts, specifically the Cubist "transformation" and the cinematic montage, are obviously more metonymically oriented. However, he sees these two modes of expression appearing alternatively due to the "bipolar structure of language."[52] Clearly, this "suppression of 'links in the chain,'

---

[51] Fenollosa, p. 9.

[52] See Roman Jakobson, *Studies on Child Language and Aphasia* (The Hague and Paris: Mouton, 1971), pp. 67-73. Here I would like to emphasize once again that Chinese poetry as represented by the T'ang poets is pre-

of explanatory and connecting matter"—T. S. Eliot's description of St.-John Perse's poetic method[53]—represents a shift from what Jakobson has called "the primacy of the metaphoric process in the literary schools of romanticism and symbolism" to a modern trend of the metonymic mode, which, through the investigation of Pound, has found some correlation in the Chinese ideogram and classical Oriental poetry.

The ideogrammic method or the metonymic mode, however, is not limited to Pound's poetry; it is also employed in some of his prose discourse. The first attempt in this direction is probably his most provocative *Jefferson and/or Mussolini* (written in 1933 but not issued until 1935 with the publishing date recorded in the Fascist manner, "Anno XIII"). There he warns his readers: "I am not putting these sentences in monolinear syllogistic arrangement, and I have no intention of using that old form of trickery to fool the reader, any reader, into thinking I have proved anything, or that having read a paragraph of my writing he KNOWS something that he can only *know* by examining a dozen or two dozen facts and putting them all together."[54] Disregarding the annoyance of his reviewers, the ideogrammic method, which is seen by Pound as his contribution to criticism (*SP*, p. 333) and is intended to scrape "the dead and desensitized surface of the reader's mind,"[55]

---

dominately in the metonymic mode. Due to its unique syntactic structure, the Chinese language can allow the subject to be absent in a complete sentential unit. This syntactic flexibility also permits the juxtaposition of, in a few cases, as many as five noun images in one poetic line without any grammatical connectives. This is perhaps the maximal case of what Jakobson has called "association by proximity." He considers this to be responsible for Pasternak's lyricism in the metonymic mode in both poetry and prose. See his "Marginal Notes on the Prose of the Poet Pasternak (1935)," in *Pasternak*, ed. Donald Davie and Angela Livington (London: Macmillan, 1969), pp. 140-41.

[53]St.-John Perse, *Collected Poems* (Princeton: Princeton Univ. Pr., 1971), pp. 675-76. This is from Eliot's preface to his 1930 translation of *Anabasis*.

[54]*Jefferson and/or Mussolini* (New York: Liveright, 1935), p. 28.

[55]*Guide to Kulchur* (New York: New Directions, 1970), p. 51.

is used even more massively in *Guide to Kulchur*. It is not surprising, then, that this treatise appears to be a slipshod "ragbag" of some motley facts and opinions. Instead of a ratiocinative exposition or a "logical" organization, it begins with a selective translation of Confucian *Analects* without supplying any elucidation of its rather unexpected initial presence; and this is followed by discussions of disparate topics simply numbered as sections and parts and placed adjacently without the usual conjoining transition.

Besides the ideogrammic method, Pound has also resorted to other less sophisticated means to arouse his reader's attention. Once he said that he would like to "invent some kind of typographical dodge which would force the reader to stop and reflect for five minutes (for five hours), to get back to the facts mentioned and think over their significance for himself, and draw his own conclusions."[56] A very crude way to arrest momentarily the reading process is, of course, the sudden capitalization of some key words, which we have already seen in Pound's estimation of Dante. The most didactic device is perhaps the sudden, authorial intrusion in the continuous flow of a text to tell the reader to "pause here for reflection."[57] Appeals of this kind sometimes are mingled with typographical emphasis, as evidenced by the closing of *Ta Hsio*: "The translator would end by asking the reader to keep on re-reading the whole digest until he understands HOW these few pages contain the basis on which the great dynasties were founded and endured."[58] In his long epic, while the ideogrammic method dominates, the typographical and the didactic have made their contributions too. There are, however, even more eye-catching elements for the reader: the parading of Greek tags, the astonishing appearance of a musical score, the striking spatial arrangement of syntax, and the occasional punctuation of the

[56] *Social Credit: An Impact* (London: Stanley, 1951), p. 17. First published in 1935, this was later included with some excisions as "An Impact" in *Impact* (Chicago: Henry Regnery, 1960).

[57] *Guide to Kulchur*, p. 34.

[58] *Confucius*, p. 89.

Chinese pictograms.

These formalistic methods, from the ideogrammic to the typographical, as our argument goes, are attempts to revitalize the reader's imagination, to invite an active, creative participation, and to demolish the addictive habit of unthinking consumption. These are noble objectives. In order to re-involve the reader's consciousness, however, there must be in the first place the existence of an audience. With the increasing withering of the audience in the modern world—in our time the situation is worsened by the diversions offered by movies, television and rock music, not to mention drugs, motorcycling, CB radio and various other fads—no matter how engaging, provoking and stimulating a poetics can be, it will certainly be futile to effect a change on a massive scale. This poetics may be theoretically sound and workable; but to believe that by promoting it a mentality and a situation caused by some external factors can be rectified inevitably will end up as a shattered dream. What is more, by flaunting its obscurity and difficulty in the face of its bourgeois reader, by hoping to negate a reading habitude through a formalism grown out from a fragmentation itself, this poetics and poetry merely backfire and further aggravate the whole situation, for the audience has either ignored or condemned such practice. In the end, perhaps the only function these Poundian efforts have served is the crystalization of the artist's dilemma in the modern world.

An illusory impression some contemporary students of Pound and the brief Edwardian period actually have, is the almost pastoral order of that twilight era and the concurring triumph of avant-garde art. That the former idea is a wishful mythologizing can be easily proven by perusing the records of unemployment, labor trouble and financial crises of that period.[59] As for Pound and the movements, the publicity they had was an extremely limited one. The Poundian drives for funds to help Joyce and Eliot might easily lead one to a wrong conclusion of Pound's

[59] See David Thomson, *England in the Nineteenth Century 1815-1914*, vol. 8 of the *Pelican History of England* (Middlesex, England: Penguin, 1950), chs. 9, 10 and 11.

own well-being; but in fact Pound was then just one step ahead
of starvation. In 1914, for instance, his entire income from writing
was a meager £42. "My American royalties," he wrote in 1916,
"amount to one dollar 85 cents per year." In order to pay his
bills he had to depend on his father's subsidy and his wife's
annuity.[60] The situation was not ameliorated by Pound's deter-
mination to make a living out of writing. But even by overworking
himself under pseudonyms (as B. H. Dias for art notes and as
William Atheling for music criticism), he could hardly make ends
meet. According to one count, he made at least 73 contributions
to periodicals in 1917, 124 in 1918, 90 in 1919, and another 90
in 1920.[61] Not all the essays, however, received payment. Some
of the more memorable ones now available in collections and
studied by critics—e.g. "Notes on Elizabethan Classicists,"
"Henry James" and "*Dubliners* and Mr. James Joyce"[62]—were
actually donated to *The Egoists* and *The Little Review*. Needless
to say, the poetry of those years always went free. Years later,
re-reading the prosaic profusion of those years, he stated in his
typical manner that "what I had written as a free agent, say for
the *Little Review* was the solidest; what I had written at a guinea
a short for Orage was worth gleaning; but no article for which I
had been paid three or five guineas was worth a hoot."[63] Despite
such prolificacy, he still had to receive money from literary
patrons when they were available—John Quinn, a New York

---

[60] Michael Reck, *Ezra Pound: A Close-up* (New York: McGraw Hill,
1973), pp. 29-30.

[61] See Donald Gallup, *A Bibliography of Ezra Pound* (London: Faber &
Faber, 1963). I have only recorded the numbers in accordance with section
C of the bibliography.

[62] For his article on Joyce, Pound privately made this apology: "My article
on you is very bad, but I simply can't afford to rewrite articles for the *Egoist*.
One can do only a certain amount of work unpaid. I wish it were better."
Pound/Joyce, ed. Forrest Read (New York: New Directions, 1965), p. 30.

[63] *Polite Essays* (London: Faber, 1937), pp. 100-101. Clearly the same is
also true about young Eliot, and Pound states: "A number of Eliot's essays
might never have been written if there hadn't been a skulking anonymity in
the background holding out much-needed lumps of fifteen guineas."

city lawyer, for example, for a few years after 1915 had been steadily sending money to Pound.[64]

In spite of such difficulty, had his efforts to educate the public been more successful, he probably would have never concluded that any fundamental alteration of the consciousness could not be achieved without change "at the root." With the dissipation of the Vorticist movement and the lifelessness and stagnation of the British literary scene, he was even more restive and unhappy. Cantos 14 and 15, "the hell cantos," as he admitted much later, "are specifically London, the state of English mind in 1919 and 1920."[65] That the solution, instead of a cultural one which had failed, was to be a change of the economic base began to sink in gradually. Since 1911 Pound had been writing for A.R. Orage in *The New Age*, which eventually became a forum for the "Social Credit" theories of Major C. H. Douglas. According to Pound, Douglas "is the first economist to include creative art and writing in an economic scheme, and the first to give [the artist] a definite reason for being interested in economics; namely, that a better economic system would release more energy for invention and design" (*SP*, p. 232). After his meeting with the Major in Orage's office in 1918,[66] Pound had finally found a solid theory to work with and champion for. He had embarked on a course "sailing after knowledge," culminating in the embracing of Confucianism. But evidently his voyage had started long ago when he hoped to alter, by his ideogrammic formalism, the bourgeois mentality and its anesthetizing reading habit entirely on the cultural level.

[64] Reck, p. 30.

[65] *Letters*, p. 239.

[66] Noel Stock, *The Life of Ezra Pound* (New York: Pantheon, 1970), p. 221.

ANDERSSTREBEN: CONCEPTION OF MEDIA AND INTERMEDIA

Wai-lim Yip

The arts have indeed "some sort of common bond, some inter-recognition."

—Pound

There is another sort of poetry where painting or sculpture seems as if it were "just coming over to speech."

—Pound

To recover the notion of a kind of unique language half-way between gesture and thought . . . they [media] can occur in a sort of central expression without advantage for any one particular art.

—Artaud

The idea that one art medium is capable of expressing the "world" of another medium is proverbial both in the East and in the West. Many treatises have been written about it, the most notable example in recent decades being Irving Babbitt's *The New Laokoon*, in which he examines the changing attitudes toward poetry as a norm before and after Lessing's famous distinction between poetry and painting. Babbitt was arguing his case in terms of the incompatibility between classical and romantic art and concludes that Romantic literature was a result of the confusion of the functions of the different media.

Why another exploration into the concept of *andersstreben*, or the esthetics of one art passing into the condition of another? Why still another rehearsal of the different responses to Lessing's distinction when Babbitt has already given us a full review of the historical forces that have gone into the making of the new Laokoon? Such a rehearsal would be unjustified had it not been for the huge corpus of modern poems and paintings which demand understanding, not according to their own norms, but in terms of the potentialities of another medium. Indeed, much of modern poetry and art proceeds from an obsession of "the inter-recognition" of the arts, requiring the reader-viewer to apperceive them with constant reference and cross-reference to the other mediumistic models. The total esthetic experience would be incomprehensible without our using the "perceptual eyes" of one model to see or feel the operative dynamics of the other.

As such, the implications of this change in modern esthetics have gone beyond the bounds of the *New Laokoon*. The present examination of the esthetics of "Andersstreben" is different from the traditional account of *ut pictura poesis* in yet another way. Many studies of the convertibility of arts aim at mapping and tracing the art motifs in poetry or poetic themes in paintings, particularly in the case of such amphibian artists as Rosetti and Swinburne. While such studies no doubt still belong to the domain of "andersstreben" esthetics, they hardly touch upon the structuring activities of each mediumistic norm, nor the implied function and meaning of such interchange and synthesis. This essay begins, therefore, with a brief, but highlighted rehearsal of Lessing's description of the potentialities and the limitations of the media, clarifying the esthetic implications therein through the responses from subsequent estheticians to his distinction, and thus seeing, in what particular ways, modern artists and poets, partly consciously reacting against it, partly urged by the media themselves, achieve a change in attitude in their perceiving procedures. One must be thankful to Joseph Frank's famous essay, "Spatial Form in Modern Literature," a general overview of this change. It has, in many ways, prepared for my exploration into the subject. But due to the special nature of his aim at generalities, he has bypassed many of the fundamental esthetic dimensions implied in the subsequent responses, and, consequently, not enough consideration has been given to the ways in which mediumistic revolution works out its own artistic raison d'etre. Among the many possible perspectives leading into Lessing's argument, the Chinese esthetic horizon provides for certain illuminating entrances into the working dynamics of such cross-fertilization of mediumistic models. Beyond the practical purpose of widening the possibility of the appreciative act, there is, in the last analysis, still the temptation for us to probe into the *why* of this obsessive change. The present paper also anticipates, then, the other panel of this work (not presented here), namely, the meaningfulness of returning to some deeper cultural ideal that has been long lost to modern man—in which the cooperation of all art forms as a homogeneous entity is an important part of lived experience.

Historically, Lessing's distinction between poetry and painting (linguistic forms and plastic forms, including sculpture) was occasioned by Winckelman's *Thoughts on the Imitations of Greek Works in Painting and Sculpture* (1755), which is a study of the Laokoon set of sculpture recently unearthed at that time. The part that spurred Lessing into his long treatise runs:

> The general and distinguishing characteristics of the Greek masterpieces of painting and sculpture are . . . noble simplicity and quiet grandeur, both in posture and expression. As the depths of the sea always remain calm, however much the surface may be agitated, so does the expression in the figures of the Greeks reveal a great and composed soul in the midst of passions. . . . Such a soul is depicted in Laocoon's face . . . this pain expresses itself without any sign of rage either in his face or in his posture. He does not raise his voice in a terrible scream, which Virgil describes his Laocoon as doing; the way in which his mouth is open does not permit it. . . . The pain of the body and the nobility of soul are distributed and weighed out as it were, over the entire figure with equal intensity.[1]

[1] Johann J. Winckelmann, "Thoughts on the Imitation of Greek Works in Painting and Sculpture" (1755), in *Literary Sources of Art History*, edited by E. G. Hólt (Princeton: Princeton Univ. Pr., 1947). Reprinted in Holt, *A Documentary History of Art* (New York: Doubleday, 1958), p. 349.

To Lessing, this conclusion has missed a most important aspect of the esthetic act: to be precise, Laokoon's mouth was half-open; this was not due to the classical Greek ideal of restraint, but chosen to be this way because sculpture as a plastic form, spatial by nature, has its mediumistic limitations and hence cannot express the entire spectrum of the agony in the total action—the progressive nature of which can only be achieved by poetry. It was here that Lessing began the now famous distinction, which, in a subterranean way, is still possessing artists and poets of the present. To further clarify the comparison and contrast that follow, let me quote this part again:

> There is this essential difference between them: one is a visible progressive action, the various parts of which *follow on another* in *time*; the other is a visible station-ary action, the development of whose various parts takes place in *space*. ... If it be true that painting employs wholly different signs or means of imitation from poetry,—the one using forms and colors in space, the other articulate sounds in time,—and if signs must unquestionably stand in convenient relation with the thing signified, then *signs arranged side by side can represent* only *objects existing side by side*, or whose parts so exist, while *consecutive signs can express only objects which succeed each other*, or whose parts succeed each other, *in time*. Objects which succeed each other, or whose parts succeed each other in time, are *actions*. Consequently, actions are the peculiar subjects of poetry.
>
> All bodies, however, exist not only in space, but also in time. They continue, and, at any moment of their continuance, may assume a different appearance and stand in different relations. Every one of these momentary appearances and groupings was a result of a preceding, may become the cause of a following, and is, therefore, the center of a present action. Con-sequently, *painting can imitate actions also, but only as they are suggested through forms.*

Actions, on the other hand, cannot exist independently, but must always be joined to certain agents. In
so far as those agents are bodies or are regarded as such,
poetry describes also bodies, but only through actions.[2]

Lessing is arguing here that the main function of poetry, using
language or articulated sounds temporal in structure, is to describe
actions—an action being a linear succession of objects or
moments containing a beginning, a middle and a following.
Painting, on the other hand, using lines, colors and forms, spatial
in structure, is to give forth simultaneously visual bodies of
objects, static and co-extensive units, in one single moment.
Poetry is not capable of presenting the corporeal qualities of
objects; they can only be approximated by suggestion, one
luminous property at a time, and they are visible, but not physically visible and complete as in paintings. A round, red, shiny apple
is one simultaneous impression in visual representation. Meanwhile, painting is not capable of describing a successive quality of
actions; they can only be approximated by *one* selected instant
that most suggests the progressive extensions of an action.

Lessing's esthetic assumptions contain many loopholes which
have continually attracted criticisms from later theoreticians,
Herder and Pater (to be discussed in full in the second panel of
this essay) being among the most interesting ones. Before we
attack these esthetic ramifications and their relevance to modern
poets and artists, it might not be out of line to test, briefly, the
validity of Lessing's arguments by some Chinese examples.

Lessing argues that the main function of poetry is to describe
action consisting of successive moments. Let us see how it applies
to these three poems from China, one of folk origin and two by
cultured poets, Wang Wei and Liu Tsung-yüan.

1.   South of the river: to pluck lotus.
      Lotus leaves drift, drift.

[2] Gotthold Ephraim Lessing, *Laocoon*, trans. by Ellen Frothingham
(Boston: Roberts Brothers, 1887), pp. 90-92.

Fish sport, midst of lotus-leaves.
Fish sport, east of lotus-leaves.
Fish sport, west of lotus-leaves.
Fish sport, south of lotus-leaves.
Fish sport, north of lotus-leaves.
——Anon. (Han Dynasty)

江南可採蓮。蓮葉何田田。
魚戲蓮葉間。
魚戲蓮葉東。魚戲蓮葉西。
魚戲蓮葉南。魚戲蓮葉北。

（ 樂府古辭 ）

2.   High on tree-tips, the hibiscus
      In the mountain sets forth red calyces.
      A home by a stream, quiet. No man.
      It blooms and falls, blooms and falls.
      ——Wang Wei (701-761)

木末芙蓉花，山中發紅萼。
澗戶寂無人，紛紛開且落。

（ 王維「辛夷塢」 ）

3.   A thousand mountains—no bird's flight.
      A million paths—no man's trace.
      Single boat. Bamboo-leaved cape. An old man
      Fishing by himself. Ice-river. Snow.
      ——Liu Tsung-yüan (773-819)

千山鳥飛絕，萬徑人跡滅。
孤舟蓑笠翁，獨釣寒江雪。

（ 柳宗元「江雪」 ）

The absolute distinction between time and space evaporates here.
There is spatialization of time in all three poems: an instant of
experience ("fish sport") is expanded spatially and directionally
to give the vivid impression of the activities of the fish, time and
space inseparable; a moment of quiet activity ("hibiscus blooms
and falls") is *arrested* as in a static picture; two visual moments
(cosmic mountain scene and a single fisherman) are presented

simultaneously as in a painting. No doubt, embodied in language, the objects are presented successively, but they are not joined by a story line of development as in a dramatic action; rather, they are juxtaposed as spatial units first and our total consciousness of the moment is not completed until all of them are simultaneously projected onto the screen of our perception. The objects exist not only in co-extensive relationships; these spatial units are temporalized by the mobile point of view of the perceiver. More importantly, none of these moments of esthetic experience can be termed "actions" in the sense Lessing describes them. Lessing had in his mind only one prototype of poetry: the epic or narrative poetry; he had bypassed the entire compositional reality of the lyric. We will return to this point when we come to Herder's criticism of Lessing.

Next, let us try Chinese paintings. Lessing's "one-moment" theory, the classical Western concept of perspective, would also be out of key. In almost all the Chinese landscapes, we see scenes not only from the front, but also from the rear, from the sides, from above and from below; not one moment from a specific perspective, but many moments from many spatial viewpoints. The Chinese artist proceeds from the belief that art should be a sort of tuned correspondence with the vital rhythms of Nature. He should, first of all, literally live with the "total" mountains and "total" rivers, to know and feel first-hand the living reality of these mountains and rivers by roaming in them for years, viewing them and experiencing them in their different moments of appearances, in their various climatic and temporal pitches (seasonal and diurnal changes) and from all vantage points (e.g. an imposing mountain seen from looking up offers a majestic quality quite unlike mountain ranges seen from flat land, etc.) After having lived with these experiential moments, he recreates them all in one picture, avoiding one static compositional axis but offering simultaneously many axes to constitute a total environment into which the viewer is invited to roam about and to commerce with the *living* moments captured in corresponding vital rhythms. Therefore, the viewer is not restricted to see it from one static location *selected* arbitrarily for him by the painter. The viewer revolves, as it were, with the multiple perspective available to him.

Now, if we turn to Herder's response to Lessing, we will have a wider esthetic horizon against which we can understand the implications of his criticism. Herder believes that the essence of poetry is not actions as understood by Lessing; the essence of poetry is *Kraft* (force, power), which operates from space (objects made sensual) in time (through a succession of many parts into a poetic whole). He argues that Lessing's conception of "actions" is superficial and incomplete:

"Objects which succeed one another, or the parts of which succeed one another, are actions." How? I cause things to succeed one another as much as I please, let them be bodies or still views; nothing becomes action through succession. I see time flying, each moment chasing the next—does this mean I see action? Various aspects of nature appear before me: singly, they are still; in succession, do I see action? P. Kastell's color-organ, with its successive presentations of colors, even in wavy or snaky lines, can never portray actions. A melodious chain of notes can never be called an action. . . . The concept of succession is only half the idea of action. Action is *succession* through *Kraft*. I think of an entity which operates through temporal succession, I think of transformations which through *Kraft* of one substance are consequent upon another: this is how action occurs. And I bet that if action is the object of poetry, this object can never be determined from the dry concept of succession: *Kraft* is the center of the sphere . . . poetry operates through energy: never with the intention to present in all completeness a de-tailed image or painting (even successive), but rather that, at the same time as the energy, the entire *Kraft* must arise and be felt.[3]

---

[3] Johann Gottfried von Herder, *Sämtliche Werke* (Zurich: Georg Olms Hildesheim, 1967), III, 139, 157. I am indebted to Mr. Frank Langer for the present translation.

In Herder's opinion, Lessing's account of mediumistic potentialites and limitations does not touch upon the essential fact of our esthetic experience. The esthetic object of a poem, a painting or a piece of music does not reside in the peculiar charms made possible by a certain medium's potentialities; it resides in something else, in *Kraft*, a power or life-force unrestricted by mediumistic differences. Take dance, for example. Dance has all the potentialities of temporal sequence and spatial extension, but not all gestures and movements can be called the art form of dance. Any attempt to define the core of an art experience should proceed from outside mediumistic characteristics.

Interpreting Herder, René Wellek pushes the issue further by the example of cinema. The movie has all the advantages of all media, temporal sequence, spatial extension, corporeal authenticity and ideational function of words. In other words, it is a medium that can approximate experience most fully. And yet, not any sequence of images taken by a camera—in fact, not any succession of moments (action) can make a movie of artistic import. The esthetic core of experience must be defined outside the consideration of the potentialities of the medium,[4] or, as the New Critics would put it, the esthetic object must be seen in the unique way in which a structure of experience is promoted, not by the medium itself, but by the artist's manipulation of it. This typical formalistic position is, no doubt, different from Herder's original obsession. Herder's *Kraft* refers particularly to the Romantic emphasis upon the boundless organizing power of the poet's soul and to its empathetic power of enlivening the objects that come into the orbit of his perception. This obsession with subjectivity made Herder react against Lessing's classical formulation. Indeed, Lessing's conception of poetry and the subsequent array of the essentials of poetry was based only on the epic or the narrative tradition of poetry. The so-called sequential make-up of beginning, middle and following or conclusion was directly transposed from Aristotle's *Poetics*, which was a poetics of dramatic works, i.e. essentially narrative structures. When Aristotle

[4] Rene Wellek, *A History of Modern Criticism* (New Haven: Yale Univ. Pr., 1955) I, 186ff.

referred to poetry, he meant chiefly the epic; he never discussed the structure of the lyric. One essential fact about the lyric, whether in its melic stage or in the later subjective variety, is that it does not emphasize sequential time. Often, in a lyric, the poet promotes the stimulus of an emotion or an experience of a scene at a certain heightened pitch. The motivation of an action and the contour of a linear development, often found in a narrative poem, are ambiguous and not fully accounted for in a lyric (even in a story lyric such as "Edward, Edward") or submerged in the background (as in Rilke's Orpheus sonnets). A lyric is the texture of the emotional stimulus pushed to the front. Quite often, a lyric is a moment of time arrested at its most pregnant instant— pregnant in the sense of suggesting the multiple lines of development that precede this instant and the possible lines of development that might follow. It is an instant, a point, not a period of time, in which temporal sequence does not hold an important role. The linguistic sequence in the poem is the spatial expansion of the interior of an instant. It is as if we reach out from the center to the circumference. Or, in its melic stage and structure, a simple outburst of emotion or statement of emotion is built up into an impact by incremental repetitions and variations through musical emphases and interplay. While Poe's dictum, brevity as a necessary condition of a lyric, and his attack upon the narrative element, are, no doubt, a later theoretical rationalization, many ancient tribal songs and most Chinese poems, all brief and without the burden of narrative sequence, lend support to his formulation.

This is no place to go into a full discussion of the lyric; we only want to heighten here certain essential features of the lyric which constitutes a significantly large portion of the total output of world poetry, to make us understand more fully the limitations of Lessing's theoretical premises.

The emphasis on the lyric by Herder is at root Romantic also; it was linked to the power of the "soul." This is clearly different from the formalist position, and yet Herder's discussion of *Kraft* in conjunction with mediumistic considerations points toward a theory central in modern poetics. Modern poets and estheticians argue that poetic meaning does not reside in the words, but out-

side them (Wimsatt[5]), and the poet's ideal should be to strive
beyond poetry just as the later Beethoven strived beyond music
(Eliot[6]), and preceding them, Valery: "A poem is really a kind
of machine for producing the poetic state by means of words."[7]
This theory, which is the very basis for Abbe Brémond's theory
of pure poetry, reaches back to Mallarmé's poetic "bouquet"
that rises musically from the words. The poetic state, ineffable
by normal discourse, is evoked by a unique manipulation of words
in such a way that when the reader reads the poem, he is no longer
aware of the words as such, but, as in a flash, he is transported
into the "world" suggested by the words. Words are pointers into
an ineffable, complex state of feeling. As Pound puts it, "a thing
outward and objective transforms itself, or darts into a thing
inward and subjective."[8] Following the Symbolists, and Mallarmé
in particular, Pound conceives words as a form of inspired
mathematics, an equation of emotion, mood or ineffable state of
mind, and, as Eliot slightly alters it, they form an objective correlative, a formula of words and events that evoke the emotion.
Post-Pound and post-Eliot poets and critics continue to elaborate
on this concept: that words have both immanent and transcendent

[5] W. K. Wimsatt, "Comment on 'Two Essays in Practical Criticism,'"
University Review, 9 (Winter, 1942), 141.

[6] In an unpublished lecture quoted in F. O. Matthiessen's *The Achievement
of T.S. Eliot* (New York: Oxford Univ. Pr., 1958), p. 90. The whole paragraph suggests further parallels, at least in phrasing if not exactly in content,
to Pound and Yen Yü discussed later in this essay. The relevant part reads:

> This speaks to me of that at which I have long aimed, in writing poetry;
> to write poetry which should be essentially poetry, with nothing poetic
> about it . . . or poetry so transparent that we should not see the poetry,
> but that which we are meant to see through the poetry, poetry so
> transparent that in reading it we are intent on what the poem *points at*,
> and not on the poetry, this seems to me the thing to try for. To *get
> beyond poetry* as Beethoven in his later works, strove to get *beyond
> music*.

[7] Paul Valery, *Art of Poetry* (New York: Bollingen/Pantheon, 1958), p. 79.

[8] Ezra Pound, *Gaudia-Brezeska: A Memoir* (London, 1916; New York:
New Directions, 1970), p. 103.

meanings, and the very highest ideal of poetry resides in its power to leap out alive to the readers, freeing itself from the fetters of words.

In my Chinese book of criticism, *Order's Growth*, I use the traditional Chinese esthetic ideal, *hsien-wai-chih-yin* 弦外之音[9]— sounds beyond the strings or music beyond the notes on the strings, with strings representing the words or medium—to discuss this concept. The phrase comes from Ssu-k'ung T'u whose esthetic horizon can be traced to Taoist-Buddhist origins. Without going into the long history of the morphology of this esthetic horizon in China, it is sufficient to say this: distrusting the potentialities of language (or any human-invented medium of communication) to represent Phenomenon (the totality of all forms of beings in their continuously changing conditions), the Taoist estheticians offer the suggestive function of language to achieve a flash-like perception of total Phenomenon. The key phrases from Chuang-tzu that gave rise to all later variations of this concept run:

> It is for the fish that the trap exists. When we get the fish, we can forget the trap.... It is for *i* [meaning, sense of things rather than propositional meaning] that words exist; when we get the *i*, we can forget the words.[10]

> 荃者所以在魚，得魚而忘荃。⋯言者所以在意，得意而忘言。

The other familiar phrases, *i-tsai-yen-wai* 意在言外 (*i* exists outside words), *hsien-wai-chih-yin* (music beyond strings), *yün-wai-chih-chih* 韻外之致 (extreme interest beyond rhythm) and the art theory that, in painting, it is not resemblance, but "the vital rhythm" (*ch'i-yün sheng-tung* 氣韻生動) or *i* 意 (sense of things, i.e. not the things themselves) that counts—all these could be considered variations of Chuang-tzu's embryonic phrases. Following the Taoists, the Chan Buddhists equally distrust linguistic

---

[9] *Chih-hsu ti sheng-chang* 秩序的生長 (Taipei: Chih-wen, 1970), pp. 215-18.

[10] *Chuang-tzu chi-shih* 莊子集釋, ed. Kuo Ch'ing-fan 郭慶藩 (Taipei: Ho Lo, 1974), p. 944.

communication and offer an *a*logical and intuitive approach to experience. Thus, in the now famous *kung-an* 公案 *(Kōan)* ritual, we have the following question and answer:

> Q: What is the general idea of Buddha's law?
> A: Spring comes, grass green by itself.

The words here do not explain, but, like sparks in the dark night, they help to make us see, in a flash, the meaning beyond the words. It is as if we were brought to the edge of possible perception of total meaning of Phenomenon. This "flash of interest" "lit up by the spotlight of words" becomes the central concern of much later criticism. (See my "Yen Yü and the Poetic Theories in the Sung Dynasty,"[11] and "The Taoist Aesthetic."[12])

When we introduce here the Chinese esthetic positions for comparison, we are not ready to equate *Kraft* with *ch'i-yün sheng-tung* (vital rhythm), or "meaning outside the words" (Wimsatt and others) with *i-tsai-yen-wai* (sense-of-things, often intuitive apperception of an aura of meanings and rhythm outside the words). The full chord of convergences and differences between the two esthetic traditions are rather complicated for the present purpose. Between the two, however, one thing is clear: both emphasize a *certain something outside* the physical poem as the esthetic object. This *something outside* puts the question of convertibility of arts in a totally different light, as we will see later. The emphasis is on the word *outside*, i.e. the power of words in *extending beyond themselves as signs* to offer us either a glimpse into the state or activity of an experience, now structured because of the contour etched out by the words, or an evolving process with which we perceive, step by step, the growth of an experience. Two examples from Chinese poetry might be useful here:

High on tree-tips, the hibiscus

[11] *Tamkang Review*, 1, No. 2 (Oct. 1970), 183-200.

[12] *New Asia Academic Bulletin*, 1 (1978), 17-32.

In the mountain sets forth red calyses
A home by a stream, quiet. No man.
It blooms and falls, blooms and falls.

—Wang Wei

木末芙蓉花，山中發紅萼。
澗戶寂無人，紛紛開且落。

（王維「辛夷塢」）

A lone sail, a distant shade, lost in the horizon

—Li Po

孤帆遠影碧空盡

（李白「送孟浩然之廣陵」）

The flash-of-interest by being nature-and-thus-natural in these
examples is effected by the fact that the cuts and turns of the
poem (through syntactical divisions of phases of perception and
appropriate pauses and speed) *coincide* with the cuts and turns
of nature's disclosure of itself or our experiencing of nature. When
such coincidence happens, we are enabled to leap, as it were,
beyond the words themselves and be spatially liberated from the
sense limitations of the words to enter into the rhythm of nature
or into the fluctuations of experience. In the first example, the
objects (the hibiscus etc.), their activity (continuous blooming
and falling) and the condition or atmosphere (quiet, no man) are
captured in their actualities uncontaminated by ideational fabrication, and such a scene, arrested at its moment of greatest suggestiveness, is suddenly opened up to us as they rehearse themselves uninterfered. In the second example, the words, as signs,
recreate the visual curves and gradations of our perception. The
function of words is analogous to the art of miming. As I have
explained elsewhere, a mime, in order to reflect an event that is
not visible, forms gestures and moments, highlighting them to
suggest the energy flow that originally supports that event. To
realize a moment's vital rhythm, language must move exactly
the same way the moment originally moves the perceiver. As
Su Tung-p'o (1036-1101) puts it:

My writing is like water gushing out from an ample,

deep spring. . . . It can move on a thousand miles a day
without effort and turns with mountains and rocks and
shapes itself according to the objects it encounters.[13]

吾文如萬斛泉源。不擇地而出。……雖一日千里無難。及其與
山石曲折隨物賦形。

（蘇東坡「經進東坡文集事略」）

In his essay "Projective Verse," Charles Olson talks about the
kinetics of a poem:

A poem is energy transferred from where the poet got
it . . . by way of the poem itself to, all the way over to,
the reader. Okay. Then the poem itself must, at all
points, be a high-energy-construct and, at all points, an
energy-discharge. . . . FORM IS NEVER MORE THAN
AN *EXTENSION* [italics mine] OF CONTENT . . .
ONE PERCEPTION MUST IMMEDIATELY AND
DIRECTLY LEAD TO A FURTHER PERCEPTION.
It means exactly what it says, is a matter of, at *all*
points . . . get on with it, keep moving, keep in, speed,
the nerves, their speed, the perceptions, theirs, the acts,
the split second acts, the whole business. . . . USE
USE USE the process at all points, in any given poem,
always one perception must must must MOVE, IN-
STANTER, ON ANOTHER.[14]

Both Su and Olson (as well as Creeley) single out energy flow
as the necessary condition of good art. But Olson, still under the
influence of the Romantic-Symbolist conception of language,
implies that language orders and creates art experience *at all points*
and the words so structured do not necessarily reflect an experience identifiable with external reality. It is at root an ex-

[13] Su Shih, *Ching-chin Tung-p'o wen-chi shih-lüeh* 經進東坡文集事略 in *Ssu-
pu tsung-k'an* 四部叢刊, Vol. LVII, 335.

[14] Charles Olson, *Selected Essays* (New York: New Directions, 1966),
p. 17.

pressive theory. To Su, language is also expressive, but only to the extent that it is structured according to the measure of the objects as they exist and operate *as they are* in Nature. He is at once mimetic and expressive.

It comes to us as no surprise that Su Tung-p'o should be the first Chinese critic to pronounce the covertibility of poetry and painting: *shih chung yu hua, hua chung yu shih* 詩中有畫，畫中有詩 (In poetry, there is painting; in painting, there is poetry).[15] As an art critic, he expounds Hsieh He's concept of *ch'i-yün sheng-tung* (vital rhythm) in art, and furthers the development of *wen-jen-hua* 文人畫 (painting of the literati) and *hsieh-i-hua* 寫意畫 (paintings of poetic meaning). Briefly, he values the esthetic state of objects created rather than their outward verisimilitude. ("To discuss painting in terms of verisimiltude is next to the level of a child's mentality."[16]) He asks for grasping the spirit of the horse, and not the detailed copying of its skin and hair. Literati painters avoid outwardly realistic details and capture the primary vital rhythm of the objects. Poets avoid discursive commentaries and promote our entry into the "state" of the objects in their actualities. They both seek to extend beyond their media and point toward the common domain of "poetic world" or "esthetic state."

Su's formulation of "vital rhythm" in painting is sometimes not unlike Roger Fry's. In "Post-Impressionism," Fry says:

> Particular rhythms of line and particular harmonies of colour have their spiritual correspondences and tend to arouse one set of feelings, now another. . . . Rhythm . . . is the fundamental and vital quality of painting, as of all the arts.[17]

In fact, Su's view points toward Fry's friend, the esthetician Clive

---

[15] Recorded in Chao Ling-chih, *Hou-ch'ing-lu* in *Chih-pu-tsu chai ts'ung-shu*, XXII, 8.9a, compliled by Pao T'ing-po, preface dated 1776 (Shanghai: Ku-shu liu-t'ung ch'u, 1921).

[16] Conveniently in Lin Yü-tang 林語堂, *The Chinese Theory of Art* (London: William Heinemann, 1967), p. 92.

[17] *Fortnightly Review*, 95 (May 1, 1911), 862-3.

Bell. Su discourses on form in an intriguingly similar way:

> I have been of the opinion that men, animals, houses
> and furniture have a constant form. On the other hand,
> mountains and rocks, bamboos and trees, ripples, mist
> and clouds have no constant form *(hsing)*, but have a
> constant inner nature (*li*, inner law of their being). . . .
> When a mistake is made with regard to form, the mis-
> take is confined to that particular object; but when a
> mistake is made in the inner nature of things, the whole
> is spoiled.[18]

余嘗論畫：以爲人禽，宮室，器用，皆有常形。至於山石，竹
木，水波，烟雲，雖無常形，而有常理……常形之失止於所失
而不能病其全。若常理之不當，則舉廢之矣。

While Su never employs Clive Bell's term "significant form," his
li has part of that implication. And it is even more intriguing that
a modern attacker on the distinction between media, Susanne K.
Langer, should start with an amplification of Bell's "significant
form." In her essay "On the Significance of Music," Langer is
also concerned with positing the esthetic object. She believes that
the esthetic value of a work of art resides not in the feeling, but
in the "morphology of that feeling." By morphology, she means,
no doubt, the process of growth or activity of the "feeling" to
be contained in a work of art. Thus, like Herder and Su and other
neo-Romantic estheticians, Langer thinks the distinctions between
mediumistic characteristics are superficial. Poetry, using a tuned
progression of words, painting, using a design of the interaction
of colors and forms, and music, using cordial and melodic
structures of notes—all attempt to approximate the activities and
growth of feeling. This is the only way in which music can be
properly appreciated. This definition of the art object will also
help to solve the riddling question of why sometimes the same
piece of music could arouse in the listener two diametrically
opposed responses: both happy and sad feelings. This is possible,

[18] Lin Yü-tang, pp. 94-5.

Langer argues, because in certain cases, both happy and sad feelings take on the same form of morphology. Here one is reminded of the sophisticated music theory of Hsi Kang 嵇康, a fourth-century Chinese poet, in which he argues that notes themselves do not have or give feelings:

> Taste may be classified as *sweet* or *bitter*. Now Mr. A is virtuous, so I like him. Mr. B is foolish, so I dislike him. Liking and disliking issue from me; virtue and folly belong to Mr. A and Mr. B. Can we say, then, because *I* like Mr. A, he is a *man-to-be-liked*, and because *I* dislike Mr. B, he is a *man-to-be-disliked*? Can we say this is a *happy* taste because *I* enjoy it and that is an *angry* taste because *I* rage over it? This is displacement of names [this and that, I and thou] and functions [inner and outer]. Sounds and notes should be classified mainly as good or bad; they have nothing to do with happiness and sadness. Happiness and sadness issue from the basis of our feelings; they are not attached to sounds and notes.[19]

> 夫味以甘苦爲稱，今以甲賢而心愛，以乙愚而情憎，則愛憎宜屬我，而賢愚宜屬彼也。可以我愛而謂之愛人，我憎則謂之憎人，所喜謂之喜味，所怒謂之怒味哉。由此言之，則外內殊用，彼我異名，聲音自當以善惡（好壞）爲主，則無關於哀樂，哀樂自當以感情而後發，則無繫於聲音。

Music proceeds in terms of different tempi, different manners of acceleration and relaxation, sound and silence, notes and rests, superimpositions, repetitions, reverses and variations etc. to approximate the activity of feeling. The notes themselves do not make statements of *ideas* and *emotions* as such. But—
  can we say the same things about words, one of whose main functions is to give out meanings (ideas and emotions)? They cannot be, or perhaps should not be, treated like musical notes.

---

[19] *Hsi-k'ang-chi*, edited and collated by Lu Hsun 魯迅 (Hong Kong: Chung-hua, 1978), V, 2ab.

Here lies the difficulty of modern theory of art and poetry. In
order to arrive at the morphology of feelings or ideas (Here, in
fact, we are already talking about Pater's "condition of music,"
the full extent of which will be treated in the second panel of this
essay), poetry will have to de-emphasize the meaning function of
words, and it has to rely on a structure or process explainable only
in terms of that of music or painting. Modern·poetry, notably
that of Pound, Eliot, Williams, Stevens and the Black Mountain
Poets, attempts to break away from the limitations of words and
aspire to the condition of music, using repetition of leitmotifs,
themes and counterthemes, variations, silences and rests, etc., and
to the condition of painting, using synchronic structure rather
than diachronic progression. We will examine examples of these
changes in modern poetry and art in the second panel of this
essay. For now, it is sufficient to note that these changes come
from the obsession of arriving at what Artaud called "a sort of
central expression," "half-way between gesture and thought"
between language and notes or brushstrokes.

> The arts have indeed "some sort of common bond,
> some inter-recognition."[20]

> There is another sort of poetry where painting or
> sculpture seems as if it were "just coming over into
> speech."[21]

> Every concept, every emotion, presents itself to the
> vivid consciousness in some primary form.[22]

This central expression, as Donald Davie explains in conjunction
with Pound's poetry, "aimed to express not ideas . . . but rather
a state of mind in which as it were tremble on the edge of ex-

---

[20] Pound, Gaudier-Brzeska, p. 96.

[21] *Gaudier-Brzeska*, p. 95.

[22] *Gaudier-Brzeska*, p. 101.

pression."[23] Pound himself puts it in almost mysterious terms:

> We appear to have lost the radiant world where one thought cuts through another with clear edge, a world of moving energies . . . magnetisms that take form, that are seen, or that border the visible, the matter of Dante's *Paradiso*, the glass under water, the form that seems a form seen in a mirror.[24]

It is interesting that this passage almost reads like the Taoist-Chan-Buddhist-oriented Chinese critic Yen Yü (fl. 1180–1235) who also emphasizes arresting such a luminous world beyond the words.

> The highest kind of poetry is that which does not tread on the path of reason, nor fall into the snare of words. . . . The preeminence of the poets in the flowering T'ang Dynasty [721-755] lies in the interest which can be likened to the antelope that leaves no traces, hanging its horns. The excellence is in their transparence and luminosity, unblurred and unblocked, like sound in air, color in form, moon in water, image in mirror. Words have limits, but *i* (sense of things) are endless.[25]

所謂不涉理路、不落言筌者，上也。……盛唐詩人惟在興趣，
羚羊掛角，無跡可求。故其妙處瑩徹玲瓏，不可湊泊，如空中
之音，相中之色，水中之月，鏡中之象，言有盡而意無窮。

（嚴羽「滄浪詩話詩辨」）

The striking resemblance between Pound and Yen Yü here

[23]Donald Davie, *Ezra Pound: The Poet as Sculptor* (London: Routledge & Kegan Paul, 1964) p. 218.

[24]Ezra Pound, *The Literary Essays of Ezra Pound* (New York: New Directions, 1954), p. 154.

[25]*Ts'ang-lang shih-hua chaio-chih* 滄浪詩話校釋, annotated by Kuo Shao-yü 郭紹虞 (Hong Kong: Chung-hua, 1961), p. 23. See Yip, "Yen Yu . . . ," p. 191.

is amusingly irritating. Both Yen Yü and Pound want the poem
to spark off a flash of revelation of an ineffable state of being,
variously called "marvelous state," "spirit," "energy" or
"rhythm." Yet, everything else Yen Yü postulates could be
considered the severest criticism of modern poetry, Pound and
Eliot in particular, if so applied. Yen Yü was criticizing the Kiangsi
School of poets in the Sung Dynasty who made poetry out of
scholarship. Prior to propounding his ideal poetic state, which
should be luminous, unblurred and unblocked, Yen Yü says:

> Poetry depends on a particular talent, not on books,
> [alternate reading: scholarship.] It depends on a
> particular "interest," not on proposition of principles
> . . . the moderns [i.e., the Sung poets, referring particu-
> larly to the Kiangsi poets] . . . want to write poetry
> with words, with erudition or with disquisitions.
> Though they are well used, indeed, they are not yet
> the poetry of the ancients . . . they employ many
> allusions, ignoring the gusto. They hardly use a word
> or rhyme whose usage cannot be traced back to some
> precedents. But to read such a poem, no matter how
> many times, will lead nowhere.[26]

夫詩有別材，非關書也；詩有別趣，非關理也。……近代諸公
……以文學爲詩，以議論爲詩，以才學爲詩。以是爲詩，夫豈
不工，終非古人之詩也。……且其作多務使事，不問興致；用
字必有來歷，押韻必有出處，讀之終篇，不知着到何在。

（嚴羽「滄浪詩話詩辨」）

Both Pound and Eliot talk about a "special talent" and a unique
sensibility or interest emerging from the poem, but both of them
have no doubt also committed the sin of writing poetry "with
words, with erudition," "with allusions," if not exactly "with
disquisitions." What are we to make of the intriguing convergence
of their poetic ideal? Or do they converge at all? Part of the
difference between the two theoretical attempts have been slightly

[26]Kuo Shao-yü, p. 23.

touched upon in our discussion of Su Tung-p'o and Olson. What is involved here is the "world" created in the poem and the question of impersonality. A brief summary of Yen Yü's position might be useful here. (For a detailed historical discussion, see my "Yen Yü" essay referred to above, p. 167, n. 11.)

Yen Yü is concerned with a kind of free activity, a spontaneous expression of a special "interest," not to be trapped in words, a mode of existence, traceless, transparent, luminous, unblurred and unblocked. This mode of existence is suggested rather than stated. Words are employed in such a way that we are no longer aware of the words themselves, but a purely wordless state emerges from the words. Reading or scholarship, to Yen Yü, can be beneficial only as a cultivation of one's sense of what good poetry is all about, namely, to know that the best poem is always one that is unblocked, unblurred and unencumbered by particular phrases and strange words. This understanding has to become part of the poet's natural make-up, as it were, a cultivated "bosom," so to speak, in which and from which words emerge in a sort of fairly spontaneous order which follows the cuts and turns of the measure of things with little or no deliberate linguistic or formal sophistication on the part of the poet. The concept of *tzu-jan* (be nature-thus-natural), must necessarily reject formal sophistication, particularly that which builds, grows and complicates within a system of words outside the measure of things. De-sophistication is the first step in the cultivation of this "bosom," an intuitive grasp of the expressiveness of *tzu-jan*, prior to taking up the pen. A poet's personal fabrication of language complexes is, therefore, an obstruction to the free flow of order of things and is to be avoided.

There is no question that Pound and Eliot's ideal poem (under the influence of Symbolism) is one in which obvious traces of ratiocination must be withdrawn so as to leave the poem in a sort of autotelic existence to speak to us for itself without the aid of the poet's discursive elaboration and commentary. On one level, this ideal poem converges with a large group of Chinese poems (as ideal poems for Chinese estheticians) in which the scenery speaks for itself without the garrulous commentary of the poet. (This is what Pound values most in Chinese poetry.) There is little question about Pound and Eliot's advocacy of impersonality: their whole emphasis upon concrete presentation demands the absence of the poet. And yet, the paradox in the modern apologists is clear: the so-called extinction of personality is a special form of asserting the poet's presence because it is a conscious, and perhaps over-conscious effort to turn language to his special use. The manipulation of words, such as the dislocation of syntax (a Mallarmean heritage), the isolation of phrases or objects from their natural environment for special musical and gestural functions, and the juggling of themes and events (personal, mythical and historical) to form *new* wholes and *new* structures, is (I must repeat this word) a *special* form of individualism playing against the natural measure of things. To begin with, there is little or no attempt in Pound or Eliot to submerge himself into the energy flow of things in the phenomenal world, except for some of their earlier short imagist poems. Rather, they *select* moments from their experience of the phenomenal world and *construct* a world or a sequence of events that reflect the energy flow of their *selves*. It is a structure of words that approximate the cuts and turns of their individualistic way of perceiving the world, and this world, so created and believed to be autonomous and autotelic, need not be identifiable with the objective world. This is, of course, the working out of Mallarmé's motto: "Everything in the world exists to eventually culminate in a book"; that is, Nature is at the service of the poet. It is here that we find Roland Barthes' criticism of Mallarmé cogent:

> Modern poetry destroyed relationships in language and reduced discourse to words as static things. This implies a reversal in our knowledge of Nature. The interrupted flow of the new poetic language initiates a discontinuous Nature, which is revealed piecemeal. . . . Nature becomes a fragmented Space, made of objects solitary and terrible, because the links between them are only potential. . . . The poetic word is here an act without immediate past, without environment, and which holds forth only the dense shadow of reflexes from all sources

which are associated with it.

"Is there any poetic writing?"[27]

With all the emphasis of striving beyond the words as medium to enter into a "poetic world" to be shared by works of other media, with all the possibilities of having words edging over to musical and gestural expressiveness, Chinese poetry does not give one an impression of the reversal of Nature. Similarly, in spite of a certain structural resemblance to Cubist esthetics (e.g. multiple perspective, depth), Chinese landscape paintings remain natural and not mechanical; complete and not fragmented; real and intimately recognizable and not artificially strange. There is no need of distortion and defamiliarization. For the Chinese poet and artist, the priority is given to the things in Nature, and his foremost job is to capture them as they are. Meanwhile, Pound, Eliot and the Projectivists are fundamentally expressionistic, with roots reaching back to the Romantic emphasis of the poet's organizing power and the Romantic-Symbolist ordinance of the magical power of words, believed to be order-generating and world-creating, which, in turn, has given rise to a special obsession of the making of art language as opposed to seeing language as a means to approximate and disclose Nature. The central expression developed by modern poets, the art of edging into the potentialities of another expressive medium, achieved through the alienation of words from their limitations, must now be viewed from this expressionistic obsession. In this obsession the mimetic impulse (which is equally important in the Chinese works) has to be downplayed, if not exactly ex-communicated, and the possibility of putting totality in view is replaced by new wholes constructed out of fragments that bear little or no resemblance to our original correspondence with Nature.

[27] *Writing Degree Zero,* trans. by Annette Lavers and Colin Smith (New York: Beacon, 1970), pp. 49-50.

A PROSPECTUS FOR CHINESE LITERATURE
FROM COMPARATIVE PERSPECTIVES

John J. Deeney

"When you are up to your ass in alligators, it is difficult to remind yourself that your initial objective was to drain the swamp." So goes the snappish saying on my office bulletin board. The alligators which infest the comparative literature swamp all seem to possess two rows of fine teeth which threaten to grind us between their jaws: impressionistic subjectivity//scientific objectivity, intuition//analysis, relativism//absolutism, subjectivism//objectivism, generalization//specialization, and even American School//French School.

There are many ways to drain a swamp and any number of perspectives have been applied to get to the bottom of it. The danger is that we risk restricting ourselves to a single one and thus lose the larger perspective. Horst Frenz has pointed out that, "in the area of literary criticism, there will probably never be a consensus of opinion" nor a "critical theory which will be congenial to Asian and western comparatists alike." A. Owen Aldridge concurs and stresses that, "while the study of Chinese-western relations is a worthy enterprise, . . . there is no preferred manner of going about it."

Nor is it sufficient—though certainly desirable—that a balanced selection from a pluralism of critical approaches be applied. There have to be some fundamental coordinates which enable us to plan out the best courses of action, for such coordinates underlie all the perspectives which make the swamp habitable for Chinese-western comparatists. I would suggest four such coordinates: Consolidation, Cooperation, Criticism and the China Complex.

Consolidation

Much of the very basic groundwork for solid Chinese-western comparative literary study remains to be done. Such work is tedious and time-consuming, but it is the foundation upon which the entire edifice stands or falls. First of all, we must supply ourselves with a complete range of modern research tools and equipment (including computerized bibliographies, indexes, concordances, etc.) and constantly updated library holdings. Otherwise, we shall never have the resources and facilities to pursue many comparative literature questions in real depth.

In the realm of publications, there is still a critical need—in both Chinese and English languages—for glossaries of critical concepts and comparative literature terminology. It would also be helpful to have bilingual editions of literary works, histories of national literatures, translations (theory and practice) and anthologies (suitably annotated) from different national literatures, which would give a fuller representation of genres, periods and themes across two or more literary traditions. This new type of anthology would present literary texts more comparatively than chronologically, for the texts chosen would be illustrative of the principles and methods of the comparatist.[1]

Another aspect of consolidation is the need for the comparatist to acquaint himself more systematically with interdisciplinary studies, the pitfalls and highpoints of which are neatly summarized in an American Comparative Literature Association report:

> They have a salutary role to play in reorganizing our patterns of knowledge: we should be able to learn from them as well as contribute our own perspectives. But we must also be alert lest the crossing of disciplines involve a relaxing of discipline. Misty formulations, invisible comparisons, useless ingenuities, wobbly

[1] For some practical tips on how such an anthology might be compiled, see Robert J. Clements, *Comparative Literature as Academic Discipline: A Statement of Principles, Praxis, Standards* (New York: The Modern Language Association of America, 1978), pp. 228-29. Cf. my forthcoming review-article of this book, *Tamkang Review*, 11, No. 1 (Fall, 1980).

historiography plague all fields in the Humanities including our own: cross-disciplinary programs are not
immune from them. As participants, we need to muster
the theoretical sophistication, the methodological
rigor, the peculiar awareness of historical complexities
our special training affords us.[2]

Interdisciplinary areas which seem particularly promising for
Chinese-western comparative literature studies are, literature and:
painting and calligraphy; linguistics and stylistics; sociology and
political science and the history of ideas (especially in the light
of China's extraordinary mid-century developments which have
affected all the arts). Another pedagogical device which seems to
have been neglected in overcoming the formidable barrier to cross-
cultural communication, is the professional use of sophisticated
audio-visual materials.

Cooperation

Comparatists interested in promoting Chinese-western
literary relations may often feel, indeed, that they are caught in
quicksand. The mainstream of comparative literature activities
seems to pass them by while, at the same time, they are fending
off attacks from traditional scholars of the Chinese Literature
Department. Most comparatists have managed to extract themselves from this slough of despair and are happy to note much
progress in both areas. The international community of comparative literature scholars has to be met on its own grounds, not
by berating its benign neglect of Chinese-western comparative
literature studies. The active collaboration of Chinese literature
scholars has to be sought out, so that their rich literary legacy may
travel beyond its own limited boundaries and feed into the mainstream of world literature reaching the wider readership it
deserves.

Another report of the American Comparative Literature
Association urges every sort of cooperation: cross-departmental
freedom of enrollment, cross-listing of course offerings, exchanges

[2] In Clements, p. 181.

of instructors, borrowing of staff for oral examinations as well as their use as co-jurors or even co-directors of theses, their assistance in administering language examinations, their participation in colloquia, panel discussions, conferences and similar activities. The report goes on to say, of other literature departments:

> We should not be living up to our standards unless we are also fulfilling theirs; and that, if we succeed, we shall be realizing together the richest potential of the humanities.[3]
>
> Collegiality is implicit in the very term *university* as well as *college.* Without this spirit of fraternal participation in a common humane endeavor, Comparative Literature cannot thrive; indeed it cannot exist as a dynamic enterprise.[4]

It is my personal conviction that the ultimate success of comparative literature studies in China will depend upon full participation in the joint effort by Chinese literature scholars and their western counterparts. There is a sense of urgency here, for scholars schooled in the long-arduous training of traditional Chinese are a fast-vanishing generation.

Of almost equal importance for comparatists is the need for increased cooperation on the regional level. It is not altogether fortunate that literary scholars in the East seem to know more about western languages and literatures than those of their own region. But, surely, the literary traditions of the East will have a more profound and far-reaching effect on the world community of comparatists, if their scholarly contributions arise out of intra-Asian contexts rather than variations on conceptual frameworks and critical terms imported from the West. If we encourage more regional conferences and exchange professorships, subscribe to each other's journals and newsletters, engage in personal correspondence and sharing of papers, we may indeed, discover—

[3] In Clements, p. 266.

[4] In Clements, p. 269.

as the story goes—"Acres of Diamonds" in our own backyards.

It is difficult to develop a global perspective if the comparatist only views one side of the East/West fence. One must never confuse a particular national, or even regional, literature, however rich, with the entire wealth of world literature. Nor should one fear that taking such a world-wide direction will inevitably lead to a uniform acceptance of some common poetics. On the contrary, it may well bring us to a better understanding and appreciation of "universal literature." As A. Owen Aldridge understands the phrase in both its quantitative and qualitative dimensions, "universal literature" is:

> the sum total of all texts and works throughout the world, or the combination of all national literatures. . . . From the perspective of content, universal literature may refer to any work which reflects attitudes, situations or experiences which are felt or understood by human beings in all cultures. . . . [Furthermore,] the techniques of comparative literature succeed in relaxing the tension between nationalism and internationalism by recognizing cultural differences as a basic premise, but at the same time calling attention to similarities, which reflect the universality of psychological and esthetic reactions. The revealing of parallels in human relationships described in individual works in various literatures seems both to reconcile nationalism with internationalism and to increase the mutual understanding of Eastern and Western cultures. . . . The study of comparative literature rests upon the assumption of the fundamental unity of all mankind . . . [and] the recognition of common human elements in the human race to which all literatures conform.[5]

[5] *"Bungaku ni okeru hikaku to fuhensei"* 文學における比較と普遍性 ("The Comparative and the Universal in Literature"), in *Hikaku bungaku—Nihon to Seiyo* 比較文學——日本と西洋 [Comparative Literature—Japan and the West], trans. and ed. Akiyama Masayuki 秋山正幸 (Tokyo: Nan'undo, 1979), pp. 33-60, passim.

Criticism

Despite the reservations made on the first page of this After-word about considering a pluralism of critical approaches the panacea for our comparative ills, a judicious selection of critical methodologies can be very beneficial in clarifying the relationships —real or imaginary—between Chinese and western literatures. We can be confident that Chinese literature—like all great litera-tures—will never seriously be damaged by, nor break down under, any critical system(s), for its permanent beauty always beckons us to look, and look again, for increased enjoyment and enrich-ment. Surely there is something to be said for applying Chinese approaches to its own literature over and above the commonly accepted western ones. And do we dare go so far as to hope that the hitherto one-way process might be reversed and, one day, Chinese literary scholars will be invited to formulate and explicate their traditional ways of reading works not only in Chinese litera-ture but also in non-Chinese literatures?

A phrase which I coined—"The Chinese School of Com-parative Literature"—seems to have led to a bit of confusion and, therefore, needs some qualification.[6] I am not prepared to abandon the term altogether, but Mr. Stephen Soong's suggested substitution, "Chinese Dimension," has the advantage of neutraliz-ing the hostile tone of opposing camps (French School vs. American School vs. Chinese School vs. Russian School, etc.). In fact, I would like to consider the "Chinese School" as part of the *Weniad*[7] tradition; not a warring faction, but a circle of well-informed comparatists discussing and testing different ways of reading literatures from a Chinese perspective. Chinese critical terminology such as *fu* 賦, *pi* 比, *hsing* 興, *shih-hua* 詩話, *ch'i* 氣, *ch'ing-ching* 情景, etc. have to be used more frequently and elaborated upon with explanations and examples, until they have become as familiar to comparatists throughout the world as *je ne*

[6] See "New Orientations for Comparative Literature," *Tamkang Review*, 8, No. 1 (April 1977), 232-35.

[7] See C.H. Wang, "Towards Defining a Chinese Heroism," *JOAS*, 95, No. 1 (January-March 1975), 25-35. Wang suggests that the hero in China was traditionally associated with cultural rather than martial achievements.

sais quoi, touchstones, objective correlative, *bildungsroman*, etc.
Zen and *haiku* are already part of the literary commonwealth of
expressions; why not *Ch'an* 禪 and *chüeh-chü* 絕句 or *lü-shih*
律詩?

We must not understimate the importance of clarifying our
use of terminology. As Pound delighted in quoting Confucius,
cheng ming 正名 (rectify the names) is a way of promoting stabili-
ty and progress. For a real understanding of key terms can lead
one to a closer approximation of what constitutes the distinctive
features of the Chinese "literary mind" (文心). The translation
of the literary sensibility that is indigenous to China is, perhaps,
the single most important task facing the Chinese-western comparatist in this century.

China Complex

On more than one occasion I have taken the opportunity
to describe the tremendous contributions which Taiwan has made
in developing comparative literature studies in the East.[8] Scholars
in Hong Kong have also been doing their share in that tradition.[9]
But an issue of more immediate concern to all Chinese-western
comparatists is mainland China's new openness to the western
world, and its willingness to test the waters of a great variety of
contemporary currents. There is a considerable amount of interest
and a certain degree of activity in areas closely related to comparative literature studies. This is particularly true in the field of
translation, publications dealing with non-Chinese literatures, and

[8] See my articles in the *Tamkang Review*: "Comparative Literature Studies
in Taiwan," 1, No. 1 (April 1970), 119-45; "Chinese-English Literary Relations," 1, No. 2 (October 1970), 105-39; "Comparative Literature: West
and/or East?" 4, No. 2 (October 1973), 157-66; "Comparative Literature
Activities in Taiwan," 6, No. 1 (April 1975), 189-204; "Some Reflections on
the History of Comparative Literature in China," 6, No. 2 & 7, No. 1 (Oct.
1975-April 1976), 219-28.

[9] See my articles in the *Quarterly World Report* of the Council of National
Literatures: "China: Taiwan, Hong Kong, the Mainland," (January 1976),
1-3; "East-West Perspectives: New Orientations for Comparative Study of
Literatures," 1, No. 3 (July 1978), 12-14; "Hong Kong: Cultural Cross-
roads?" 2, No. 3 (July 1979), 4-6.

even a number of American Studies centers being reactivated. But there is a shortage of trained scholars and library facilities. In fact, as Ch'ien Chung-shu 錢鍾書 wrote recently in an overly-modest response to an inquiry I made about the comparative literature scene in China,

> China's discovery of Western literature seems to be still a virgin field of study. Of course, I am speaking out of my backwoods ignorance; perhaps some well-researched work on the subject is already in existence. But I sincerely hope you will produce a definitive, even though not pioneer, book on West-East Passage, to adapt Dorothy Brewster's title. I once had had the intention of doing something along that line, and it long went the way of all intentions, good as well as bad. The only evidence for it is an article on the first Chinese translation of Longfellow's "Psalm of Life," deeply buried in an English quarterly published more than thirty years ago by the erstwhile National Central Library, Nanking.
>
> My forthcoming shapeless jumbo of a book (in 4 fat volumes!) does not come under the category of "Comparative Literature." The name does not quite fit the game. Never mind the taxonomizing, however.[10]
>
> As to "the first beginnings" of comparative literature in China, I am rather afraid that the proposed "historical sketch" would be like the chapter on the snakes in Iceland or else a pseudo-chronicle of a non-event. In a strict sense, i.e., the only sense that matters, you and your co-workers are in "the first beginning" of this discipline. Do have the courage to be dynastic founders! Need I

[10] Letter received from Ch'ien Chung-shu. 13 February 1979. The collection referred to is entitled, *Kuan Chui P'ien* 管錐篇 (Peking: Chung-hua, 1979). There is a 1980 reprint available from Hong Kong's Chung-hua Publishing Co. and a three-volume version in Taiwan.

remind you of the Ovidian tag which served Montesquieu as the epigraph of his *Esprit de Lois*.[11]

With the encouragement of such brilliant, senior scholars as this, Chinese-western comparatists throughout the world should, indeed, reciprocate by exchanging publications and ideas with Chinese institutions and scholars—a necessary and much desired extension of the Chinese dimension in comparative literature.[12]

The early generation of Chinese-western comparatists have worked hard to "drain the swamp" and clear the ground in order to plant a few seeds. Generations to come will have to see that the "tendre croppes" receive the proper nourishment, and that some Apollos are around to do the watering, lest the swamp become just another wasteland.

[11] Letter received from Ch'ien Chung-shu. 7 March 1979. The epigram referred to states: " . . . a child born of no mother," usually interpreted as a claim to originality which is based on no previous model.

[12] By way of postscript, having just completed a "Study Tour" of Peking, Shanghai, and Canton (April-May), it is interesting to note the following developments:

1) At one major university, it was the Chinese Department faculty and post-graduates (not the Foreign Language Department) who came to participate in a three-hour lecture-discussion on Comparative Literature.

2) One of the most obvious assets China offers to the Comparative Literature world is the enormous number of academics with strong backgrounds in a wide variety of languages and literatures (Japanese, Russian, German, French, English, are only the most obvious).

3) The most serious liability, perhaps, is the lack of balanced library collections, especially journals from abroad. On the other hand, it is said that over 2000 new journals and magazines, in Chinese, have been published in the past two years, 100 of which concern literature in one way or another.

4) Access to scholarship (inter-provincial as well as international) seems limited and spotty. One university journal published in 1980, included an article featuring a combination review (two pages) with translated excerpts (eight pages) of Paul Van Tieghem's *Précis d'histoire littéraire de l'Europe depuis la renaissance* (1925), probably in a Chinese translation-reprint (1951). Although the writer makes a passing reference to the popularity of comparative literature studies throughout the world—even to the French School and the American School

—his only other reference is to Frédéric Loliée's *Histoire des littéra-tures comparées des origines au xxe siècle* (1903), again, most likely in its Chinese translation (1931).

5) One senior scholar suggested that comparative literature studies of the influence variety would be most beneficial to China's comparatists at this time, for it would be a good way of getting them back in touch with what has been going on in the rest of the world, particularly during the period of the Cultural Revolution. Another outstanding translator published a book-size selection of T'ao Ch'ien's poems in 1980 without knowing of the existence of Hightower's *The Poetry of T'ao Ch'ien* (1970). On the other hand, one mainland translation magazine (Chinese to English) actively solicits critiques from foreign readers, and a university press wishes to collaborate with an American scholar in publishing a textbook on translation.

6) The Cultural Revolution did incalculable harm, to be sure, but there were some young people who, despite—or, perhaps, because of—the trying times, painstakingly shaped themselves into self-made junior scholars. The following excerpt (unaltered except for a few minor deletions) was a response to a recent inquiry about how a student who had never finished middle school got into a postgraduate program, based on a long paper, in English, criticizing translations of classical Chinese poetry.

I was in an obscure little mountain village from 1969 to 1972, some 600 kilometres away from my home town. Life was hard then, and I had only two books and a dictionary with me (*Western Literature* Vol. I. "Greece and Rome," ed. A. E. Zucker, 1934; William Swinton, *Studies in English Literature*, 1908; and Hornby's *Advanced Learner's Dictionary*). Then, I spent five years from 1972 to 1977 in a factory as an ordinary fitter. Fortunately again, I got to know some friends who managed to find quite a number of books for me, which was, at that time, not only difficult, but even a dangerous thing to do. Thus I was able to get access to great literature which just intoxicated me. I read and translated Pal-grave's *Golden Treasury* and works on history of English Liter-ature. There was no one to teach me or guide me, and my best and only teacher was book and book and book, and I read any book I could lay my hand on. I began to read Shakespeare, and read the Bible twice as great literature. Many writers became my favourite and indispensable reading, and your Washington Irving's *Sketch Book* gave me so much pleasure and enjoyment. I often read into late hours after work, averagely six or seven hours a day. That is roughly how I studied English. It has been a long and hard way, with many bitter as well as happy memories. I think it might be interesting to you as a teacher, if you want to know how some of the Chinese students tried to continue their studies in that difficult period from 1966 to 1976.

APPENDICES

ACKNOWLEDGMENTS

This publication, and the Proceedings from which it sprung, were made possible by the collaboration of virtually every level at The Chinese University of Hong Kong. It is with pleasure and gratitude that we include—as part of our endeavors—the generous testimonials of our Vice-Chancellor, Ma Lin 馬臨; the Director of our Institute of Chinese Studies, Ching-ho Chen 陳荊和; and the Director of the Comparative Literature and Translation Centre, Stephen Soong 宋淇. Each in his own way has not only expressed genuine interest in our work, but actively supported us in the smooth organization and warm hospitality accorded to our participants. We should also like especially to single out the presence, at the Conference, of our present and former deans, Professor D.C. Lau 劉殿爵 and Mr. John Gannon.

Two of the discussants, William Tay and Donald Wesling, also favored us with full-length papers. Although there was no opportunity to give a formal presentation of these papers, because of their pertinence to the Conference theme, the writers kindly agreed to allow us to include them here. All the discussants are to be congratulated for enlivening the Conference with their candid critiques and insightful comments, many of which were incorporated into the revised versions of the position papers. A special debt of gratitude is owed to Stephen C.K. Chan 陳清僑 and Judy Leung 梁麗娟 of the Comparative Literature Division for the cheerful and efficient way they saw to all the practical details of the Conference and this publication. We also wish to thank Ms. Carla Kim-yang Lim, for her meticulous copy-editing.

Finally, we wish to acknowledge the enormous benefit we have received from two scholars whose efforts at directing traffic along the literary lanes between East and West can never be praised too much. We are particularly pleased that Professor Horst Frenz and Professor A. Owen Aldridge consented to join us in this volume with their lucid remarks in the Preface and Foreword respectively. Both have made their presence felt through constructive criticism at virtually all major Chinese-Western Comparative Literature conferences from their inception in the early seventies. It is a pleasure to close with an acknowledgment of their contributions, past and present, and an optimistic assurance that they and comparatists like them will be with us in the future.

WELCOMING AND CONCLUDING SPEECHES

Welcoming Address from Professor Ching-ho Chen, Director of the Institute of Chinese Studies, at the Opening of the Conference on East-West Comparative Literature, August 14, 1979

The brochure describing the Institute of Chinese Studies states in its first paragraph that a "broad but unified concept of Chinese Studies" is "characterized by its comparative approach." It is therefore fitting that the Comparative Literature and Translation Centre of our Institute should sponser this first Hong Kong Conference on East-West Comparative Literature. It is my pleasure to welcome you here, particularly those who have come a long way, and to wish you every success in your collective endeavors toward finding meaningful approaches in East-West comparative literary studies.

To formally open the Conference, it is my privilege to introduce to you one who has taken more than an ordinary interest in personally supporting this event as well as other activities relating to comparative studies—Professor Ma Lin, Vice-Chancellor of the Chinese University of Hong Kong.

Welcoming Address from Dr. Ma Lin, Vice-Chancellor of The Chinese University of Hong Kong

Friends and colleagues, I take great pleasure in welcoming you to The Chinese University of Hong Kong for the occasion of the Conference on East-West Comparative Literature.

As a scientist, my role here is less participation than congratulation; as an educator who oversees, with the assistance of many able hands, the day-to-day operation of an institution of higher learning in implementing its educational goal, I am, in spirit, a humanist and thus share with you the interest in advancing the cause of human understanding.

Often superficial observation of the distinction between the discipline of humanities and that of science is that the former focuses its attention on the abstract and philosophical, and the latter on the concrete and real. Sir Francis Bacon used the fable of the Sphinx to illustrate the dichotomy between the two disciplines, and to demonstrate how one solved the problems raised by the other. The physical appearance of the Sphinx—with the face and voice of a virgin, the wings of a bird, the claws of a griffin—implies the beauty and charm of science when first confronted, the freedom it may bring when properly mastered, and the terror it threatens when out of control. Such a creature of diametrically opposed possibilities was finally conquered by Oedipus, the proto-man, who, having solved the riddle of the Sphinx, became king of a nation. The twofold condition attached to the riddle suggests (a) distraction and laceration of mind, if one fails to solve it, and (b) a kingdom, if one succeeds. The story brings out the mutual dependency of science and humanities, and shows two kinds of concerns: one concerning the nature of things and the other concerning the nature of man; and the mastery over both promises man his kingdom. By such affinity between the two disciplines, I feel a certain kinship with you.

There is another meaningful connection between a scientist and a humanist; they all share the same loyalty—to solve the

problem of misunderstanding. The scientist brings man understanding of his world; the humanist, of man. It is through the
combined efforts of both that a more livable world is made possible. This brings us still closer to each other.

I also feel the particular meaningfulness of holding the East-
West Comparative Literature Conference at our University site, as
the University claims itself to function as the cultural exchanging
ground between the East and the West. May the success of your
conference be symbolic of the convergence of the East and the
West through mutual understanding and cooperation.

Thank you.

Concluding Address from Mr. Stephen Soong
Director of the Comparative Literature and Translation Centre
August 16, 1979

I was told by one of our honorable guests that "Hong Kong
is the most natural and the ideal place to conduct the study of
Comparative Literature, since it is a bilingual society, where cross-
fertilization of two great cultures takes place in all its activities."
I took his words both as a compliment and as a statement of fact.
If our conversation had not been interrupted, I would have continued to speak to him in the following vein: "In Hong Kong, the
ideal place to conduct Comparative Literature studies is The
Chinese University. In The Chinese University, the ideal place
to conduct Comparative Literature studies is the Institute of
Chinese Studies. In the Institute of Chinese Studies, the ideal
place to conduct Comparative Literature studies is the Comparative Literature and Translation Centre. And in the Centre,
the ideal place to conduct Comparative Literature studies is the
Comparative Literature Division, composed of a group of young
and energetic scholars, whom Rudyard Kipling would call "men
of infinite sagacity."

The key words are "young and energetic." That is why we
are profoundly grateful to the participants, especially those from
abroad. The presence of these eminent scholars provides the
Comparative Literature Division with the necessary impetus to
develop new directions of research, to refrain from too much
inward looking, to respond to fresh ideas and eventually to achieve
a new synthesis of eastern and western cultures. Professor Frenz
denied the existence of an American school, thus implicitly doubt-
ing whether there is a Chinese school. Perhaps the choice of the
word "school" is unfortunate, for it reminds one of rigid depart-
mentalization, whereas the study of Comparative Literature calls
for an integrated and interdisciplinary approach. I would like to
suggest here, if I may, that we use the word "dimension." Surely,
Comparative Literature has enough room for a Chinese dimension.

In using the term "dimension," we must refer to The Chinese
University. It was established in 1963 and it is now 16 years

"young." At first, it was suggested that The Chinese University should serve as a bridge between the East and the West. To the University, however, this was inadequate. Any Chinese university can be such a link, for every modern university, in the real sense of the term, should serve as a link between its own cultural heritage and that of the outside world. In order to fulfil its unique and distinctive mission, The Chinese University has developed a two-pronged thrust over the years: (1) the collection of Chinese data through the assimilation and application of Western methodology, and (2) the incorporation of a Chinese dimension in all the disciplines. There are now three centers or units which possess a comprehensive collection of Chinese data: (1) Chinese Medicinal Material Research Centre, (2) the Art Gallery of the Institute of Chinese Studies, and (3) the Chinese Music Archives. The Comparative Literature and Translation Centre is also contributing its share to the unique mission of the University. The Translation Division provides Chinese data to the students of Chinese studies, especially those interested in Comparative Literature, through its journal, *Renditions*, through its publication of *Renditions Books* and *Renditions References*. With the help and support of the Institute of Chinese Studies, it will develop a new Chinese-French Translation Stream and a new Chinese-German translation Stream within the next two years. The partner of the new venture— Chinese-French Translation Stream—will be Prof. Ruhlman and his colleagues. The Comparative Literature Division, incorporated last year, has already begun to compile (1) *A Glossary of Literary Terms* (E-C and C-E), (2) *A Reference Book of Chinese Literary Critical Terms* (C-E), and (3) *A Companion to Comparative Literature: Chinese-Western Literary Relations*, all to be completed within the next two years, not to mention various research projects conducted by individual members. Besides providing Chinese data, the major objective of the Division, however, is to study Chinese literary theories and gradually to formulate an alternative way of viewing literature. After all, Chinese civilization is the only existing civilization with an unbroken tradition from the earliest origins, and there must be methods and techniques in Chinese classical works which would contribute to modern methodology. It is hoped that with the aid of Chinese data, a

Chinese approach will be formulated so that it can go beyond national confines. Undoubtedly, the Occident would welcome a new *Orientation*.

LIST OF CONTRIBUTORS, CHAIRPERSONS, DISCUSSANTS AND PARTICIPANTS

In the following list of names, "Co" stands for Contributor, "Ch" for Chairperson, and "Di" for Discussant.

Aldridge, A. Owen, Department of Comparative Literature, Foreign Languages Building, University of Illinois, Urbana, Illinois 61801, U. S. A. (Co, Di)

Chan, Ping-leung 陳炳良, Department of Chinese, University of Hong Kong. (Di)

Chan, Stephen C. K. 陳清僑, Comparative Literature Division, Comparative Literature and Translation Centre, The Chinese University of Hong Kong.

Chang, Han-liang 張漢良, Department of Foreign Languages and Literature, National Taiwan University, Taipei, Taiwan, R. O. C. (Co)

Chen, Ching-ho 陳荊和, Institute of Chinese Studies, The Chinese University of Hong Kong.

Cheung, Dominic 張振翱, Comparative Literature Program, University of Southern California, Los Angeles, California 90007, U. S. A. (Di)

Cheung, Yat-shing 張日昇, Comparative Literature and Translation Centre, and Department of English, The Chinese University of Hong Kong.

Chi, Ch'iu-lang 紀秋郎, Department of English, Tamkang College of Arts and Sciences, Tamsui, Taipei Hsien, Taiwan, R. O. C. (Di)

Chou, Ying-hsiung 周英雄, Comparative Literature and Translation Centre, and Department of English, The Chinese University of Hong Kong. (Co)

Chu, Limin 朱立民, Department of Foreign Languages and Literature, National Taiwan University, Taipei, Taiwan, R. O. C. (Ch)

Deeney, John J. 李達三, Comparative Literature and Translation Centre, and Department of English, The Chinese University of Hong Kong. (Ch)

Fokkema, Douwe 佛克馬, Institute of Comparative Literature, Ramstraat 31, Utrecht 2501, The Netherlands. (Co)

Frenz, Horst, Comparative Literature Program, Ballantine Hall 402, Indiana University, Bloomington, Indiana 47401, U. S. A. (Co, Di)

Gannon, John 關寧安, Department of English, The Chinese University of Hong Kong. (Ch)

Hou, Chien 侯健, Department of Foreign Languages and Literature, National Taiwan University, Taipei, Taiwan, R. O. C. (Ch)

Ibsch, Elrud, Department of General and Comparative Literature, Free University, Amsterdam, The Netherlands. (Di)

Lau, D. C. 劉殿爵, Institute of Chinese Studies and Department of Chinese, The Chinese University of Hong Kong.

Lefevere, André, Department of Germanic Philology, University of Antwerp, BE 2610, Belgium. (Di)

Leung, Gaylord 梁佳蘿, Comparative Literature and Translation Centre, and Department of Chinese, The Chinese University of Hong Kong. (Di)

Liu, Shu-hsien 劉述先, Department of Philosophy, The Chinese

University of Hong Kong. (Di)

Luk, Thomas Yun-tong 陸潤棠, Comparative Literature and Translation Centre, and Department of English, The Chinese University of Hong Kong. (Di)

Ruhlmann, Robert 于伯儒, Uninversity of Paris, 7 Rue Laromiguiere, 75005 Paris, France. (Ch)

Soong, Stephen C. 宋淇, Comparative Literature and Translation Centre, The Chinese University of Hong Kong.

Sun, Phillip S. Y. 孫述宇, Department of Chinese, The Chinese University of Hong Kong. (Ch)

Tay, William 鄭樹森, Comparative Literature and Translation Centre, and Department of English, The Chinese University of Hong Kong. (Co, Di)

Wesling, Donald, Department of Literature, University of California, San Diego, La Jolla, California 92093, U. S. A. (Co, Di)

Wong, Wai-leung 黃維樑, Comparative Literature and Translation Centre, and Department of Chinese, The Chinese University of Hong Kong. (Di)

Yip, Wai-lim 葉維廉, Department of Literature, University of California, San Diego, La Jolla, California 92093, U. S. A. (Co)

Yuan, Heh-hsiang 袁鶴翔, Comparative Literature and Translation Centre, and Department of English, The Chinese University of Hong Kong. (Co)